15.95

HQ
438
6
P76
1982

SO-AUD-760

Colo. Christian University Library
8787 W. Alameda Ave.
Lakewood, CO 80226

Those Strenuous Dames

Nell Brown Propst

TO THE LANDMARK WOMEN
IN MY LIFE:

Leila Williams Brown, my mother, who gave me life and some of her incredible energy.

Antoinette Sparks Holroyd, beloved professor, who opened new doors.

Grace Benson Propst, mother of my husband, whose home was a magic place of fun and creativity.

Anna C. Petteys, the catalyst who stimulated.

All have measured themselves against unseen standards.

Those Strenuous Dames

OF THE COLORADO PRAIRIE

NELL BROWN PROPST

PRUETT **P** PUBLISHING COMPANY
Boulder, Colorado

© 1982 By Nell Brown Propst

All rights reserved, including those to reproduce this book, or parts thereof, in any form, without permission in writing from the Publisher.

First Edition
1 2 3 4 5 6 7 8 9

Printed in the United States of America

Library of Congress Cataloging in Publication Data

Propst, Nell Brown.
  Those strenuous dames of the Colorado prairie.

  Bibliography: p.
  Includes index.
  1. Women—Colorado—History. 2. Frontier and pioneer life—Colorado. I. Title.
HQ1438.C6P76   1982   305.4'09788   82-12304
ISBN 0-87108-627-1

CONTENTS

Foreword

Since settlement of the West first began, stories of the men who took part in the frontier movement have proliferated; except for a handful of outstanding or notorious characters, little has been written about the women who played an equally important part in that great westward movement. Here, in a fast-moving, well-written book, Nell Propst has provided exciting information on the lives of a surprisingly large number of the hardy, courageous women who came to eastern Colorado in the early days. Either by choice, or through the force of circumstances, they stayed to leave an enduring mark on the state. Others born on the prairie in those rigorous times fought their way to success and prominence in many fields, then left their imprint on other states and areas. Of many races and nationalities, these Colorado-bred women eventually excelled in medicine, athletics, art, education, literature, politics, business, aeronautics, rodeo and other fields, all in a period when women were still strictly relegated to "home and children" and were not welcome in those traditionally male realms. In time they won the respect and admiration of all. This fine book is long overdue.

NELLIE SNYDER YOST

A NOTE ABOUT THE DAMES

Those Strenuous Dames is the story of plains women etched against history—the homestead migration, the historic march to the vote, the quest of thousands of immigrants, the successful climb into business and the professions, and the startling accomplishments in the arts or athletics or rodeo or the military.

It is not the final word. There must be many additional heroines out there on the prairie. The two hundred or more in this book are a sampling.

The criteria for inclusion are simple. The women were a part of historic scenes; their stories were compelling; or they took steps unusual for a woman. Sometimes they had no choice. Often they just wanted to prove that they could do a certain thing. But usually the motivation was an insistent need to enter a particular field.

A modern woman, to be included, must have unusual accomplishments and recognition on at least a statewide level. No one is listed simply because her husband or father was a prominent man. She has to have a story of her own.

My strenuous dames were doers. That "my" is admittedly possessive, but I love them—most of them—with pride as I love the prairies. I believe that they were shaped by the prairie, that a unique love-hate relationship with that relentless environment brought from them qualities that might have stayed dormant elsewhere.

In many ways, this book owes its birth to the Delta Kappa

Gamma International, a professional honorary organization for educators, and particularly to the Sterling chapter under the leadership of Joan Shoemaker, president, and Maureen "Billie" Barnett, chairman for the 1981 state convention in Sterling. They asked me to speak, and in keeping with the theme of the meeting, Reapers of the Prairie, *Those Strenuous Dames* was born. The enthusiastic response and subsequent requests for the speech led to realization that here was virtually an untapped subject for a book.

I had written about several of the women in articles for magazines and anthologies: *The Alaska Journal, The Colorado Magazine, The Colorado Woman Digest, Empire, Health Horizons, Methodist History, Prairie Prints, Roundup, Senior Voice,* and *True West.* Remembering the response of a woman in Denver to a story about Doctor Portia in *Empire —* "I had no idea that such unusual people lived out there" — I began to realize that many in urban areas must have a limited knowledge of what women on the plains have done with their lives.

For that matter, those of us living in eastern Colorado probably do not realize the astounding stories that have taken place all around us. Even though I felt proud of my original gallery, who were the basis for the speech, further search has led to dozens of additional adventurers and has kept me in a state of wonder and excitement. The women on the prairie *are* strenuous — their exploits required energy — but they are breathtaking as well.

Further appreciation is due the Colorado chapter of Delta Kappa Gamma for permission to use as a resource their excellent book, *Up the Hemline.* Edited by Margaret J. Lehrer, it is a compilation of members' experiences while teaching in Colorado.

Several other books have been of especial help: *The Crowley County History,* edited by Gwen Schroeder for the Crowley County Heritage Society; *The History of New Raymer* by Franklin M. Jones; *The Merrells* by Pat and Jim Merrell; *Pawnee Country,* compiled and edited by Ernestine Koenig, assisted by the Pawnee Historical Society; and *Wo' Wakita,* edited by Emily Lewis.

I also received assistance in research from the Overland Trail Museum, Wilma Dillon, curator, and Viola Bringelson, assistant; and from the Sterling Public Library, Betty Kenyon, head librarian, and staff.

Special help has come from friends: Marguerite Sherwin Donovan, generous research and encouragement; Gladys Fairhead of Merriman, Nebraska, assistance with the story of Mary Red Kettle; Opal Lingelbach Houghton, sharing her collection about The Buttes area; Catherine Byrne Hume, who searched for the stories of teachers; Sue Josties, encouragement, advice, and expert proofreading, as well as the use of a stanza of her poem, "Prairie Children"; and Amy Dickinson Worthley, a ninety-year-old dynamo, who not only told her own story but did considerable research of other people and of homestead laws.

Most of all, I am grateful to my husband Keith, who is always vitally interested in each writing project and who has the gift of being able to analyze a problem and find a solution that makes everything fall into place.

It has been my joy to know so many of the strenuous dames and to present this gleaning of their stories.

Do not think of them as returning,
No matter how far they have travelled,
No matter how high they have climbed.
Born and bred of the prairie,
They have taken it with them —
They part of it,
It part of them,
Engrained in their being forever.

From "Prairie Children"
by Sue Baker Josties

UP AGAINST THE PRAIRIE

The sound came from somewhere out in the dark, and she awoke instantly. She lay in the painful stillness that fear brings and tried to hear what it was that had brought her out of a deep sleep. Her heart beat so strongly that for a moment she was a child again, terrified at night by the books she read by day, translating the rapid beat into the galloping midnight ride of a headless horseman. She raised her head slightly to get away from the pounding of her own heart.

And then she heard them, footsteps falling steadily on the prairie grass and coming unmistakably to her shanty.

She was a homesteader, and she was a woman alone. By day she convinced herself that there was nothing to fear. A mile or so away in each direction were other sod houses, and the people in them were decent and good. But when night came, those miles were enormous distances. And who knew what strangers might stalk the prairie in the dark?

It is a myth that young women traveling alone is a modern phenomenon. In the early 1900s, the plains of eastern Colorado were speckled with the soddies or tar paper shacks of single women. They were not like some mountain heroines who achieved fame — or at least appreciation — by taking in washing, kicking up their heels in a saloon, or shooting a faithless lover. These were single, respectable women living far from a town in the most primitive of conditions.

What were they looking for? The same things that the men were: land, adventure, perhaps romance that had escaped them

1

in sedate hometowns. Ads all over the United States urged them to come to the South Platte Valley. One, published in an Illinois newspaper in the early 1900s, told of "government land to file on."

"Be independent," the promoter urged. "Make a life of your own; fine climate; rich soil, best market; near railroads, churches, schools. No saloons."

Playing his trump card, the promoter stressed the number of "wife-hungry bachelors" that single women and young widows would find.

Perhaps unconsciously, the girls were looking for something else that the West provided. That something is best illustrated with a description by a Coloradoan of his favorite view in the state. He came over a hill one evening at dusk and saw the huge expanse of the San Luis Valley laid out before him. Soon he saw a light blinking ahead. It was no doubt at some ranch, and he would reach it soon. But it seemed that the light was always ahead of him. This newcomer to the state loved the scene because it dramatized the enormity of the western landscape.

Perhaps the view would have had a different significance for some of the early women. When they looked out at the myriad of lights in their home cities, who could tell which lamp belonged to whom? But everyone in the San Luis Valley knew the solitary beacon of that old rancher. He was not just part of the crowd. He did not need fame to make him stand out. Everyone knew who he was.

The plains have an indefinable pull which escapes many modern travelers racing through on interstates. When one can stand on a hill and see all the way to the edge of the world, it seems, one becomes a part of the country. One feels as if this country—all that he can see—belongs to him.

The openness and unbroken land of the Colorado plains must have had a particular appeal for women who were not accustomed to feelings of individuality and power. Some of them came to visit relatives who were homesteading and decided to stay and settle on their own claims. Others arrived in later years, searching not especially for land but no doubt for the freedom that the West offered. Their accomplishments cover a surprising range.

Did they come because of a hunger within them? Or did the

bigness, the blinding vistas of the Colorado prairie and sky, imbue them with the courage to strike out on new paths for women?

"The Homesteader," clay sculpture by Jessie Scott.

Chapter I

THAT AIN'T NO HOMESTEADER — THAT'S A LADY

In the early 1900s, the big homestead migration was on. Towns seemed to spring up overnight. In eastern Colorado, some were located near the Arkansas and South Platte rivers, others on open prairie along the railroads, and still others where there was no particular reason for a town to grow.

Girls came west to visit relatives or friends and found a bustling, optimistic world. Reservoirs would water the prairie, everyone said, and make it a garden; newly built beet factories and the revolutionary feedlots would provide markets for the crops and perhaps part-time work in the off seasons.

In both 1909 and 1910, almost four thousand people took out either homestead or desert claims or made final proof in the Sterling Land Office alone. Receipts topped $118,000 each year. In 1914, after residency requirements had been reduced, the Sterling office processed a record 275 in only one day. By 1909, fourteen Union Pacific and Burlington trains connected the South Platte Valley with Denver and the East. And whenever a train stopped, someone new, searching for his fortune, stepped off. And very often, that someone new was a woman.

Early 1900 was a joyous period in American history. The Wright brothers had freed a generation from the shackles of the earth. Exuberant young men tackled the mystery and unknown terrors of the Arctic and Antarctic. Looking over the vast expanse

5

The first landmark of a new town. *Courtesy, Lulu Belle Propst.*

of the prairie, exulting in their new freedom, the women home-steaders must have felt a kinship with the "birdmen" who had taken to the skies.

The homesteaders were mostly young people, very often single, and they knew how to have a good time. Almost every night, they gathered somewhere. They poured into the towns for base-ball games, and many of them belonged to a team. They were seldom mere spectators. They went to ice cream suppers or to socials at the newly organized churches. They had dances in one-room schools so small that onlookers had to stand outside, peer-ing in the one door and window. They planned elaborate parties with decorations for the barns and soddies. At one major social event, the place was "fairly ablaze with beautiful Japanese lan-terns across the porches and through the yards."

They dressed fit-to-kill, entertained with their own music, and worked hard to come up with new tricks. One was the "sheet music" stunt: a couple of young men lay on the floor, covered themselves with sheets, and snored loudly. When a town staged an annual celebration, all others obligingly closed businesses and attended.

The revelers could often snatch a nap on the way home. Roads were formed by heading straight across the prairie, and soon ruts were six inches deep. Sarah Barber Claypool, who grew up near the Wyoming Border, told that once you settled your wagon into the ruts, you could "lean back and rest or even go to sleep; the horse would follow the trail on home."

In the town of Merino, which for years had only one store, thirteen carpenters were suddenly at work in 1907. A doctor came to town, a druggist, a newspaper editor, and a "veterinary dentist" who seemed a grand step upward from the blacksmith dentist of past decades.

A brass band was highly successful. Twenty-two people ordered instruments and rehearsed twice a week. When someone new arrived, it was not particularly important that he worked on the section or painted new houses. The big news was that he was a snare drummer. When the veterinary dentist returned to Iowa, the paper lamented his loss as one of the best ball players and a member of the band.

In the summer, a big party of young people usually attended Cheyenne Frontier Days, camping out for a week or more. Their chaperones were the young couples already married. It was no wonder that girls like Ida Watkins, who came out to visit relatives, could not bring themselves to return home. Soon they were settled on claims in their own little houses.

But reality quickly set in. Jobs were necessary during proving up time, and transportation imperative. And the girls had to pull their own weight. Accustomed to riding in buggies or walking about a small town "back East" (which was any state beyond Colorado's eastern borders, beginning with Nebraska and Kansas), they now had to learn to ride horses. And it was up to them to care for the horses, to saddle them, to catch them in the first place, and to get a bit into an often reluctant mouth.

There were other not-so-romantic aspects of homesteading. Amy Dickinson, who came with her parents in 1910 to an area east of Sterling, was stunned by the mosquitoes, "a size we had never seen or experienced," and the lack of trees. She remembers sitting down on the prairie some distance from the house and asking herself despairingly, "Oh, how can we get out of this place?"

But she never said anything to her family, nor did the others voice their doubts. "We were all in it together, and our complaints would just have added to the discouragement of the others."

There is evidence that the homesteaders did, in fact, paint a rosy picture to entice others to the West, and that those who responded, though shocked, were soon a part of the conspiracy and practiced the same arts on other friends and relatives.

Ida Watkin's homestead was on high ground several miles to the north of Merino. She found a job on a ranch to the south of the river and made a twelve-mile round trip almost every day because the homestead law required that the prospective land owner actually live on the claim. Ida was terrified by her horse, and the twelve miles were pure hell for her.

When she arrived safely each night, her relief was short-lived, for as darkness settled in, she listened to the howls of coyotes and gray wolves and the other mysterious sounds of the prairie, and she imagined many an attack. The morning sun brought little relief, for then she faced another struggle with the horse.

But there were compensations, and she became such a good rider that she won a silk dress in a pony race at the Fourth of July celebration. The editor of the *Merino Breeze* liked to watch the young couples and speculate about romances, anticipating engagements. It was no secret that Ida was wild about "the most handsome young man on the frontier," Ben Ladd, and though the *Breeze* had at times noted Ben's attentions to some other "pretty young lady" or a "musical girl," it was Ida whom he married in 1910. Life was no longer lonely.

Vesta Keen came to homestead in 1911, all the way from Spencer, West Virginia. She was alone, and that was exactly the way she wanted it. Vesta was part Cherokee, was thirty-three years old, and was tired of some of the niceties connected with women's lives in the East. She wanted to ride astride, and she had heard that some women in the West had long ago freed themselves from side saddles. Moreover, Colorado women had been

Ida Ladd in her wedding dress. *Courtesy, Birdie Ladd.*

voting for almost twenty years, and Vesta longed to express her opinions at the polls.

Vesta homesteaded in Washington County. She was a practical nurse, and right away, she found her services needed. And she found herself needed in another way, too. Before her first year in Colorado had ended, she had married Curtis Mollohan, who had several children, one of them older than Vesta.

Years later, after her husband died, she bought a 1600-acre ranch in the High Plains area to the north of the South Platte. Fifty-eight years old at that time, she ran her place and fixed fences, carrying posts on her saddle horse. "I had cattle, horses, hogs — anything that could make a noise — on my ranch," she said, "down to a guinea."

Vesta had only six months of formal schooling, but she had been taught at home by her mother, and she was an enthusiastic reader. And she was proud that she put a niece through college.

Other women had come to the plains many years earlier, and, like Ida, some found romance. Sarah Frost, the twenty-three-year-old daughter of an Englishman who had settled his family in Nebraska, was sent to eastern Colorado in 1893 by her brother to prove up a homestead for him. Soon bored by the long days alone on the homestead, Sarah took a job as a waitress in the Sterling Hotel. On the very first day at her new job, a big blond cowboy came into the dining room. He was James W. "Blondy" Arnold, and he had just helped to drive a herd of cattle north from Amarillo for Jared L. Brush, owner of the large JB Ranch. Blondy ordered his meal and studied the girl who served it. He liked what he saw and asked Sarah if she would sit down and eat with him. Since he was the only customer, Sarah couldn't see why not. She liked what she saw, too.

Blondy quickly lost interest in the trail herding business and decided that it was time to settle down. Three months later, he and Sarah were married, and they, too, homesteaded, three miles above Pawnee Pass in a little rock house which was unique among the usual soddies.

It was a tough time to start a marriage. Drought and the Panic of 1893 were starving many people out. Whole communities that had homesteaded during the 1880s gave up and returned to their home states. Coxey's Army came down the river on the way to the big protest in Washington, D.C. In 1895, only 114 people made homestead entries or received their final papers in the Sterling Land Office. But Sarah and Blondy eventually prospered on their farm. He was elected sheriff of Logan County and helped to found the first fire department. She operated a bakery for a time.

Other women had come to the plains even earlier, and they had not found the social life that so excited Ida Watkins. Moreover, they had faced some very real dangers. Elizabeth Gordon was twenty-eight years old in 1885 when she fulfilled a lifelong dream by coming to Weld County, which was then all of northeastern Colorado. She filed on a timber claim south of where Haxtun was later located on the high prairie east of the South Platte. Elizabeth did not have the nerve to live alone; fortunately, the only requirement for a timber claim at that time

The tiny shacks were a pitiful defense against the enormity of the prairie. *Courtesy, Marguerite Sherwin Donovan.*

was the planting of ten acres to trees. Elizabeth spent many back-breaking days of digging holes in the prairie and planting those trees. But her work was only beginning. By the time she had run water down little ditches from her well, the ground was baking again and the trees were drooping, and she had to start her shoveling and watering all over.

But she succeeded, and the next year she decided that if other women could live alone on a claim, so could she. She pre-empted 160 acres, which meant that she could buy the land for only $1.25 per acre if she built improvements and lived on the place for six months. Her sisters and their husbands, the B. F. and W. H. Moores, and a brother were also homesteading in the area, and they helped "Lizzie" to build a little eight-by-ten house with one door and one window. Lizzie wryly described the house as having modern built-ins: a cracker box over her bed for books and one over the table for dishes. The bed and table were planks, also built in, anchored to the floor and wall. Lizzie's only other furniture were a little stove, two small chairs, and a large Saratoga trunk.

The trunk was an important item because when Lizzie wedged it between the bed and the door, it gave her a feeling of security. And she put it there every night.

She didn't fear her neighbors, of course. Several were her

family, and the rest were good people. But the closest one was a mile and a half away, and it was the thought of strangers that frightened Lizzie, even though there were no automobiles or even roads at that time, and it was not likely that many strangers would be wandering through that remote area.

Nevertheless, Lizzie took precautions. She never lit her lamps at night, no matter how much she wanted to read. She did not open the window after dark, not even in the summer. She got fresh air by taking the lids off the stove and creating a reverse draft. This meant, of course, that she could not have a fire for cooking very late in the day. Lizzie also had a pistol which the men in the family taught her how to use.

One night as she lay in the bed, she heard footsteps approaching. Long days and nights alone had sharpened her hearing, and she knew that those boots out there did not belong to anyone whom she knew. There was something peculiar about the way they struck together. Lizzie lay in the bed, so paralyzed that she did not even reach for the revolver. The man knocked. Lizzie summoned up her voice and thought that she carried it off quite well. She directed him to the home of her brother-in-law, B. F. Moore, and the man departed. Lizzie felt that she had passed her first real test.

Later she learned that the man said, "I guess there must be a woman alone in that shanty northeast of here. Her voice sounded like she was scared to death."

Lizzie had other fears. Once, during the annual roundup, she saw thousands of cattle coming toward her house. She had heard of a steer running straight through one woman's soddy. She closed her door but felt certain that if the cattle should stampede, they might flatten her little shack. But even more frightening, a cowboy suddenly rode toward her place. She had heard some pretty terrible things about cowboys and what they might do to homesteaders, particularly female ones.

"My heart was in my mouth," Lizzie said. But the cowboy simply asked a question about the area, and he was very courteous.

Lizzie's greatest fright came from a different source. February 1887 was beautiful and mild, so mild that she was having some plowing done on her claim. She was getting ready to make proof.

People who live for any length of time on the prairie are suspicious of extremely good weather in the wintertime. They come to know that conditions can swing very suddenly from one extreme to the other. But Lizzie had no anxiety. She reveled in the prairie sunshine. She felt that spring was on the way. She thought that the Colorado plains certainly did have an "Italian climate," as some romanticist had proclaimed. Just before she shoved the trunk against the door that night, she noticed that there was only a pail or so of coal in the house. But she could get more tomorrow. Perhaps it would be some time before she would even need a fire.

She was awakened in the night by the sudden howling of the wind, and she was cold. She pulled the covers closer, but soon she felt something wet. The storm was blowing with such force that snow was coming through cracks that she did not know were in her house. The wind became stronger, relentless, beating against the little wood shanty with the greatest force she had ever experienced. She reminded herself of the earth that the men had banked around the house. Surely it could not blow down.

Cold began to eat into the room. She struggled out of bed and built a fire. Perhaps if she fed it slowly, the coal would last until morning. But as she started the flames, the wind whooshed down the pipe and sparks flew all over the room. Terrified, Lizzie ran to put them out. She closed the damper of the stove, smothered out the fire, and replaced the lid.

The awful thought came to her: "I could die. I may freeze to death."

Already her body shook uncontrollably. Her fingers were stiff and her toes aching. She dug into the trunk and brought out woolen socks, gloves, caps, sweaters, and coats. She pulled on layer after layer and put every quilt and coverlet on the bed. Her big winter coat she spread across the foot of the bed to try to warm her ice-cold feet. Gradually, her shivering stopped, and Lizzie began to realize that she probably could survive the storm, that if the house had not blown away by now, things could not get worse. When morning came, the sun would come out, as it always did in Colorado.

Once she had settled herself in the bed, her thoughts turned to her family. Then she remembered that her brother, a brother-in-law, and friends had taken a tent and gone some dozen miles away to work on the open prairie. How could they survive in a tent? The wind would surely blow it and them away.

Hours dragged by, and Lizzie could not sleep. She kept thinking that morning must come soon. She fixed her eyes on the window, praying for the first gray light to hit the panes. But morning did not come. And the wind blew. She thought of Indians circling frontier outposts two decades earlier, and she felt an identity with those people barricaded against danger. Outside, the wind circled her house. Around and around it swooped, and its wailing voice seemed to hurl threats at her, to mock her. She tried to sleep, to tell herself that there was no danger, that she could wait this out. But then her thoughts would return to her family. This threatening being screaming outside the house would have no trouble getting to them.

She memorized a song, "Rock Me to Sleep, Mother," but there was no one to rock her, and there was no sleep. After awhile her eyes ached with the weariness of the long hours. Her body turned stiff and sore, but she dreaded changing position to gain a little relief. Each time she rolled over, no matter how carefully, the cold settled in and she had to start all over creating a warm nest.

The hours dragged on. Finally the wind stopped blowing. But it was still dark, still cold, and she continued to lie in the bed and worry.

Then suddenly a faint shaft of sunlight came through the window and spread its thin finger across the room. She stared at it, stupefied for a moment, then rushed to open the curtains wide. But still only the tiny ray of sun pierced the blackness within. Lizzie rubbed the frosty inside of the window, then hurried to push open the front door. It would not budge.

Then she realized that morning had come but that she could not get out until the snow melted. She ran joyfully to the stove and built a fire. Surely her coal would last until the snow cleared from her door. The stove belched smoke back into the room, and Lizzie knew that her ordeal was not over. Snow no doubt covered the top of her house as well. Lizzie was entombed in the little shack.

But her gloom did not last long. Neighbors who had managed

to get out of their houses came to shovel the snow from Lizzie's door. When they finally opened it to the sparkling scene outside, Lizzie said, "That was the longest night I ever spent."

"What do you mean, night?" asked one of the men. "This has been going on for *two* nights and a day."

Later, word came that when the blizzard had first started, her family and friends out on the prairie had grabbed their collapsing tent and huddled beneath it, letting the wind create an igloo in which they survived.

Soon Lizzie went to the land office in Denver to make proof. An agent of the Lincoln Land Company was on hand, and no sooner had she completed her business than he made an offer to buy. Her claim was one of the quarter sections that the Burlington and Missouri Railroad wanted for a town site. In July 1887, Lizzie sold half of her homestead to the land company for the marvelous sum of $1,000. But when she observed that lots in the projected town of Holyoke were going for $1,400 each, Lizzie decided to hold on to her other eighty acres. Her canny business sense paid off. In September, she received $6,000 for the last half of her place.

Now the budding businesswoman decided to build a two-story hotel, the Gordon House, in Holyoke. It was operated by her sister and brother-in-law, the W. H. Moores, and was known for its "eats, tidyness, and good accommodations."

"No liquor was to be served," Lizzie decreed, as she observed that the brand new town already had nine saloons, and she boasted that her hotel served "only the better class."

W. L. Hays, deputy county surveyor, had an interesting story about the first hotel in Holyoke, which he said was under construction within a month after he had completed surveying the area in that year of 1887. But he called the hotel the Pennsylvania House, perhaps because Lizzie and her family were from Pennsylvania. And his account of the crowds of people in the hotel is evidence that perhaps it could not always be so discriminating as Lizzie liked.

Hays said that the crush of land seekers made it necessary to press the dining room into multiple use: an eating house by day, a dormitory at night. The "rooms" consisted of mattresses rowed along the walls. Under such circumstances, the clientele was not always the better class. Hays told of being kept awake by two drunks sharing a mattress. One accused the other of hogging the covers.

That one replied, "You have got all the mattress. I am lying on the floor without a damned thing under me but my ear."

While Lizzie was in Denver making proof on her claim, she filed to homestead another 160 acres, about two miles southwest of where the new town was to be. But a young man heard of her intentions. When she returned to the prairie, she discovered that he had rushed to put up a shack, saying that he had prior rights because of possession. He planned to contest her right. Lizzie was not one to give in easily. The man's house was on the east side of the claim. She put up her shanty on the west side but in sight of his place so that she could keep an eye on him.

Soon Holyoke was flourishing with three banks, the nine saloons, Lizzie's hotel, and the railroad. A road developed west from the town, connecting with Sterling on the South Platte River. And Lizzie faced new anxieties, for her house was very close to this road.

"One beautiful moonlight night," Lizzie told, "I heard a racket that I could not understand." She looked out her east window and could see a lot of men around the young man's shanty. "I supposed they were drunks and pilferers and would soon be at my place."

She brought out her pistol, loaded it, and prepared to defend herself. But as the commotion increased, she lost her nerve, slipped out of the house, and ran through the dark to a neighbor's house.

"This was another time I crossed the bridge before I got to it," Lizzie said. "A lot of the good men of the neighborhood had decided this young man was only pretending to live on the claim, and to prove it, they turned his shack over, and as there was no floor inside, the furnishings were exposed outside."

Next morning, it was evident to all who indulged their curiosity by riding past the scene that there was only a bed in the house. The young man was actually living with his parents on an adjoining claim. When the dispute was tried in court, there were plenty to testify about what they had seen when the house was

16

upended, and Lizzie won the case.

But she chastised herself severely when she thought of her preparations to use the pistol. "I judged the wrong parties, you see. It was my friends making the disturbance."

Some women homesteaders were not fortunate enough to have relatives and friends nearby to help them. A Mrs. Townsend was a destitute widow when she came to the South Platte in 1903 and took out a claim midway between Iliff and Sterling. Like most of the newcomers, she could not afford to bring lumber from the mountains for a dwelling. (At that time, only one frame house, that of Christie Merrell, stood along the twelve- to fifteen-mile stretch of road.) Mrs. Townsend did not have the strength to cut or lift the three-foot-long sod "bricks" to build a soddy, as most of the homesteaders did.

But she dug dirt out of a sand hill bluff, about eight to ten feet high, and cleared a tiny six-by-eight-foot room. She wedged poles across the top to make a roof that slanted down over the front of the dugout, and she built a front wall and door with scraps of wood and junk. Grass and dirt piled on top kept out the worst weather, but rain always leaked into the little shelter, and dirt constantly sifted down. Perhaps that didn't matter, for the floor and walls were also dirt. In that hole in the ground, she lived like a human prairie dog.

She was brave and resourceful, but her story has a sad ending. The Bravo Ditch, which she had counted on for irrigating water, could not supply the higher ground on which her claim was located. She was unable to survive on the place and finally rented it to another woman alone, Christie Merrell, who used it for pasture.

Catherine Lingelbach, who had come to the United States from Germany when she was seventeen, had more help than most women without a husband. She and twelve of her fourteen children, the youngest only a year old, homesteaded in the Pawnee Buttes area in the 1880s. She left her husband and two married daughters behind in Ohio. The husband was a heavy drinker, and Catherine—after fourteen children!—had finally had enough.

Catherine cooked at the depot house in Grover, the only station along the little Burlington railroad that ran from Sterling to

Catherine Lingelbach:
there was nothing
that she couldn't do.
*Courtesy, Opal Lingel-
bach Houghton.*

Cheyenne. After she homesteaded, she and her sons captured
wild horses in a box canyon. A daughter-in-law told that
Catherine expected all of her sons' wives to work at anything
that she did—and there was nothing that Catherine couldn't do.

Catherine's neighbor, several miles southeast, was married
only a short time and spent the rest of her life alone on her homestead. Martha Sabrowsky Hallett once said that civilization
"brings hurt with every joy. I have yet to hear a more comforting
sound than horses chewing hay."

In 1893, when Martha was fourteen, she took part in the
Oklahoma land rush with her Prussian father. In 1906, she
claimed the Colorado homestead near a natural spring and lived
alone in a two-room dugout. From her front door, she could
look 4.8 miles east to the nearest neighbor. She could look west
to the Buttes and the Rocky Mountains.

In 1916, Martha took a husband, an American soldier named
John Hallett. The marriage lasted only a week or so. One day
as they worked on a fence, something that he did hit her wrong.
According to neighbors, she shot him in the leg, and he departed
forever.

18

Martha continued to live alone, milking cows and shipping cream on the little *Prairie Dog Special* railroad. Tony Fogale, who worked with her for the Harris Ranching Company, said that she was as good a rider and horse breaker as any man.

As Martha aged, she resisted all efforts to get her to move — "What would I do in town?" — and worked her cattle until she was seventy-nine. When she was eighty, she said:

> Teddy Roosevelt gave me this original five-acre homestead where my house sets . . . Some people would like to put me in a home but. . . . I think a person's got a right to live and die right where he pleases, as long as he earns the right.

Martha had earned the right, and she died on her homestead.

Hattie Belle Graves Rothwell also homesteaded without a husband. In 1910, she helped her fifteen-year-old son claim land at Dearfield, the colony for black people established near Masters on the South Platte River.

Hattie's parents, who had been slaves, were half white. She had married Henry Rothwell, a Cherokee Indian, in Kansas City and had moved with him to Denver about 1889. Rothwell worked in construction, helping to build the Brown Palace Hotel, the original Denver General Hospital, and the Grant Smelter in Globeville. But the marriage broke up when he began to drink and became abusive. Hattie took in washing, and she saved her money. She was among the few who benefited from the Panic of 1893. The rich English people in the Montclair area lost everything, and Hattie was smart and invested some of her savings in lots that sold for the taxes due, usually only about five dollars each.

She was a determined woman. In 1912, when an effort was made to take her property away from her, she went to court to prove that she owned the lots and that she had faithfully paid her taxes. When Denver water lines were extended through the area and she was not allowed to hook on, she drilled a new well on her property. But then the city accused her of bringing up contaminated water. Once again Hattie's spunk came to the surface. She took a sample from her well to an independent tester, who pronounced it purer than "Deep Rock," and the Denver Water Department backed off. This second effort to push her out of Montclair also failed.

"Own the ground, own the ground," she always said. So it was only natural that when her son Charlie began to talk of homesteading, she investigated thoroughly. She talked to O. T. Jackson, who was starting the colony for black people out to the northeast of Denver. And, characteristically, she was not afraid to invest in the venture. She borrowed five hundred dollars on the Denver house and bought horses at the Elephant Corral and chickens. She had two cows, one of them given to her by an employer. She bought secondhand lumber. She was never one to go into a situation unprepared.

She and Charlie, with all their animals and supplies, made the trip to Dearfield on the "immigrant train," as it was called. By the time they arrived in Masters, however, the worst blizzard of the winter was raging. The section boss of the railroad treated the Rothwells as the railroad did all immigrants, with complete cooperation. He brought a heater, fuel, food, and hay and allowed the mother and son to stay in the boxcar for three weeks until the ground cleared.

Hattie and Charlie built their one-room house, which was nine and one-half by twelve feet, in one day. The ground was dry land at first, and the prospects did not look too good. Then, when work began on Empire Reservoir, just above their claim, Hattie discovered some of the crew tearing down the fence that she and Charlie had laboriously erected. The men evidently intended for part of the reservoir to be on the Rothwells' property. Charlie was as determined as his mother. He roped the surveyor's instrument and dragged it through tall sagebrush and "tore it all to hell."

The reservoir was a blessing, however. Seepage water created two lakes on the homestead, and they were able to irrigate. Charlie farmed and Hattie raised turkeys and guineas, which, in her usual self-reliant manner, she marketed in Denver.

And they had a good time. Many black people settled Dearfield, and as in most homestead communities, the settlers maintained an active and creative social life. Hattie got along with most of the whites as well.

But making a living on 160 acres was never easy, and Hattie helped by doing housework for white families in the area. Later she tried to work in beet and onion fields but got pneumonia and had to return to Denver in 1912. When Charlie was drafted for World War I, Hattie went back to the homestead to complete the proving up of a tree claim on which he had filed. By that time, he had accumulated forty milk cows, nine horses, and about forty-five hogs. But before he returned from service, the Great Depression had already begun on the farms, and Hattie had been forced to sell most of the cows for next to nothing.

Dearfield, like many other homestead areas, witnessed a general exodus during the following years of drought and depression. It was a repeat of the tragic 1890s. Eventually, all of the black people lost their land at Dearfield.

All but Hattie and Charlie. Years after Hattie was gone, Charlie still owned some of their land.

"Own the ground," Hattie always advised. "Own the ground."

The oldest woman homesteader was said to have been Emily G. Warner. She proved up in 1914 two days before she became eighty-nine. She lived on her homestead in northern Colorado until her death at 100.

And then there was Minnie Palmer. She came alone in 1887 from Manhattan, Kansas, to homestead on Frenchman's Creek in the newly created Logan County, which at that time included all the northeastern corner of the state. She built a nice little frame house, dug a well, planted trees, and fenced about ten acres. It was back-breaking work, and Minnie must have felt proud of herself. By that time, it was winter, and since the requirement on her claim was only six months of residency per year, she went to Denver for several months to work and earn money before planting time in the spring.

When Minnie returned to the homestead, she was shocked to find a big blond young man living in her house. He spoke mostly German, but he understood her message—that it was her house, that she had built it, and that he must get out. However, the German had no intention of getting out. He had homesteaded the land himself six weeks before, he claimed.

"By shimminie," he told Minnie, "I vill hold dot land."

Arguments did not work, so Minnie turned on the charm. Looking helpless, she asked, "Well, could I just look in my trunk for something I need?"

The German had won. He could afford to be magnanimous.

"Of course. Of course," he said.

Minnie hurried inside before he could change his mind, and just as he started to follow her, she slammed the door in his face and locked it. He raced around to the window, pushed it up, and was lifting one leg over the sill when Minnie found the "something" hidden in her trunk. It was a six-shooter, and the surprised imposter took a slug in his left shoulder. Before he could hit the ground, a second bullet caught him in the hip, and as he tried to get away, a third one gave him a new part in his hair.

It was evident that this woman meant business, and she had three more bullets. The German begged for mercy. It was then Minnie's turn to be generous. She bound his wounds, which were not critical, dragged him into her wagon, and hauled him to a neighbor's house, three miles away, where he recovered.

Word of Minnie Palmer's successful defense spread far, and the *Denver Republican* expressed a sentiment that seemed to be general: "We would like to see a thousand Minnie Palmers on as many claims in Logan County."

In a country with so much free land available, the frequency of conflicts over claims was astonishing, and chivalry toward women did not seem an inhibiting factor. The Elmer Sheaffers homesteaded a piece of ground that interfered with the expansion plans of a cattleman named Sam Rice. Stories circulated regularly about shoot-outs between Mrs. Sheaffer and Rice's cowboys. Finally, in a trial, it was alleged that she hid in the hayloft of her barn and ambushed one of Rice's men. Mrs. Sheaffer had the sympathy of most people.

Amy Dickinson filed for a claim when the government eased requirements on homesteading of sand hill rangeland. A 1909 law allowed 320 acres of semiarid land per person, and an additional 320 acres were allowed by a 1916 law. One object was to encourage the production of cattle, which was impossible on the smaller plots of 160 acres. Unlike previous dryland homesteading, these were not tree claims, nor did they require the running of water over the land, as in desert claims. They were enthusiastically sought by settlers who realized that their former free range would soon disappear. Moreover, the outbreak of World War I soon created such a demand for wheat that even marginal land looked good to new arrivals.

Amy began her adventure to help her family secure some of the pasture on which they depended for their cattle herd. She went early — but not early enough — to file her claim. A man was waiting ahead of her for the land office in Sterling to open, and he wanted the same acreage. He leaned arrogantly against the door, his arms folded across his chest, and stared grimly at her. When the clerk inside suddenly opened the door, the man sprawled flat on the floor. Amy really had the last laugh when it developed that his papers were not in order. Hers were, and her claim was approved.

At the same time, Amy's younger sister also filed on 320 acres, but later she was married and did not want to continue homesteading. Under the 1916 law, Amy could take up her sister's relinquishment. But again she was challenged. All during her homesteading days, she also taught school in Sterling, and it was not always possible to make the long trip back and forth, even after her family acquired a Ford Model T. Sometimes, when the weather was bad, Amy stayed in Sterling or at her family's home on the north side of the South Platte. But she regularly managed to ford the river, either driving a team or riding horseback. Nevertheless, when time came to prove up, a neighboring man challenged her as not a bona fide resident on the homestead. But the Sterling Land Office decided in favor of the young woman because she used the land for herself, with her own herd of cattle grazing on it.

The vast pasture land south of Fort Morgan and Brush was also opened to homesteaders by the 1910 law. In an effort to help her father establish a ranch, Lillian Schulz claimed a homestead near the new community of Adena, and she soon succeeded the first teacher, Lura Groves.

Most of the women homesteaders proved up and became the owners of at least 160 acres, but when they faced the work involved in farming that 160 acres, perhaps they echoed the rueful sentiments of many a man:

"Maybe the land possessed us."

Chapter II

WINNING THE WEST
WITH A MCGUFFEY READER

That great civilizing vanguard—women teachers—was a part of the settlement of the plains. Quite often, the school marms became homesteaders as well; or conversely, women homesteaders were urged into the classroom. One of those was Kate Lester. Her partner in the 1913 venture, Eleanor Hartnett, stayed on the claim northwest of Padroni to slop the hogs, milk the cows, and even drive a four-horse team. Kate provided cash by teaching at the nearby Valentine School. She later taught at Peetz and Sterling and was elected Logan County superintendent of education.

Another county superintendent was Flora Allison. A graduate of Grinnell College (then Iowa College), she was a veteran of twenty years in the classroom when, in 1911, she decided to do something different and go west to homestead. Flora was soon teaching again. Her schools included Peetz, Padroni, Two Buttes, and Elder, and she was superintendent of schools of Logan and Baca counties.

Beulah and Onetah Kringle learned about homesteading while visiting a ranch near Bennett. Instead of returning to Iowa, they filed in 1907 on claims in the remote Pawnee Buttes area near the Wyoming border. Onetah then taught at Grover, and Beulah started the first school at Sligo. Both of these tiny communities sat alongside the *Prairie Dog Special.* Running from Cheyenne to Sterling in the morning and the other way in the afternoon, the little train provided a link for the girls between the vast open country and the rest of the world.

College degrees were not necessarily important for early prairie teachers. In fact, they were rare. Sometimes a teacher had not even finished high school. If a woman — or even a quite young girl — could pass the teaching test, she could take over a one-room school. Alice Dawson, a teacher in Las Animas, tells that her mother taught school, married, bore twelve children, and only afterwards attended college. Occasionally, even passing the test was not required. A school was extremely important to a new community trying to establish itself, and sometimes what mattered most was simply keeping the school open.

Certificates were based on the number of years of experience and schooling. A "third" was the lowest. A "first" assured a position and a higher salary and one of the better schools — in a town! Therefore, young women flocked to Greeley in the summer to take courses at the teachers' college.

The real pioneers taught in sod huts. In the early 1870s, Mrs. Rasmus Nelson of Buffalo was so dedicated to the cause of education that she donated part of her already cramped soddy for a school. Emma Eubanks taught at South Platte in 1876 at old Fort Wicked, on the trail to Denver, and a couple of years later, Mary Isom was teacher at the former American Ranche Stage Station.

Carrie Ayres was only fifteen in 1875 when she accompanied her mother to homestead in old Sterling and opened the first school there. She had twenty pupils, several of them older than she. Her salary was twenty-five dollars a month. Rent for the fourteen-by-sixteen-foot soddy with dirt floors amounted to ten dollars for the entire term of ninety-six days. Add thirty-eight dollars for furniture and supplies, and the total cost of Carrie's school that first year came to $158.75. Budget strain was avoided by each pupil bringing his own seat.

In 1881, the settlers moved their town site to New Sterling, three miles distant on the Union Pacific Railroad. Carrie and her pupils settled into the luxury of a frame building on Main Street. But one day, a prairie wind lifted the building from its foundation and blew down the chimney. School resumed in a

Willa Clanton's bed was in the wall of the parlor.

dugout until an airworthy structure could be built.

The pretty Carrie was extremely popular, and cowboys came from miles away to school functions. Even spelling bees attracted a standing-room-only crowd. A few years later, Carrie wed the much respected young tenderfoot doctor from Harvard, J. N. Hall. It was in her name that he established the foundation that provides funds for state historical markers.

Another early teacher, Willa Clanton, finished her high school credits in midterm 1898 and went out to a school on Cedar Creek. Her pupils did their sums on little slates. Each child was equipped with a rag and a bowl of water for erasing. Willa lived with the Diffendarfer family and rode to school on a horse with their little boy perched behind her. The next year, when she taught at the Burdette School in Washington County, she traveled in a little more style. The young son of the George Stockhams, where she boarded, drove the teacher to school in a wagon. But at night,

Willa shared a bed with the little daughter of the family. More-over, the bed let down from the wall of the parlor.

Willa taught music in Denver schools until she was eighty years old and then substituted until age eighty-five. An expert in cap-turing the interest of young people, she was designated special assistant in music and was sent as a troubleshooter wherever the music program was in difficulty. Before the tiny teacher's long career was completed, she had served in almost every school in the city, from first grade through high school.

Today, Willa Clanton holds what must be a unique position in the Columbine State's history: she was born in a sod hut near South Platte in 1877, one year after Colorado became a state. They have shared over a century together. Now in her 105th year, Willa lives alone in Denver and cares for herself. She dresses stylishly, still has her own teeth ("My dentist says there is no money in my mouth"), and wears glasses only to read. She is a delight to all who know her.

Willa is rather in awe of her own age. Once she remarked, "Can you believe I'm over a hundred years old? My gosh! Isn't that something?"

It is something, especially when a centenarian is as vibrant, independent, and charming as Willa Clanton. Entertaining in her pretty living room one day, Willa lifted her expressive brows and said, "I attribute my long life to my rewarding years of teach-ing and associating with young people. They helped me to keep a youthful outlook. It is magnificent to grow old if one keeps young."

And she wouldn't change anything—not even sharing the bed in the parlor with a little girl when she taught at that long-ago prairie school.

Conditions were almost as primitive for young women who taught on the plains many years after Willa's experience. Teacher Grace Dawson wrote of her friend Rhoda who got a school at Lone Star in Washington County during the 1930s depression. The community was so remote that Rhoda journeyed there on a horse. Like Willa, she had a landlord's child, Alfie, riding "rum-ble seat" to school on her horse every morning.

Rhoda considered herself lucky to get a job in the middle of a depression year. Some schools had run out of money and had been forced to close. But after Rhoda's first night of almost freezing in a lean-to bedroom where the wind blew freely through the walls, she was not so sure of her luck. Her solution was to bring her featherbed from home, and when she sank into the luxurious folds of that mattress, she was able to stay snugly warm. But next morning, her landlady asked, "You know, Alfie complains about being cold all the time. Would you mind his coming in with you, just until the weather warms up?"

"It's a good thing I like children," thought Rhoda. For now she had seven-year-old Alfie not only riding behind her every day on the horse but snuggled up in her bed as well.

Edith Brummer, whose 1929 teaching job was thirty miles east of Deer Trail in Adams County, did not have to sleep in the lean-to. Her bed was a couch in the main room of the house, and it was next to the stove. But snow still came through the walls and piled on her covers. In the middle of one of her first nights in the house, Edith was blasted out of a sound sleep by loud and terrifying reports. The family had to convince her that she had not been shot, simply that some of the bottles of home brew, stored on shelves near her bed, had exploded. In time, Edith could sleep through the explosions as calmly as the family did.

The first day of school brought panic when a nest of rattlesnakes was discovered under the building. But Edith's seven young pupils were calm and killed the rattlers in a matter-of-fact way.

Flora Allison slept with a revolver under her pillow, but it failed to shoot on the one stressful occasion when she needed it — the sunny day that she heard a noise at the door and discovered three large rattlers coiled there.

Both women fared better than Mary Johnson, who taught in the Roberts district on Cedar Creek in 1901. One day Mary and her sister Minnie, who was visiting her, went out on the prairie to pick up cow chips for the school stove (one of the many extracurricular duties of teachers in those days). The girls laughed and talked as they absentmindedly picked up the dried chips. Suddenly, too late, Mary heard a chilling buzz, and a rattlesnake, coiled under a sagebrush, struck her on the hand. She screamed, and before she could move, he had bitten her again.

Mary Johnson, victim of a hazard peculiar to prairie schools. *Courtesy, William H. Olson, nephew.*

Minnie managed to get Mary into the schoolhouse and then rode over the prairie to the nearest neighbor, Claude Roberts, who sent whiskey with the prescription to administer it freely while he made a dash on horseback to Sterling miles away. By the time Dr. L. E. Stanton arrived, Mary's hand and arm were badly swollen, and, unaccustomed as she was to liquor, her head was in doubtful condition as well.

Mary's large and loving family hitched up their wagon and hurried to her. They found her in grave danger, and as the hours went by, all hope was given up. Then, suddenly, after a few days, the healthy young woman began to rally, and after a time, she recovered.

Prairie boys and girls, accustomed to rattlesnakes, often had little fear of them. About 1885, when Maud Clark taught at Platteville, south of Greeley, her forty dollars a month hardly seemed adequate for some of the extracurricular activities. The boys in the class, several of them older and taller than neat little Maud, brought a snake to school with the request that the teacher preserve it in alcohol. Maud took the snake by the string which the boys had tied about its "neck" and coiled it on her desk. Then, to the disappointment of the class, she calmly proceeded with the lesson.

But a few minutes later, the boys and girls got more excitement than they had bargained for. When Maud saw her pupils' eyes bug out in the direction of her desk, she looked around to discover that the snake had revived and was crawling toward her. Her instinct was to scream and head for the far horizon. But Maud was being tested. With a bravery that she didn't know she had, the little teacher picked up a ruler and pulled the string to her. As soon as she tightened the noose, the snake passed out again. Maud carried it at arm's length down two flights of steps, put it outside, then walked into the classroom, completely in charge. She found that her "roughneck" pupils had not moved, that they were more frightened than she was. Maud ordered the boy who had brought the snake to kill it.

And so did one little school marm gain control of her class.

The teachers were tested in many ways. Simply getting to school was a challenge. Etta Shannon walked three miles every day to her classes north of Proctor. She had had good training, however. When her family had first homesteaded in 1887 on the table land north of Padroni, she and her sisters and brother

Etta Shannon graduated in a class of five and then taught in a prairie school on a terrain as trackless as the ocean. Members of her class, back row: John and Pearl Henderson; seated: May Perkins, John McClure, and Etta. *Courtesy, Overland Trail Museum.*

had to walk five miles each morning to a little ten-by-twelve school and, of course, make the return trip in the afternoon. The route was across open prairie. There were no landmarks at all, no roads, fences, or railroads. They might as well have tried to make their way across an ocean. But their father plowed a five-mile furrow that they followed to avoid getting lost.

When Etta started teaching, she was more familiar with the subtleties of plains topography and made her way without a guiding furrow "across unfenced prairies where range cattle roamed."

"I started my own fires," she told, "carried coal, kindling, and did janitor work in general. At night I slept in the same room with the family where I boarded."

But Etta was luckier than her sister Mattie, whose first teaching job was at Willard. Mattie walked seventeen miles to Sterling, carrying her telescope (as suitcases were called in those days). Transportation for the remaining fifteen or so miles to Willard was provided by the school board.

Living conditions were always a problem. Some of the teachers slept in caves dug into hills near their schools. In 1933 to 1934, when Maude Linstrom taught at Box Elder School in eastern Adams County, she and the other teacher lived in the coal room attached to the school. The walls had so many cracks that the young women nailed cardboard over them to try to shut out the icy blasts. At night, they routinely wore all their heavy clothing to bed.

Helen Fuller, who taught that same year at a one-room school eighteen miles east of Brighton, told that for a dollar a day, she boarded and roomed with a very fine family, but she noted, "indoor plumbing was not one of the accommodations," and since the outhouse had large cracks, "it was sometimes necessary to brush off the snow before the facilities could be used."

Edith Brummer said that the worst thing about having a bed in the keeping room of a house was the lack of privacy, which was afforded appropriately by the outdoor privy. When the young teachers visited each other, they carried on their conversations out in the toilet.

"Our families must have sometimes wondered about the seriousness of our stomach disorders."

Sometimes the adventures were more intense. Grace Benson

was only eighteen in 1910 when she came with her homesteading parents to the Graylin community. One of her sisters, Ruth, taught in the sod schoolhouse built on the parents' claim. Grace had to look for a job elsewhere. She got one near Peetz, high on the table land above Chimney Canyons.

She found the country a wide-open, mysterious place, so different from her native Wisconsin that it was intriguing. But it was also frightening. At night, she heard the howl of the gray wolves and felt fortunate to be safe in the Kraxburger home where she boarded. Sometimes as she walked to school, she saw the wolves slinking along in the distance and wondered what she would do if they ever came close. Most of the time, she was happy to make the trip in a buggy with the young son of the family.

She heard stories, and it was difficult to separate legend from fact. Again and again, people said to her, "Have you ever seen the woman in the white dress walking along the rim of Chimney Canyon?" Grace tried to tell herself that this was only a ghost story, but as she heard mysterious accounts of the solitary figure wandering, distraught, on the edge of the high country, she felt a strange unease.

Others talked about Al Cochran, who had been sent away to prison for murdering a cowboy. The chatter did not alarm Grace until one day the students came to school in high excitement with the news that Al Cochran was out of prison. Someone pointed out his buggy racing along the prairie road. But after a time, the gossip died down, and the community began to accept Al Cochran's presence. Grace put him out of her mind. She did not often let worries darken her days. But sometimes, as she taught her pupils, a cloud of dust would appear in the distance, and the children would watch the rapid approach of a buggy, and finally one of them would say, "Here comes Al Cochran."

As the man neared the school, he would slow his horse and stare intently toward the little building.

Then one afternoon, when the children departed for home, Grace remained to do some work for the next day's lessons. Busy with her studies, she did not notice the cloud of dust far up the road. At first, she did not hear the rapid approach of the buggy. When she looked out the window, a wave of fear swept over her. He was close and already beginning to slow down. She pressed up against the wall, hoping that he would not see her, but she felt the burning eyes staring at the window, and she heard the voice call to the horse, "Whoa."

The school was one room. The door and window both opened to the south. Outside, the prairie stretched in every direction, treeless, open, immense. No place to hide. Only in Chimney Canyons, miles away. The image of the woman in white flashed through Grace's mind.

Terrified, she saw him get out of the buggy, saw him tie up the horse, waited while he came to the door. He was a rough-looking man. He would have been frightening even if she had never heard the stories. He stared at her with that intent look, and Grace stared back. Then slowly, a smile spread over his face.

"All alone, ain't you?" he said. He looked around. "Kids all gone home." His eyes came back to Grace, who had not moved. He started toward her.

She had lived a protected life, surrounded by a loving family and friends. Their days had centered on the Methodist Church. Never before in her eighteen years had she been really frightened. But now, here she was alone in this room with a convicted murderer, and the nearest of her new friends was miles away. Nothing in her life had prepared her for defending herself.

He came another step or two, the smile still on his face, the smile the most frightening thing about him, and his eyes moved over her slim young body. Grace could only think, "I have on a white dress."

He was almost to her, and still she could not move. Terror caught in her throat. Her mouth opened. She wanted to scream. The great choking fear in her throat pushed tears to her eyes, but no sound came from her.

And then beyond him, she saw something. He read it in her eyes, and he turned. Another cloud of dust was on the road, this one whipped up by a buggy going faster than Grace had ever seen before. The horse swerved into the yard, and the driver was out of the buggy before it stopped.

"I've come to take you home, teacher," the boy said.

He was only a young fellow. He could no more prevail against Al Cochran than she could, but he stared at the man as if he were capable of anything. And Al Cochran muttered something and stepped around them and went out to his buggy.

The boy had seen Al Cochran drive by and had raced to his teacher's rescue. Grace never did know whether the danger was real that day. She never did know what was behind the story of the woman in white. Perhaps it was simply someone's imagination, turning the scream of a lynx cat, which sounded like a terrified woman, into a haunting story.

But whenever Grace saw a wolf or heard a cry in the night, or when she thought of Al Cochran coming into her school that day, she had a fleeting image of herself as the woman in white, stumbling along the rim of Chimney Canyon, trying to escape the terrors of that big new country.

A person wonders why the young women subjected themselves to such difficult conditions. The answer was that the girls felt lucky to have a job at all, especially during the severe depressions. Sometimes, even when they had teaching positions, districts would run out of money, and checks could not be cashed.

They were not alone, for obviously the people with whom they lived and whose children they taught were experiencing the hard times. Teresa Lee, who taught at La Junta during the 1930s, said that some children could not come to school because they had no clothes, especially shoes. In an earlier crisis, up at Hereford near the Wyoming border, the daughters of Mr. and Mrs. James Newton Vertz took turns wearing the one good dress to school. When a cow wandered up to the homestead one evening, Mrs. Vertz looked upon her arrival as a gift from God and milked the visitor.

The young teachers helped to collect shoes and other necessities in their home communities and donated them to the children. Catherine Byrne Hume, who taught at Padroni in 1929, had a weekly "If it fits, it's yours" party in the classroom. Donations were brought from Sterling, and the local families contributed items outgrown by their own children.

Catherine also began a Soup Bar. Noticing that some of the children had only a couple of cold biscuits or "rubbery pancakes" for lunch, she went down to the local telephone switchboard and asked the operator to call everyone at once. When all the receivers had been picked up, she told the parents that if they would be willing to take turns sending vegetables or whatever they could spare, she would prepare a soup pot each day. She talked a store into giving her broken crackers.

During the last period each day, the older boys and girls peeled and diced potatoes, carrots, parsnips, and other offerings. Next morning, when Catherine arrived at school, the custodian already had big canning kettles with boiling water on the stove, ready for her to start the soup of the day. (Catherine was one of the few teachers who did not have to build her own fires, but she gladly took on the job of cook.)

When hungry, dirty people came through Sterling during the 1930s, principal Myrtle Pantall began an unusual service at Lincoln School. She installed a bathtub in the basement. Many a time she had to cut the clothes off a child. Then she bathed him and completed the enrollment process with a good meal. She collected food, clothing, and hundreds of pairs of shoes for the unfortunate victims of the depression.

Nadine McCormick Chapman went even further. While teaching in Illinois her first year after college, Nadine adopted a six-year-old girl from an orphanage. It was, of course, almost unknown for a single woman to be granted custody of a child. A few years later, Nadine came to La Junta and married the sheriff, who had been a childhood friend. He was a widower, and she assumed care of his four children. Then, in 1948, when she was sixty years old, she adopted a little boy.

One example of women doing good deeds where they happened to be is that of Deborah McNary, widow of a doctor, who homesteaded with her son Frank northeast of Sugar City in Crowley County. She and a Lawrence family pooled their supply of books and established a little library from which people throughout the drylands of eastern Colorado could borrow.

Beryl Foster, teaching in rural Weld County in 1933 and 1934, found that the school was lucky to stay open and that library books were counted as frills and were very low on the priority list. One day as Beryl walked to school, she watched the beet trucks lumbering along the road to the dump, swaying with their top-heavy loads. Invariably, when the trucks hit a chuckhole or rounded a curve, some of the beets toppled off. And Beryl got an idea. Why couldn't the children pick up those lost beets, which

35

would go to waste anyway, and sell them to the sugar company?

The pupils entered the project with enthusiasm. Those riding horseback to school brought along tow sacks to fill, and those walking carried as many beets as they could. The children fortunate enough to be driven to school were able to deposit dozens of beets every morning. And sometimes, the walkers or horseback riders made several trips to bring in all that they had piled along the way.

At the end of the harvest, one of the parents hauled the beets to the dump, and the school received a check that paid for a "considerable number of exciting and interesting books." Best of all, the children, who had worked for the money, appreciated the books far more than if they had just magically appeared.

Some of those beet trucks were used as school buses during the 1930s depression. Clella Rieke, who attended Padroni School, recalled that the kids would be so cold upon arrival that the waiting teachers would grab them and start rubbing their hands. Even the trucks were an improvement. In earlier days, children had been transported to some schools in open wagons.

One imaginative young woman, Violet Du Bois, who was fourth and fifth grade teacher at Padroni, turned even a dust storm into a positive situation. "See," she said, "you don't have to go outside in the cold and wind to play." Under her leadership, the kids organized marble tournaments in the sand that piled on the floors of the school.

Bertha Wedemeyer Boomer taught at Grover in 1893. When she built a fire after a blizzard, water began to drip through the ceiling. She found that the attic was blown full of snow, and she and the children spent the remainder of the day hauling it out.

Bertha was only a teenager, and she cried herself to sleep many nights. One day she witnessed a tragedy that she never forgot. A student, Peter Nelson, casually wound his horse's hackamore about his wrist as he stood talking to other children. A sudden gust of wind blew his slicker into the air and frightened the horse into a run. The boy was dragged to death.

The young teachers found that humor was their best weapon against hard times. Edith Brummer told one of the stories that made the rounds: a mother, anxious to have a good dinner when teacher came to visit, put her bread dough under the warmth

Fae Stanley (Oram).
One serving of prairie
dog stew was enough.
*Courtesy, Auriel Oram
Sandstead, daughter.*

of bed covers so that it would rise well.

Fae Stanley (Oram) did not relish rabbit and jackrabbit sausage which many Buttes people served the visiting teacher during the depression, but she ate it. There came a day when she was snowed in with a family and had her first serving of prairie dog stew. It was the main course, and Fae ate it in the interest of politeness and a new experience. However, the one experience was enough to satisfy her curiosity.

The Rhoda of Grace Dawson's story laughed with friends about young Alfie sharing her bed, and she told how the family asked if she'd mind doing chores while they went away on a trip. For two weeks, Rhoda fed the hogs and milked the cows, hoping that her cooperation would gain a good recommendation for her next teaching job. Sure enough, the recommendation was written, but a board member in the new community told Rhoda that she had been hired despite the letter.

"All he said," the man told her, "was that he didn't know much about your teaching, but you sure could milk cows."

Edith Stout, who taught in southeastern Colorado, lived in the only bedroom of a three-room house owned by a young couple and their two little children. The wife had come from New York City and was well educated and talented, but she had never cooked, and Edith said that not once did the woman prepare a meal without burning something. But the young wife had the bigness to provide for her boarder what she no doubt would have liked for herself. Every morning, before Edith arose, the fires were started in all three rooms, and every morning, coffee was served to Edith in the luxury of her bed.

The young women were included in all dances and social events, and they were popular. The girls had a good time, espe-

Left: Living conditions were tough on the prairie . . . and (below) privacy nonexistent in the little houses. *From Auriel Sandstead Collection.*

But the school marms had fun.

Lulu Belle Rand and a
beau.

Harvest Festival Days
. . . and a horse race
at Keota. From *Auriel
Sandstead Collection*.

Left: Fae Oram and her horse. Right: Lonnie Pippin riding a different kind of horse. *Courtesy, Lulu Belle Propst.*

cially after they learned to ignore an occasional whiff of manure from a cowboy's boots. Edith Brummer told that some cowboys had actually acquired cars, and the girls were always delighted to accept a ride home. The pleasure of a fairly warm Ford made even the inevitable "wrestling match" with the cowboy worthwhile.

When the cowboys observed that homesick Edith always went out to meet the mailman on his twice-a-week rounds, they filled out all the magazine coupons in her name, and for years, Edith received free samples of cattle and sheep medicine.

Not all the teachers got along so well with the community. Louise Hagen had the town of Sterling buzzing in 1907 when she resigned from the high school faculty and went home to Boulder after friction with the school board. But she later returned to Sterling and became an institution, teaching there for half a century. One of the schools was later named for her.

Nor did the pupils always show proper respect. Once after Flora Allison sang in a mixed quartet, a little girl said, "I was at church yesterday and heard you sing."

Pleased, Flora answered, "You were?" and waited for the child's comment.

"Yes," the little girl continued, "You were the one who screeched so."

An incredible number of schools were established at various times on the plains of eastern Colorado. The first at Akron in Washington County was started in 1882 with Hattie Irwin as teacher. Mary Pratt began a school in Yuma in 1885. Like many an unmarried woman, Mary had helped out in first one relative's home and then another. But she found time to speak on women's rights, and in 1885, she struck out to do something for herself. She was fifty years old when she arrived in Yuma County to homestead. She is said to have brought "culture and learning" to Yuma. Her little school accepted pupils from ages five to twenty-five. The following year, the first tax-supported school opened in the lumber company with Mary Elmore as teacher.

The first teacher in Grover, Marion Howard, went there in 1886. She was the daughter of Oliver Howard, superintendent of schools for Weld County, which still included all of northeastern Colorado. Marion was also the niece of Dolly Grover Donovan, the first woman in Grover. The town had been named for her family, and the name stuck even though the railroad tried to change it to "Schotooge," an Indian name.

Julesburg, though the earliest town in northeastern Colorado, had no school for years. "And there was no talk of a school," according to Edna Weir Westlake, who lived there in 1880 when the town was already over twenty years old. Some children were sent to Sidney, Nebraska, thirty-odd miles northwest. Finally, in 1885, Miss Amelia Guy opened the first school.

In 1979, Margaret Garner and Charlotte O'Connell headed a Sterling Arts Council project to move a one-room school, Stoney Buttes, from northwest Logan County to the grounds of the Overland Trail Museum, where the building could be preserved as an example of those many little centers so vital to their communities. In her search for information to be housed in the building, Mrs. O'Connell learned that at least one hundred one-room schools had been located in Logan County alone.

There were thirteen high schools in the county during the 1930s. Sterling, the largest, had literature classes the first semester, and then the books were used by all the remaining schools during the second term. Other books and supplies were shared the same way.

In order for Flora Allison to make regular visits to all one hundred schools under her supervision from 1915 to 1931, she finally bought a Ford runabout. Inevitably, she was criticized for speeding, but she said, "When I got up to 25 miles per hour, I could feel my hair rising on end at such speed."

Most of the one-room schools had a small student body, giving the teachers a chance to provide the best of a basic education. Sometimes, though, the enrollment was surprisingly large. David Hamil, who was Speaker of the Colorado House of Representatives, had attended one of those schools near his family ranch at Proctor. He said that at times the little building was crowded with as many as sixty children.

Etta Shannon (Monroe), who taught not only at Proctor but at several other one-room schools in Logan County, said, "There were always fifty or sixty in my rooms. And one time, when they were erecting the new building, I had around a hundred."

But often, the problem was not enough pupils. In the early 1900s, Christie Merrell, the youngest mother on the south side of the Platte between Iliff and Sterling, added her name to the list of students in order to have a big enough enrollment for a school district. When the Nas Litch School, up river, faced closure, the board hired a woman to teach her child in it, and he was the only pupil. That situation lasted for a term, and then the community faced the disappointment of losing its main identity.

The early schools reflected the fact that homesteaders had come not only from throughout the United States but from the world as well. In the remote Grover area, before the turn of the century, the settlers arrived from England, Scotland, Germany, and Czechoslovakia. There were Germans from Russia, and the Scandinavian countries were represented.

John Carsten, an early rancher, came from Germany. When his four brothers joined him in the United States, a girl, Ida

Schluter, came with them to marry John. One of their daughters married John Bradley, an Englishman, who managed the historic Oasis Ranch south of Grover.

Czechs and Scandinavians also settled in the Willard area. Along the South Platte could be found all of the above, plus Japanese, Italians, and later Mexicans. Throughout southeastern Colorado, the same ethnic groups were represented.

A colony of two hundred Jews came from the East Coast and South America to settle at Atwood in 1896. They built little frame houses, all alike, all painted green. Their experience was not happy, and many Jewish babies were buried in the cemetery. Single men predominated and were restless, and the people began to move away. By 1910, most of the houses were occupied by Germans from Russia.

Frances Swedensky Garfield once had sixty-five German-from-Russia children in an Iliff classroom. None could speak English. In the 1920s, Esther Stogsdill landed a job at Granada in Prowers County and then discovered on the first day that all the children were Mexican. Not one spoke English, and Esther knew no Spanish. For some time, teacher and pupils used sign language until they began to understand each other.

Clella Rieke told that when she entered first grade at Padroni in 1928, about twelve or fourteen pupils spoke English, and about the same number spoke Italian, Spanish, or German. The teacher, Gail Mettner Grauberger, announced, "At the end of the school year, we will all speak the language of the Constitution — English."

The children later told that they took their books and tablets home at night, and entire families learned the lessons of the day. Gail Grauberger now lives with her husband, Jay Apley, on a ranch in Poudre Canyon. For several years, foreign educators visiting Colorado were sent to observe Mrs. Apley's teaching.

Some gifted teachers presided in those early schools. Effie Anderson Brown was shaped by the prairie. Her first school was Capitol Hill out on the high country north of the South Platte. Most of her life was spent teaching in the little town of Merino. Yet she brought to her students the big outside world, the world of dreams and ambitions and the will to make them happen.

In 1913, when Effie arrived as a child in the boom town that homesteading had created at Merino, she thought it was the worst place in the world. Sixty years later, she recalled:

> We had to stay at the hotel for several nights. The first night I was standing in the door and saw a drunk fall off the sidewalk. That was the first drunk man I ever saw. The folks had a room across the hall and down several doors from ours. That night the drunk man kept running up and down the hall trying to get in our room. We kids were scared to pieces. One of us held a chair against the door all night. Later this man used to sleep in our livery stable, and he would come along and throw us kids a dollar. At night he would come back asking if he could have a dime to buy a loaf of bread.

Despite the bad first impression, Effie was to say, "After I lived there for over fifty years, I thought it was wonderful and everyone in it."

That acceptance helped Effie to bring a sense of belonging and pride to her students. In a way, the livery stable was responsible for one aspect of her later inspired teaching. A Mrs. Spence, an art teacher from Chicago who lived in the homestead town for awhile, bargained with Effie's father for regular use of a team and buggy to take rides in the country. In exchange, she gave art lessons to Effie.

Several generations of children remember the circuses and trips to Eskimo land that they experienced with Effie. With such creative events, she taught a practical application of arithmetic, reading, and writing. And she led the boys and girls to use their imaginations. She was years ahead of her time.

Her most famous student was Ralph Edwards, radio and television star of "Truth or Consequences" and "This Is Your Life." For years, he talked about Miss Effie on his broadcasts. When he returned to Merino in 1950 for a homecoming and national broadcast, he called his second grade teacher onto the stage and made her take the consequences of a trip to Europe.

"She brought the world to me," he said. "I want her to see part of the world."

In 1930, Flora Allison entered a national contest, "How Radio Can Be Used in Education," and was a first-place winner. Her prize: a trip to Europe, an awesome adventure in those days.

Catherine Byrne Hume was a guest teacher of the Art Publication Society in St. Louis. A specialist in music, she visited con-

Effie Brown with Ralph Edwards: "She brought the world to me. I want her to see part of the world." *Courtesy, Ralph Edwards.*

vents in eleven states. When her father became ill, she came home to care for him and then began her career of creative teaching in Logan County. She was especially talented in using drama in her work with young people.

The 1957 Teacher of the Year in Logan County was Gladys Shull Brewer, who had begun her career immediately after graduating from Atwood Union High School in 1918 and did not earn her college degree from the University of Wyoming until 1942. For twenty-four years, she attended college during summers and took extension courses in the winters while teaching at rural schools.

Gladys had thinned beets as a girl, and her hatred for the work contributed to her ambition. She had a strict upbringing. Her

Catherine Byrne Hume. She gave her students everything from soup to skits.

father threatened, "If you ever get a whipping at school, you'll get another at home."

"I did, and I did," said Gladys. He also vowed that if he caught her dancing the "Grizzly Bear Rag" at the Atwood Jewish Dance Hall, he'd send her home. "He did, and he did," Gladys said.

Teaching was heaven. With her first check, she bought a fifty-dollar Liberty Bond, a ten-dollar hat, and had ten dollars left. But her second school, the Sherwin, was rickety, and the Sherwin house where she boarded, "wild looking with buffalo and big steer heads on the wall. I wasn't keen about it and said I would stay a week and see."

The Sherwins had sixteen hired men at the bunkhouse and a nurse, a hired girl, and a cook. Gladys filled the kids' lunch pails each morning and drove the children to school. She made hot soup on a pot-bellied stove. In return, she was provided with free board and room and — wonder of wonders — a car.

"After a week," she said, "you couldn't have pulled me off the place."

But teaching did not exactly liberate her. "Teachers in those early days didn't know much," she said, "but board members often knew less." When she returned to teaching after several years of marriage and an imminent divorce, her contract specified that it was "subject to the completion of your plans for divorce." Married women were not allowed to teach, but as long as she was being divorced, that was okay.

In 1952, Gladys was one of fifty teachers in the United States who were chosen by the National Education Association and the country of Denmark to make the first Scandinavian Life Experience Tour to Europe. She later served as a delegate to the NEA Conference in Chicago. But her greatest honor came as a result of a paper written by a former student. Because of that nomination (among thousands submitted), she was one of eight Colorado teachers who received 1959 awards from the NBC radio program "Quiz Kids" as "The Teacher Who Helped Me Most."

Richard Dunlap, a fifth grader, wrote: "I was a big boy for my age in third grade. . . . I didn't know how to use phonics or spell or read. . . . Mrs. Brewer said I could get to the top of the class." Within a month, the boy was doing third-grade work, and by the end of the year, he was indeed at the top. "She gave me the foundation that is helping me to do good work every day in school."

Marie Stratton Greenwood of Stratton in Kit Carson County was a teacher and postmaster for twenty-nine years. In 1976, she was honored as an American Mother of Achievement, 1776–1976.

The woman who was undoubtedly the most accomplished teacher from the Colorado plains (and perhaps from the state) was Madeline Veverka, a native of Czechoslovakia who crossed the ocean and then the continent of North America with her parents and her mother's three sisters and their families in the early 1880s. The clan homesteaded near Willard. Their great adventure brought them not only land ownership for the first time but also the opportunity to attend free schools.

Madeline grew up with a deep appreciation of those schools. Even before she graduated from high school in 1895 (at age twenty-two), she passed the test and began teaching in a one-room soddy. She constantly urged her many young relatives,

Graduation picture of
Madeline Veverka.
She had a rare appre-
ciation of prairie
schools. *Bernice Sanders
Collection, Overland
Trail Museum.*

and other children as well, to stay in school and to learn everything that they could.

Madeline followed her own advice, for she earned bachelor's
and master's degrees at the state normal school in Greeley, though
she spent several years of alternate teaching and studying to do
so. She became superintendent of education in Logan County
and principal of Lincoln School in Sterling. She designed and
established a kindergarten program at Las Vegas Normal University in New Mexico. Later she taught the eighth grade and
was assistant principal in a school in Los Angeles. Then she was
called by Teachers' College in Greeley to develop a rural
education department.

Her own quest for education continued. She studied summers
at the University of Chicago with the famous educator, John
Dewey. Then, again in the summers, she earned second
bachelor's and master's degrees at Columbia University.

Los Angeles appointed her the head of kindergarten–primary education, and during years of phenomenal growth in that city, Madeline sometimes had to cope with thousands of unanticipated pupils on opening day in the fall. The ability to deal with such problems led to her appointment as director of all elementary education in Los Angeles. She wrote two sets of textbooks that were widely used, and there was great demand throughout the United States for speaker and visiting professor Dr. Madeline Veverka.

For she had also earned a doctorate. In 1930, Columbia awarded her a scholarship to study in Europe. Madeline chose Charles University in Prague. Because of the advantages that she had found in the United States, she took her most advanced degree in her native country, Czechoslovakia, where, as a citizen, she would probably not have been able even to graduate from high school. It was beautifully ironic and appropriate.

These teachers cut their teeth in one-room schools. Is that significant? There was no time for malarkey in a one-room school; no bureaucratic hiding place for an incompetent; no guess work as to who did or didn't do her job. The atmosphere apparently was not only good for the child—it was superb training ground for teachers. As Margaret Garner said in her speech when the Stoney Buttes school building was presented to the Overland Trail Museum:

> These were the seats of learning for rural America. Out of them came statesmen, distinguished clergy and educators, men and women of letters, and a large body of citizens who knew how to read, write, and spell better than many of today's college graduates. Most of them had a better understanding of English grammar than many of today's radio and TV announcers.

Etta Shannon Monroe once recalled the hardships of those early days of homesteading and teaching and how a family used every honorable means to add to the resources. If this meant walking seventeen miles to get to a new teaching job, then so be it. "We existed," said Etta, "without any county help, A.A.A., P.W.A., W.P.A., or other governmental alphabet agencies, but assisted ourselves by A.O.P. (Aid of Perseverance!)."

In the long run, the teachers with their *McGuffeys* outgunned the six-shooters.

Chapter III

PRAIRIE NIGHTINGALES

G reat numbers of people came to the plains of Colorado for their health. The "lungers" (tuberculosis victims) made a desperate journey to the land of sunshine and clear skies in the hope of saving their lives. And many of them found the elixir for which they searched. Others were doomed to disappointment. Some started too late and died on the way.

It was said in the early days that if a lunger, on his pilgrimage west, could survive Akron, Colorado, he had it made. That was no slur on Akron. The town is located on the high plateau between the South Platte and Republican rivers. Soon after passing through it, travelers dropped to the lower altitude along the South Platte, and the pressure on their lungs was relieved.

They found, however, that despite the healing qualities of Colorado's climate, there were disadvantages for the sick. For a long time after permanent settlement began during the 1870s, there were virtually no doctors. Occasionally, a "two-year man" appeared, like J. G. Ivy, who practiced at Sarinda for a time in 1878. It was not until 1883 that a full-time, qualified doctor, J. N. Hall, settled in Sterling. At that time, he was the only physician between Evans, south of Greeley, and North Platte, Nebraska. He alone served an area of roughly eight thousand square miles. It was no wonder that his predecessors had not stayed long. One had, understandably, dropped dead.

Even after the turn of the century, when most towns had at least one doctor, there was little that they could do to combat the ravages of diphtheria, typhoid fever, pneumonia, scarlet fever, and other deadly diseases. As always in the long story of man's history, people frequently lost their babies at birth or their young children to the frightening illnesses. Mothers often did not survive childbirth to care for their young ones, or a man was struck down in what we consider today his most productive years.

One of the few weapons — and it was defensive — was the quarantine. People hated it. Once a doctor quarantined a family in the Grover area for scarlet fever and then, casting about for other possible precautions, instructed the wife not to ship her cream to market on the *Prairie Dog Special.* Instead, she was advised to dump it in the hog trough. The furious woman snatched up a cream can and upended it on the poor doctor instead.

Enforcer of quarantine laws in Greeley was Dr. Ella Mead, who was the only woman in the 1901 medical class at the University of Denver. She established a nursing service in Weld County; did all her own lab work; and, in the 1920s, helped to start a birth control clinic, one of the earliest in the United States. For her contributions to medicine in Weld County, she received nationwide attention and the Florence Sabin award (given in honor of the accomplished woman scientist who was born in Central City, Colorado).

Dr. Florence Fezer was another Greeley resident who became a physician. She specialized in the new field of anesthesiology and was medical examiner for women in the physical education departments of the teachers' college in Greeley and of Colorado A and M at Fort Collins.

Despite the heroism of the country doctors, who regularly risked their lives by battling blizzards to reach desperately ill patients, getting medical help was a chancy proposition. Mary Catherine Close, a German from Russia living in Crowley County, hung a sheet on a clothesline as a signal for her husband to fetch the doctor when her birth pangs began. But often by the time a doctor could travel the long distances to ranches or homesteads, it was too late.

Therefore, people frequently owed their lives to another group. They called them prairie nightingales, and the name was given in respect and gratitude. They were the nurses, many of whom lived out on the prairie. Some (like Vesta Keen in Washington County) were homesteaders, too, and they could reach the scene of a crisis before a horseback rider could even notify a doctor in town.

Some of them were simply midwives with no training except what they had learned through experience. Mrs. Johnny Doughty "borned" the babies in the 1870s community of South Platte. Later, after the Doughtys moved elsewhere, one of those women whom Mrs. Doughty had attended, Belle Clanton, took on the job of helping her neighbors bring their babies into the world.

Mrs. William Elder, who with her husband homesteaded east of Hereford in Weld County in 1909, was also a midwife and assisted with the delivery of many babies. Though doctors were available by that time, with one in the town of Grover, Mrs. Elder often managed the birthing alone when the doctor's horse and buggy failed to get him to the "party" on time.

A Nurse Williams tended women with diphtheria in the Keota area. Her prescription was: "Eat lots of lemons." One woman who ate only lemons did get well.

Laura M. Wright was known as the "Angel of Bob Creek." She traveled throughout the territory now known as Crowley and Otero counties, delivering babies and caring for the sick. In winter, she drove her horse and buggy across frozen streams. Three boys in the Rusher family told that they would have starved during the winter that their mother died if it had not been for the Angel.

When Laura's buggy pulled out, often in the middle of the night, it was packed with sheets and bedding to wrap babies born to needy parents. Laura's husband added beef and other food. There were compelling reasons for their generosity. In the 1880s, Laura's first husband had abandoned her and two small children. Too proud to return to her parents' home, she took a job as cook at Hop and Bingham Ranch, near present-day Rocky Ford. There she met Watt W. Wright, foreman of the ranch, whose background had been as miserable as hers. Watt's mother had died when he was quite small, and his father was an alcoholic. One day when Watt was about six years old, his father, a butcher, took him along on a trip to the Kansas City stockyards to buy a beef. A cattle trader tousled the child's hair and said, "Why don't you give this boy to me?" And the father did.

Thereafter, the boy was shunted from one home to another. In Las Animas, the daughter of Kit Carson took him in for a time, and he learned to speak Spanish in her home. But he became frightened one day and ran away. Luckily he became friends with Senator and Mrs. George Swink, who ran a cafe in Rocky Ford. One day young Watt rode down the main street of the town brandishing two six-guns and shooting gas street lights. Mrs. Swink stepped to the door of the cafe and hollered, "Boy, get off that horse and put those pistols down." He did. Then she called, "And get in here and fill your stomach. You look as if you need it." He stayed for three years.

Not long after Watt and Laura met, they were married. When the Hop and Bingham Ranch was broken up about 1891, they bought some of the stock and the brand, the T Down Bar, and set out to homestead on Bob Creek, northwest of Ordway. They prospered and they shared, not only their possessions, but their time and Laura's nursing skills as well.

Atilla Gillette, a practical nurse, cared for patients on her homestead west of Sligo. Her husband worked in Greeley and Denver, and Atilla satisfied the residency requirement of the claim while caring for patients and working in a small "hospital" in Grover.

The hospitals of the early twentieth century were usually private homes. Though seldom operated by professionals, they met a need for maternal or recuperative care. Women living far out on the prairie stayed in those homes when their delivery time approached and so were able to avoid much anxiety. One such hospital was operated by a Mrs. Bussey in Sterling.

Edna Weir Westlake, after the death of her second husband, opened a nursing home in Sterling, though she had had no training. She cared for a woman who had a sandbur in her thumb, causing the bone to die. One woman, Mattie Clanton, spent months in Edna's hospital from 1922 to 1923 while she took X-ray treatments with a Sterling doctor. Edna reported that the treatments "made a new woman out of Mattie."

Babies were frequent patients, especially if the mother was too ill to care for them at home. Once, in 1923, a mother died, and the family brought her three-month-old son to Edna's hospital. The mother's complications had left an effect on the baby, and he needed expert, round-the-clock attention in order to survive. On several occasions, Edna tended small children whose mothers had deserted them and whose fathers could not run their farms or businesses and also care for little ones.

After the first public hospital was built in 1922, Edna remarked, "Times are not very good with me now as the new hospital takes about everything." Later she commented, "I don't want people to be sick, but I hope I get a share of those who must be."

In following years, much of her business came from people not quite sick enough for the hospital, from those taking daily treatments, or from the elderly who had nowhere else to go. One of those was Jimmy Chambers, who had been the second permanent citizen of what was to become Logan County. He came down from Denver, quite ill, and died a few days later.

Once Edna wrote to a brother:

> Oh, those childhood days when we had so few cares and were all together. Now how old we all are. My old head is white. The days and years pass so quickly. It seems that the older we get, the more demands there are on our time and strength and money. I am always up at six and never through before ten or eleven at night. I am glad because I am still able to work. . . . I haven't been on welfare yet, and I will be past crawling when I am.

Two women who were among the earliest trained nurses on the plains of Colorado were Ethel and Edith Spoor. Ethel came to Sterling in 1881 with her parents when her father was appointed the first roadmaster of the new Union Pacific line up the South Platte. When she grew up, she taught school for three years, then decided to become a nurse. Her marriage to Lewis Johnson was cut short by his death after only seven years. When World War I broke out, Ethel, then in her thirties, determined to go to Europe and serve. She was in Langres, France, when the Armistice was signed.

The worst crisis that the nurses ever had to face was the Spanish Influenza, a pandemic that spread over the world from 1917 to 1921. At first it raged through the armies fighting the

Ethel Spoor (Johnson) as a
child when her father was first
roadmaster of Union Pacific
in northeastern Colorado.
*Courtesy, Overland Trail
Museum.*

war, but soon it was hitting the towns of even remote areas of
the plains of Colorado. It struck suddenly during a beautiful mild
winter when cosmos were still blooming in backyards.

Eventually, the flu killed millions. It caused hemorrhaging
from the lungs, and lung tissue died when invaded by the virus,
for which there was no cure. Doctors and nurses could only advise
their patients to take aspirin, drink fluids, and keep the
temperature down. Oxygen was given to desperate cases, but
there was little of it to use.

Viola Smith of Ordway made a cough syrup from herbs when
her husband had the flu. It was so effective that Dr. James Edgar
Jeffery had her make the medicine for all of his patients. Some
people wore asafetida bags around their necks to ward off the
infection, but cynics felt that flu was avoided only because the
awful smell kept people at a distance.

Sarah Ayars, who drove a team to deliver mail in northern

Weld County during the war, had had nurses' training. Sometimes she stopped on her route to deliver a baby. During the epidemic, she stopped to help its victims. Sadie Mosser, a registered nurse, lived in the Iliff area. When an entire family there became ill with the dreaded flu, she fearlessly moved in to nurse them.

Often, several members of one family died, and one of the saddest scenes in eastern Colorado was that of people digging graves in the frozen prairies. Funerals were held in the cold open air rather than risk exposing people to the disease.

Hospital facilities were almost nonexistent. In Sterling, back in 1913, Dr. Fisher had built a five-bed hospital in an old house, and his nurse, Miss Wiebers, was in charge of it. But it and other nursing homes were too small to handle the emergency.

Sometime after 1914, Dr. J. H. Kellogg, while treating Belle Landrum's daughter for typhoid, discovered that Belle was a natural, though untrained, nurse, and urged her to open a hospital in her home. It was a heaven-sent opportunity. Belle's husband was a western adventurer who liked to pull up stakes and move ever so often "to see what was over the next mountain." Their daughters were then in high school and college, and Belle announced to Tom, "No more moves." She rented a two-story house, and Dr. Kellogg began to send his patients to her. Soon he, Dr. J. H. Naugle, and Dr. C. J. Latta were using one room for operations. Belle sterilized equipment and assisted.

She had a healing love of her patients. Once she persuaded a doctor not to commit a little Italian woman suffering a breakdown but to let her provide care. Belle felt that the woman was suffering from too many babies born too frequently, and she saved her for a normal life.

Then came the flu. Belle's daughters gave up their beds as the house filled with as many as nine patients. The girls cooked, washed, ironed, and carried trays. No one died in the house, not even a pregnant woman, though most expectant flu victims were especially vulnerable. Belle's only losses were a nephew whom she treated out on his ranch (he had recently had pneumonia) and a young cousin whom she nursed in Fort Morgan.

To try to conserve the strength of the nurses and doctors, Dr. Naugle and his wife, Meta, a trained nurse, took the lead in

Belle and Tom Landrum on their wedding day, 1888. He always wanted to see what was over the next hill. *Courtesy, Duane Miles, Sterling* Journal-Advocate.

Belle and two of her daughters, Mary and Alice, who helped to fight the flu. *Courtesy, Alice Landrum Reynolds.*

setting up makeshift hospitals. They borrowed mattresses and lined them up in Masonic Hall. When that was full, church basements and other public buildings were also converted to hospitals.

The doctors continued to drive to outlying ranches and farms, and many times it was the nurses who were left to care for the increasing numbers falling sick in the towns. Dr. Jack Naugle of present-day Sterling accompanied his father on one of those emergency runs in a blizzard when he was seven years old. They made the trip as far as Willard before the Hupmobile got stuck in the snow. The Will Sandstead family took the small boy into

58

their home and let the determined doctor borrow a horse for the attempt to reach the sick.

Meta, working day and night with the stricken in Sterling and anxious about her other small children, had no way of knowing what had happened to her husband and son. It was days before the storm cleared and the Sandsteads brought Jack home, and it was even longer before Dr. Naugle was able to make his way back to Sterling.

Meta Boeck was from Boise, Idaho. She had come to Colorado to attend University Nursing School in Boulder. There she met J. H. Naugle, who was studying to be a doctor. They were married and established practices in Sterling near the place where Dr. Naugle's parents had homesteaded.

Another woman who took the lead in fighting the flu was Dr. Eugenia Barney, one of the early women physicians. She and her daughter Hazel had come to Sterling in 1908. The male doctors were at first skeptical of her ability but grew to respect her skill, particularly in the care of children. She became a public school nurse. During the flu crisis, she worked closely with the nurses, and she was a heroine to the sick.

Though the pandemic reached its climax in 1918, it continued to claim victims for several years. Never before in history — and never since — has an illness swept the world with such devastating thoroughness.

When the horror was over, Dr. Barney and Meta Naugle were determined that Sterling should have a real hospital to deal with future emergencies. They were the leaders in soliciting funds and planning the Sterling Hospital, later called the Good Samaritan.

But everyone helped. Women's clubs federated in order to be as effective as possible. Virginia Landrum, who had graduated from Colorado College and taught at Iliff until the flu closed the schools, organized one of the first benefits, an evening of dance. She professed to be "completely unqualified" and said that she "boldly stole" the routines of Hazel Barney, Sterling's only dance teacher. Edna Price (Kellogg) with her "perfect ear and ability to play anything heard" was the accompanist. The show raised several hundred dollars for the hospital.

Ironically, Belle Landrum was denied permission to care for

a nephew in the new facility. Someone decreed icily: "Mrs. Landrum is not a nurse." But she had been good enough to hold the fort for years until the hospital was built.

The first superintendent of that hospital was a little woman who had also selflessly tended the flu victims. Many times as the women worked around the clock, trying to save lives, she was reminded of words that had been spoken to her years before: "What do you want to be a nurse for? Any woman can be a nurse." The speaker was a math "professor" in a Nebraska high school near the turn of the century. The girl was his most brilliant student. He could foresee an unusual future in mathematics if she would just forget this nursing business. Alice Mosser was little but determined. She tossed the red curls hanging down her back and announced that nothing could change her mind, that she had always wanted to be a nurse.

"You'll tie up your life emptying bedpans," he declared. "I'm disgusted that you would settle for woman's work."

Well, that professor might have been surprised at all that Alice Mosser accomplished in her ninety-three years. Not only was she a superb nurse for over half a century, but her philosophy of helping those around her led to adoption of four children while she was still a college student, of two more after her marriage, and to homesteading on the high open Colorado prairie, where her nursing skills were given to the people isolated in their sod huts, miles from a doctor or town.

Alice felt her calling so strongly that she broke her engagement to a classmate. He vowed, "I shall never marry until you do."

Alice was nineteen when she finished high school, a little older than usual because of a serious bout with typhoid fever. The red curls were cut off to simplify her care, and the hair grew out brown. Grateful for recovery, Alice was more determined than ever to be a nurse, and she sold the curls for seventy-five dollars to help finance her training. She worked for a time with hydrotherapy, and it added to her vision of nursing as a way to alleviate suffering.

After completing nursing school in 1908, Alice enrolled in college, which placed her in the minority of women at the time. During one summer vacation, she nursed a woman who had

had a stroke. That woman had sole care of her orphaned grand-children. Neither the doctor nor Alice could understand how the elderly patient was holding onto life. She could not speak or move. Then one day, Alice realized her torment.

"Are you worried about the children?" she asked.

The woman made a massive effort and spoke her first word since the stroke. "Ch---dren."

"Don't worry," Alice said. "I will take care of them." A look of peace spread over the grandmother's face, and that night, as if released, she died.

What was a college student to do with four orphans? With Alice, there was no question. She had given her promise. The administrator of the estate settled her and the children in a house in Lincoln, Nebraska, where Alice and the oldest boy attended college. To her pride, he became a doctor.

Everyone did his part of household chores and cooking. In the evenings, they studied and had fun. The boys and girls never forgot Alice. Even when she was an old woman, the doctor and his wife came regularly from California to visit and to thank her for keeping the children together.

In 1910, Alice and her two sisters (Sadie, also a nurse, and Bertha, who taught in a soddy) came to the Graylin area of north-eastern Colorado to homestead. The youngest child, still only fourteen years old, accompanied them on the venture. The sisters were lucky to claim adjoining land so that their soddies could be built in sight of each other and they could share one well. Alice dug the well because she was small enough to be lowered in a bucket. Day after day, she shoveled dirt in that bucket, and her sisters pulled it to the surface. Men came to look and laugh — but stayed to admire the forty-six-foot hole with perfect round walls.

The sisters had only a hundred dollars apiece to begin their new life. But that didn't matter — everyone on homesteads wore out-of-style clothes. Ironically, many years later, their former homesteads were dotted with oil wells.

When the legendary blizzard of 1913 hit, the sisters could see the storm coming from miles away and quickly gathered at Alice's hut. They survived the three-day blow. When they finally dug out, they could see only snow across the prairie. All the little

In 1910, the Mosser sisters built their soddies

. . . harvested wheat

. . . and explored Chimney Canyon with friends. *Pictures courtesy of Sidney Propst, son of Alice.*

soddies were completely covered.

Alice and her sisters made many trips across the plains to tend the sick and deliver babies. On one such mission, a blizzard caught them in their "Democrat" (a spring wagon with one seat and room to haul supplies behind it). Unable to see, they huddled for several hours under the many quilts that they always carried with them. Finally, desperate, they loosed the reins, and the horses took them home.

During the flu epidemic and throughout Alice's career, the sick would say, "All she had to do was walk in and I felt better."

In 1922, Dr. James McKnight established a small hospital in Haxtun, and Alice was his superintendent. Later she became the first superintendent of that first public hospital in Sterling. And all the time, she delivered babies, very often without the assistance of a doctor. She kept their names and birthdates in a little leather notebook. Eventually, that book listed over eight hundred of "her babies."

Alice was thirty-nine years old when she married Myron Propst and moved to his ranch near Atwood. And only then did her old sweetheart marry. When she and Myron had no babies to add to her list, they adopted two little boys, Lee and Sidney. Sid's red hair was appealing, and Lee looked like a child who needed help. He did. Not even Alice's nursing skill could save him.

In 1959, Alice was honored for fifty years of nursing, but she did not quit. For years, she continued to serve on private duty. When her husband became gravely ill, they moved to Merino, and she stayed home to care for him but continued to walk about the little town to give shots, take blood pressure, and otherwise help her neighbors. When Sid's daughter, Mina, was born three months premature, Alice, fearful of blindness from too much oxygen, took the baby home in a shoebox and nursed her to a healthy life.

As her husband became more and more helpless, Alice brought the world to him. She invited a half dozen children to come to kindergarten each morning, not only bringing entertainment to Myron but giving some busy mothers a couple of hours of freedom. There was no charge for the school, and the pupils later said, "Alice was a landmark person in my life."

The old professor would have been glad to know that she also found a use for her mathematics. When she was nearly eighty, she learned "new math" in order to help her grandchildren, and when they reached high school, she coached them in geometry and algebra.

There was a constant stream of visitors to the little house, and many of those eight hundred babies came to visit or sent greetings on their birthdays. Patients whose lives had been saved by Alice's care came regularly to thank her.

She remained absorbed in medicine, studying the latest journals and marveling over each advance. As she thought back over the early years of her career, she observed, "Doctors had no miracles in those days, and what we did as nurses very often made the difference between life and death. Nurses made the miracles a lot of the time." Then as she thought about it, she added, "And they still do. Real nursing is not just medicines. It's care."

The plains people were grateful for that care from Alice and from all of the other prairie nightingales.

THE AWAKENING

The women homesteaders were accepted on the prairie. Teachers and nurses were joyfully welcomed. But women were not content with those limited roles. They had dug wells, had driven teams to break the sod, had helped to make the frontier livable, and they were not content to slip back into woman's world. They had caught a glimpse of bigger challenges.

Courtesy, Bernice Sanders Collection, Overland Trail Museum.

Chapter IV

VOICE FROM THE FRONTIER

"If we are good enough to teach, then surely we are good enough to enter that world so accessible to our male students."

In 1891, a frontier Methodist woman wrote those words to *The Christian Advocate,* protesting in a witty but forceful manner the half-world to which women were relegated.

Missouri Powell Propst had come in 1874 as a bride to the plains of northeastern Colorado, where she was a full participant in the hard business of taming the frontier. At her childhood home in Alabama, she had played the piano and guitar, painted portraits, and otherwise enjoyed life as the daughter of a lawyer and Methodist minister. She was a graduate of the Methodist Female School for Young Women in Tuscaloosa.

But the young man that she married, Sid Propst, faced a rather doubtful future in the dreary times after the Civil War, and so together they traveled by train and covered wagon to the lost frontier of northeastern Colorado.

The hundreds of thousands who had stampeded up the South Platte River in search of gold in 1859 and the years following had seen little value in the land. But in 1874, the *Denver Times* described northeastern Colorado as "a landscape of unsurpassing beauty" with thousands of buffalo and cattle and a few little clusters of houses. The entire population along the 180 miles could not have been more than 250 people.

Missouri's first night in Colorado was spent on the dirt floor of John Wesley Iliff's Riverside cattle camp rolled up in a buffalo robe which she described as "lively" (with "beasties," the cowboy term for lice). There was one tree at this camp, and it was the first she had seen all day. The almost suffocating smoke from an old camp stove was not the only cause of her tears, and she was glad that her new young husband could not see her reaction to the place he had so enthusiastically described as the "land of milk and honey."

Missouri thought, "The fun of immigration is about up."

Their first home in Buffalo was a tent, attached to a lean-to shack, which was actually a hole in the prairie topped by a cover of wood brought from Greeley. For a more permanent home, they dug the sod and put up a hut that Missouri's artistry made into a charming sight: "a quaint little sod house with sunflowers growing on the roof."

Missouri's fingers, accustomed to artistic pursuits, helped to break the sod. She planted gardens, milked cows, made butter. She lost her first baby to the harsh frontier life and was plunged into such despair that she later wrote, "My mind became almost as impaired as my body."

But, like Sid, she soon loved the "great green prairie," and she liked the feeling of usefulness in her life. And she was crazy about Sid. When he went away to round-up, she wrote:

> I miss "Hun" so much. He is always busy and me right after him. . . . Susie (her sister) vows she would never work for any man like I do him, but I tell her it is for myself and our pleasure that I work.

The couple prospered, and in 1891 there were four talented, healthy children in the big house that replaced the soddy. Missouri had continued to use her talents, playing her instruments, painting portraits of family and friends, teaching in the Sunday school, and writing bright, sparkling letters to her Southern family.

But she was a woman of great intellect, and there must have been times when she longed to use it more fully. She helped to organize the first Southern Methodist church in the area. In 1876, when she attended the annual conference in Denver, women's contributions were limited to singing solos and participating in discussions.

The situation was little better in the larger Northern Methodist Conference. The Women's Foreign Missionary Society had begun in Colorado in 1873, but an all-male committee reported its activities. At the 1877 conference, however, the men were forced to concede that "Woman is man's equal" but maintained that the advantage of the society was that it provided a means for women to evangelize their own sex. Even the women's Methodist magazine, *The Ladies' Repository,* was edited by a man.

Actually, the chief function of women in the church, even on the frontier, seemed to be raising money by cooking meals and staging socials and choir benefits. They cleaned the parsonage before a minister arrived and helped to settle his family.

But women like Missouri longed to serve in a more meaningful way. It was a time when almost any man feeling the call could preach the word of God. Missouri's husband was one of those "half preachers," a frontier term indicating that the man undertook the ministry along with his other work.

Finally, in 1891, Missouri drafted an article of protest about women's limited rights and sent it to *The Christian Advocate.* She ridiculed man's habit of placing woman in an exalted position but at the same time making that position a prison. She noted that the elm does not "give the pine its elm ideas of what it needs to become a pine." Yet man, she said, does this to woman:

> Man, being at one and the same time the institutor of the office, the selector of the candidate, the *candidate,* the *elector,* and the *incumbent,* he proceeds according to his Mohammedan, or his Buddhistic, or his Christian, or his Hebrew, or his savage, or his civilized ideas, to mark out "Woman's Sphere," to tell her what are her duties, her needs, her capabilities, how to be womanly, how she can make him happy, what in her will meet his approval . . . how much knowledge he will let her acquire.

But man made one big mistake: "his permission to learn to read opened the big outer door and let her into the vast fields of knowledge where she was, by no means, content with browsing around the edges."

Missouri ended the article with the plea that women be allowed to make their contribution to the world:

> "It is not well for man to be alone" did not mean that man, poor fellow, was lonesome and needed woman to make things pleasant

for him, but that he needed her help in planning and working of school systems, conducting of newspapers (those going into families), the making of laws, choice of officials, caring for the poor, and by all means, man should not be left alone in the ministry.

In a world so in need of improvement, call in the reserves, Missouri cried.

Her article was not accepted. She was undoubtedly considered a radical. Within a year Missouri was dead, a victim of typhoid, contracted when she returned to Alabama to care for her dying father. Her life was ended at age forty-four, and she did not have the satisfaction, a year later, of seeing Colorado women among the first in the nation gaining the right to vote. Women of her community would very soon be elected to public office. If Missouri could have looked down through the generations to the 1970s, what satisfaction it would have given to see her great-great-grandchildren, boys and girls alike, campaigning for their mother, Mary Estill Buchanan, the first woman secretary of state in Colorado.

Just as satisfying would have been the progress of her Methodist Church. The changes did not come very soon, although four women were accepted as lay delegates to the general conference in 1896 and a new constitution in 1900 established women's rights as lay participants. But it would be another twenty-four years before Methodist women would be given limited clergy rights and 1956 before they would be fully ordained.

Missouri was ahead of her time, but perhaps her voice from the frontier was a forecast of those changes.

Chapter V

THOSE STRENUOUS DAMES

Elation swept over the state. The women could hardly believe it. The election votes were counted, and for the first time in the history of the world, men had gone to the polls to grant women the right to vote. The state was Colorado, the year was 1893, and it would be twenty-seven years before the 19th Amendment would grant all women across the nation that same privilege.

It was not the first time that the attempt had been made. Back in 1877, the Colorado Legislature had referred a proposal to the people (men, of course). In 1869, the Territory of Wyoming had written equal status for women into the organizational charter. A year before Wyoming's revolutionary action and again in 1870, Colorado women tried to get their own territorial legislature to give them the vote.

Then in 1871, some females did go to the polls. They were members of the Union Colony at Greeley, and they had the blessing of Nathan Meeker, their leader. Perhaps he had been influenced by Susan B. Anthony's visit to the state. Perhaps the credit should go to the Greeley residents, for they were generally well educated, and Susan B. Anthony often remarked that suffragists came from the ranks of cultured people. Meeker's wife, Arvilla, later served on the Women's Suffrage Committee of Colorado.

But maybe Meeker was simply playing savvy politics. The election — to nominate a postmaster — replaced the usual petition, one of which had already been circulated by a candidate that he did not favor. Meeker's candidate, Albert E. Gipson, a young lawyer, suggested that women be allowed to vote. Not to be out-maneuvered, the other man, J. B. Flower, agreed.

Election Day resembled a scene from musical comedy. Snow began to fall, and Mr. Gipson, fearful that his women could not get to Colony Hall — for surely they would vote for the man who had enfranchised them — sallied forth in a sleigh with bells a'ring-ing to bring them in. He gave elegant and triumphant escort into the building. But Mr. Flower also rented a sleigh, and not only did bells jingle, but it was decorated, if not with flowers, at least with flags and campaign posters. His ladies were gallantly handed down from the sleigh with the pomp due women being presented to society.

Then — roll the drums! — complications set in. The oldtimers mutter, "Give 'em an inch." A woman, Emily Morris, also de-clares for the job.

Though neither Gipson nor Emily Morris won (she received only nineteen votes), the women proved that they would indeed go to the polls.

A few years later, in 1876, the women of the new state of Colo-rado gained a modest victory: the privilege of voting in school elections. When Greeley colonists voted about the location of a school, Annie Green declared, "I had the honor of voting but the dishonor of being whipped." Her side lost by two votes.

Then, in 1877, the legislators put the amendment granting full enfranchisement on the ballot. Susan B. Anthony cam-paigned for the proposal. She was treated with courtesy most of the time, but many of the men, not only immigrants but also rank-and-file who were isolated from national news, did not even know what she was talking about. Some told her politely that they sure couldn't figure out what it was that she wanted them to do. So, despite support in high places — Governor John L. Routt introduced her in one mountain saloon — the proposal lost, over two to one.

By the time a second chance came in 1893, the state was in turmoil, mired in the Panic of 1893, one of the most severe depressions that the country has ever suffered. Worse, Colorado endured year after year of drought. Many places on the plains had only six inches of rain per year.

As is always the case, the depression had started years before on the farms. As early as 1883, people were having to give up land for lack of a few dollars to pay taxes. The Panic cast a pall over the settlers' exuberance at creating a new life in a new world. Each year brought more grim crises. To the indignation of the women, liquor was being sold in some of the towns where charters had forbade its sale. In 1887, Edna Weir ran for Sterling City Council to protest. Hers was a fruitless campaign, but it provided amusement for the men.

But as the long dry years continued and as the depression dragged toward its nationwide climax in the nineties, the women intensified their efforts. They flocked to support the Farmers' Alliance, later called the Populist Party, and the men, perhaps because of the impotence that the years had brought, had more insight into the position of the women. The Speaker of the House, Elias Ammons, gave his support to putting suffrage again on the ballot, and both houses tallied the necessary two-thirds yea votes.

November 7, 1893, was an unusually tumultuous election day. In Colorado and nationwide, the Populists made a strong showing. And the women of Colorado were given the right to vote! Susan B. Anthony declared, "The men in Colorado are the best in the world. . . . This act stands alone in the history of the world. No class of men has ever done as much for even another class of men."

No sooner was the vote granted than some women began to think of running for public office. Again men grumbled, but most were merely amused when Nannie Gunn and her campaigners took to the streets to urge her election as county clerk of Logan County. Their campaign uniforms aped men's wear with vests and ties and red suspenders. The editors of *The Logan County Advocate* were aghast at their abandonment of long dresses in favor of divided skirts so that they might ride "clothespin style." The paper noted that some were even taking up the disgusting habit of chewing gum.

But the candidate was highly regarded. Nineteen-year-old Nannie Pelham had come west in 1865, traveling in a covered wagon to the gold fields. She and Spencer Gunn were married in 1874 and homesteaded on the South Platte Valley near Cedar Creek. They were employed by the large JB Ranch, whose range stretched from Sedgwick to Akron. It was owned by Jared Brush, who, incidentally, was elected lieutenant governor of Colorado in that 1893 election.

Nannie cooked for the JB hands. Spence rode the range, sometimes being away from home for weeks at a time during the annual spring gathering of cattle. Periodically, he and the other JB reps would cut out cows bearing the Brush brand, and when the herd was big enough, some of the men drove them to JB headquarters. When Spence was a part of that crew, he had a chance for a brief reunion with his sweet Nannie.

Nannie was crazy about Spence. He had come into her life fairly late. Most women at twenty-eight had been married for several years and had children. While he was away, she had plenty to do around their pretty little sod house. At first, it was one of the few graced by a woman, and her care showed. Many a woman, after a miserable night at John Wesley Iliff's Riverside Ranch, felt her spirits lift when she reached Nannie's cozy little house.

Those new friends, especially the young ones, often returned to the fun that was so abundant in the little soddy. Nannie and Spence had dances with music by a young Italian boy who knew only one tune to play on his cracked violin.

Though Nannie was independent, when she saw cattle coming along the river and heard the piercing yells of the cowboys, she ran out, ostensibly to scare the cows away from her garden and flowers. But her eyes were searching for a familiar figure, and when he came close, she could see that he was watching her, too. Sometimes, if the cattle were moving well, he could stop for a drink of water, and more important, a quick kiss.

Nannie never told him of her fears when he left, but she always admonished, "Be careful now." Sometimes when she thought of the dangers on the prairie, her heart seemed to stop. And so each time that he came home safe, she gathered him into her arms with thanksgiving as well as love.

One day, a couple of years after their marriage, Nannie saw a rider coming fast. Spence had gone out with some other cowboys to work cattle not too far away. But she had not heard the bawling of approaching cows, and this rider was alone. Fear grabbed her. She ran out to meet the horseman. He was pushing his mare so hard that something had to be wrong.

Then she saw that he was W. L. Henderson, a young cowboy who was working with Spence that day. She began to run. Something awful flooded into her throat. She got to Henderson before he could get off his horse. She reached up and grabbed his arm. The horse shied away, but Nannie didn't seem to notice. She pressed frantically after him, her eyes burning into Henderson's.

"Has something happened? Is it Spence?"

He got down quickly and took her arms.

"Yes, Nannie, his horse got excited and threw him."

She moved back, turning her head from side to side, unable to speak, the words choking in her throat, fear transforming her usual calm face to a map of hysteria, her eyes glittering with tears that came from somewhere in that choking mass building up in her throat.

She finally whispered, "Is he dead?" Then the tears came. "He can't be dead."

"No, no, he's not dead. But he's hurt bad. We've got to get your wagon."

She turned and ran to the corral. Before Henderson could catch up, she was already leading her horse to the wagon. They worked without talking, and in minutes, the horse was hitched, and Nannie jumped onto the seat and snatched the lines.

Henderson grabbed the horse's head. "You've got to wear a cap and coat, Nannie. It's too cold."

She lifted the reins to slap them against the horse, but Henderson held on and shouted, "You'll need covers for Spence. He's got to be kept warm."

She jumped down and ran for the house, coming back almost at once with quilts, struggling into her coat as she hurried to the wagon. They left the yard in a run, Henderson showing the way on his horse. When he looked back, Nannie was right behind him, standing, leaning forward, shouting and urging the horse to greater speed.

Spence never regained consciousness. The next evening they buried him. The setting sun was symbolic. Nannie, still a bride, was a widow, and her brief happiness with Spence had ended.

She stayed on the ranch, continuing to work for the JB, and to the admiration of all, managing her little place quite well. Though the joyful dances came to an end, Nannie could always be counted on to care for a cowboy with a broken leg or anyone who needed help. People coming along the river continued to stop at her house for hospitality that was quieter now, and when winter blizzards hit, cowboys far from home camp knew that they could always find refuge in the little soddy.

Almost twenty years later, she ran for office. Though the campaigning of her friends was a source of merriment and though political experts declared she hadn't a chance, Nannie had male admirers who spoke up in her behalf. Others, who laughed, must have had a different attitude in the polling booth. Perhaps, as they picked up the pencil and looked at her name, their memories went back through those years that Nannie had managed alone. Perhaps, for some, the vote was a gesture to their old friend Spence who had died in the kind of accident that could strike any rider, no matter how skilled.

For when the votes were counted, Nannie had won over two respected male opponents, John H. King and John C. Scott. She was among the first women in the United States to be elected to political office.

Nannie Gunn, one of the first women elected to public office. *Courtesy, Overland Trail Museum.*

Georgia Sanders, first deputy county clerk in Logan County, and her husband, J. T. McRoberts, at their Cedar Creek ranch. It was a three-day trip to buy groceries. *Courtesy, Overland Trail Museum.*

Her deputy was Georgia Sanders, who had come with her pioneer parents in 1876. She had finished high school and then taught northwest of Iliff for nine years. Then she, too, pioneered. She studied business in Greeley and Denver and took the gigantic step of investing in that new machine, the typewriter. Since there was only one other in the town, Georgia soon had a rushing business in her public secretary office. Her clients included top businessmen of northeastern Colorado, and when the male court stenographer could not travel from Denver to Sterling, the judge called on Georgia to perform the duty.

Her skills were the frosting on the cake and helped to insure that women would hold the county clerk's office for years to come. In fact, it was 1932 before a man could again be elected. H. C. Sherman, a leading citizen, wrote to the paper in 1897 that though he had not supported Nannie, he now conceded that her office had performed the clerical work "more promptly than it was ever done by any of her predecessors." Georgia's typewriter must have been a part of that improvement, for before its installation, all deeds and most other documents had to be written by hand.

Edna Weir served in the office from 1897 until 1902. Back in 1881, when Edna was only seventeen, she had been the first woman postmaster at Julesburg. When the Union Pacific Railroad was extended to New Sterling that year, she and her husband moved their store to that town, and for several months, she was the first postmaster there. Mrs. David Leavitt had initially held the job in the original town.

In 1889, a second woman, Florence Kendall, took over the postmaster's job in Julesburg. She had been in the Postal Service in Washington, D.C., and when she and her son, Messmore, decided to homestead, she got herself appointed to the Julesburg office.

In 1895, Dollie Donovan was installed as the second postmaster at the town of Grover. A horseback rider brought the mail from Wyoming to the Donovan ranch. Sarah Ayars, the nurse who delivered mail and babies west of Grover, had one of the two longest routes in the United States. Emma Burke Conklin became postmaster in Sterling in 1907 and was in office when the first free mail delivery came to Sterling.

Daisy Littler, who homesteaded with her husband, was another early mail carrier. In 1916, she drove a team of mules to Leroy and other points east, and the round trip took most of a day.

Daisy Littler, born in 1880, drove a team of mules to deliver mail. *Courtesy, Robert Littler, a son.*

She took along her baby, Betty, stopping to nurse and care for her whenever necessary. The Littler homestead was immortalized in a book, *Hannah's Sod House,* written by another daughter, Helen Littler Howard.

There were other victories in the election booth. Sarah Emma Smith, wife of one of the first four settlers of Sterling, became secretary of the school board. Charity Ann House, who had lost her 1896 race for the office of Weld County Superintendent of Education, later served on the Greeley School Board for twelve years and was president for two terms. At Merino, Emma

Sarah Emma Smith, secretary of the school board. *Courtesy, Judy Smith Schott, great-granddaughter.*

Elizabeth Propst and Mrs. Sam Stockham were also elected to school boards.

The big boys ran things in most country schools, and one day, Emma's son Tom got in trouble. The teachers, Blanche Sheridan and her brother Paul, announced their resignations. It seems that Paul had asked a misbehaving boy to leave the classroom,

The big boys ran things in most country schools.

but he refused. When Paul attempted to put him out, Tom and other big boys intervened. It was a humiliating experience for the teachers. Hugh Davis, also on the board, thought, "Well, now, we'll see how tough a woman board member is."

Emma was tough. She decreed that only those boys who apologized and behaved themselves in the future would be allowed back in the school. Tom was the only one to do so and remained in class. His parents were easy-going until something riled them, and Tom wisely felt that life would be more comfortable in school than out.

In the early 1900s, Christie Merrell became the deputy game warden in Logan County and hauled many an offender to town for fining.

Down in Olney Springs in Crowley County, soon after the turn of the century, the women led a successful crusade to vote the town dry. But saloon signs still advertised the sale of liquor, and Mrs. M. V. Roberts and her friend, a Mrs. Newton, declared that something should be done about it. The men lightheartedly suggested that the women could take care of the job. Next morning, before dawn, the two women awakened their daughters. When townspeople began to stir a few hours later, they discovered that all the signs had been painted over.

In 1929, the women of Grover became indignant about the careless way that men were ruling that town and ran thirteen women for the various offices. And all were elected! Elizabeth Lower was the new mayor. Caroline Franklin's husband wouldn't let her sign the oath of office, but that was evidently one of the few problems. The "petticoat government," as the men routinely referred to it, did so well that the slate of women was elected to two additional terms.

But the most unusual women office holders in Colorado were May Justice of Akron and Goldie Curtis of Crowley County. When May's husband, the sheriff of Washington County, was killed in an accident in the summer of 1930, she was appointed to take his place and did so until early the next year. In June 1932, Goldie was appointed to complete the term of her husband, Gomer. Not until 1981 did a third Colorado woman undertake the job of enforcing the peace as sheriff.

Women county commissioners have been rare on the plains. Nona Thayer and Jane Steinmark were appointed to the boards of Larimer and Weld counties in 1976, and Elda Lousberg to the Logan County board in 1977. All have won subsequent elections.

Colorado women have been members of the state legislature since 1895 after three from the Denver and Pueblo areas rode to victory on the momentum of gaining the right to vote. Eighty women have been elected to that body, many for multiple terms, but fewer than a dozen have been from the plains area. In 1911 and again in 1913, Agnes L. Riddle took her seat representing Adams, Arapahoe, and Elbert counties. The first real success from the heart of the prairie was Kittie Brighton, who won election from Las Animas County for three terms, beginning in 1927.

From northern Colorado, Ruth Clark served four terms, starting in 1955, and then took Senate seats in 1963 and 1965. She and Kathleen P. Littler, who also moved up from the House, have been the only plainswomen ever to be elected to the Senate. They represented Larimer and Weld counties, respectively.

When Kathleen Painter Littler was first elected to the legislature in 1960, Weld County got a bargain package, for she was the earliest woman to represent the county; she was a resident of Greeley, the most populous city; and she had a rural background. Thus, she had an understanding of the varied problems of her constituents.

Kathleen was born in 1903 on the well-known Painter Ranch near Roggen. It had been homesteaded by her English family in the early 1880s. The grandmother who had presided over her bachelor sons' home continued to live with Kathleen's family, and many English customs were observed, especially at holidays.

The elegance in the large ranch house was balanced by the primitive accommodations of the time. There was no plumbing until 1917. Private baths were accomplished by carrying a high-backed tin tub from room to room. Kerosene lamps had to be cleaned and filled every day, and coal stoves in each of the eleven rooms needed fueling and ashes removed every morning. Groceries were shipped periodically from Denver.

There was no church until 1917, and the maternal

The well-known Painter Ranch, Roggen, 1902.
Courtesy, Kathleen Painter Littler.

grandmother, who also lived with the family, took the children out in the sand hills on summer Sunday mornings for an outdoor worship service.

There were no nearby playmates, but the children had a good time. A large dining table seated the extended family, hired men and girls, and frequent visitors. The children rode horseback to school, even in thirty-below-zero weather. Sometimes they stopped on the way home to skate on a pond, and their father created a slide in the yard. He watered it every night and let it freeze, and the children took some pretty fast trips on their sleds.

Kathleen and Stafford Painter rode their horses to school even in thirty-below-zero weather.

Kathleen went away to boarding school when she was thirteen, attended the University of Denver, and graduated from Boston University with a degree in religious education. In 1928, she earned her master's at Columbia University. Her work with the Episcopal Church and with the YWCA, as well as an active ranching life after marriage, added other dimensions to her capability in the legislature.

Kathleen was proud of her ranch background and of the rural legislators of the time. They were ". . . much more understanding of urban problems than the urban legislators were of rural problems." She feels that good legislators are not only people

Kathleen Littler during a break at the legislature.

of fairness and honesty (with the courage to say "I don't know" when necessary), but they also recognize that they are servants of the public and owe that public their most diligent efforts.

Eastern Colorado's top office holder was Anna C. Petteys. Her first public service was ten years on the Board of Trustees for State Colleges. When the Colorado State Board of Education was created in 1950, she conducted a vigorous statewide campaign for the At Large seat and won. She served three six-year terms and was vice-chairman and chairman for a total of six years. Her energetic and positive service resulted in major gains for education in the state.

Women also stepped into the pulpit in one way or another. Mary Pratt not only started the first school in Yuma but the first Sunday school as well. She was practical. Back in Ohio, she had joined in a Women's Crusade against a local saloon. But when there was no suitable building for a Sunday school in Yuma, she accepted an offer from a saloon manager to hold classes in the rear of his building. Children sat on boards laid across beer kegs.

The first pastor in the town of New Raymer was a woman,

Mrs. L. M. Sweigard. She arrived with her husband in 1910 but became ill and died two years later.

Gertrude "Trudie" Horn preached in the little towns of the Buttes area for more than twenty-five years. She and two friends came to Hereford in 1936 as the Gospel Trio to hold a revival. They were hired as regular preachers, but within a few years, the other two married and left. Trudie became known as the "Prairie Preacher." In hard times she was paid with food. She performed marriage services for over three hundred couples and became almost a part of people's families. She also turned her car into an "ambulance" in case of emergency. Once, as she was rushing a child to a Denver hospital, she was stuck in a snow-drift during a sudden blizzard but managed to find a fence post and work the car loose. When her twenty-five years were honored with a reception, more than eight hundred people came to express their appreciation.

Leila Hinkley, a native of Logan County, was for more than twenty years secretary and secretary general of the Young Women's Christian Association in China. In 1942, after the

Prairie church, north of Plattner. *From a painting by Jessie Scott.*

Japanese attack on Pearl Harbor, she was interned in Peking and was held there until after the war.

Hildegarde Kloeckner Aeschlimann of Burlington was the first woman ever to serve on the National Church Council of the American Lutheran Church. She was a lay person for ten years on that top governing board and in 1977 was chosen to represent the United States as a delegate to the Lutheran World Federation meeting in Dar Es Salaam, Tanzania.

Perhaps the most astonishing career was that of Dr. Ruth Hull Bennett, who was married to a rancher, Claude Bennett, living south of Ovid. The two, members of the Religious Society of Friends (Quakers), had met at Nebraska Central College, where he was captain of the undefeated football team and an all-state tackle. They became engaged in 1916 when Ruth was nineteen years old. But she had already committed her life to being a medical missionary, and so while Claude served in a noncombative capacity during World War I, Ruth continued to study and work

Ruth Hull (Bennett), twenty, at graduation, Nebraska Central College, 1917.

Ruth with friends at medical school.

to pay her schooling debts. In 1919, Claude went to northeastern Colorado to ranch. It was not until 1925 that Ruth earned her medical degree. Then, for three years, she worked as medical director at a women's prison. All this time, the couple were still engaged.

But Ruth could never feel satisfied without using her medical skills in the mission field. An opportunity came in India, and just before going there in 1928, she offered to break the engagement. "But," said Dr. Ruth, "he had no other plans so we continued our correspondence with each other as we had always done whenever at a distance from each other."

For seven years she ministered to Indian women "from palaces to the humblest huts." In 1935, she returned home, and in early 1936, she and Claude were married. They had been engaged for twenty years. Almost immediately, Ruth was offered a temporary position at a mental hospital in Massachusetts.

"In the depression days of the thirties, anything with money attached looked good," she said. "My husband, as usual, agreed to my desires. . . . Not until I got there did I . . . realize I might be pregnant. I was thrilled . . . for at thirty-nine, it was high time I was having a child."

The son, Claude Fraser Bennett, was only ten months old, however, when the Mission Board made an urgent request for

Ruth with her husband and baby shortly after the return to India, 1937.

Dr. Ruth to return to India. Ruth said, "It must have been a tremendous struggle for my husband to give his blessing to the ordeal, but once he had made that decision, he was more heroic even than I when it came time for the actual departure." And so in late 1937, the mother and baby arrived in India in the middle of a cholera epidemic. For three years, the family kept in touch with letters and snapshots.

Dr. Ruth and little Claude returned home in 1940. For the next twenty years, Ruth alternated her life on the ranch with relief practice for doctors of northeastern Colorado and western Nebraska when they needed to get away. Sometimes she commuted even further. During World War II, she worked in a field hospital in California, but Claude joined his wife and son during part of that time.

Dr. Ruth retired at the age of sixty-five and cared for her mother-in-law, who had helped her many times through the years. But after Mrs. Bennett died, "I got itchy feet again." She took another job in California at a state hospital for the retarded, intending to stay only six months. But she liked the work, and so Claude would join her during the winters, and she would return to Ovid in the summer. In 1967, when Dr. Ruth was seventy, she retired again—except for volunteer work back home in Ovid and Julesburg, Colorado.

Etta Shannon Monroe, the teacher, became a strong leader in the Sterling Presbyterian Church. She could not preach, but she was the next best thing. She taught Sunday school from the age of fourteen (for sixty years), was head of every organization in the church, and was in demand as a speaker throughout northeastern Colorado. It was said that her programs were always polished. She started meetings on time and ended them on time.

She was interested in history as well and once presented the seventy-five-year account of her church. She was also responsible for a big historical pageant commemorating the history of Sterling. She and Emma Burke Conklin were appointed to the board of the Logan County Historical Society, the first local historical group in Colorado.

District Judge Raymond L. Sauter once said that it was a crime that Etta's folks couldn't afford to send her to law school. With her mind and communicating ability, she would have made a superior attorney.

When the Overland Trail Museum was built near Sterling, both Etta and Emma Burke Conklin took an active role. It was Mrs. Conklin's idea to build the museum like a fort. Her sister, Phoebe Henderson, often paid bills for the usually penniless Museum Association.

Wilma Lytle Pidgeon was instrumental in organizing the Sedgwick County Historical Society and helped to establish the museum in Julesburg.

Bertha Boger Wear of Burlington won a trip to France for first place in a state 4-H club demonstration. That interest led to a long career as one of the early home demonstration agents.

Modern women have moved into other fields of service. Margaret Garner of Sterling is a piano teacher, but her broad civic interests have led to volunteer service on state review boards where citizens' input is needed. Her most significant contributions have concerned children. In 1963, Governor John A. Love appointed her to the first Governor's Commission on Licensing for Child Care Facilities. For three years she was the chairman. She spent six years on the Child Welfare Advisory Committee,

Margaret Garner's most significant contributions have concerned children.

and for two years she was chairman of the state Children's Laws Committee.

Early in 1956, when Margaret was serving on the latter, five young people in Logan County were sent to institutions of correction, and she decided that concern for youth should be a coordinated effort of schools, agencies, churches, public offices, medical associations, and law enforcement groups. The resulting Coordinating Council on Youth Services has now worked actively for twenty-five years, and Margaret Garner has been the secretary for all of those years. That work is her chief commitment to society. She feels that because of the council, "fewer children have been lost between the cracks."

Work with the clearinghouse led indirectly to her appointment by Governor John Vanderhoof in 1974 and two reappointments by Governor Richard Lamm to the state Health Facilities Review Council. The seat had to be filled by a representative of a nongovernmental agency in the northeastern part of the state. As

Naioma Felzien Benson was asked, "Can you harness a horse?"

a nonmedical member of the council, Margaret looks at applications from the citizen's point of view. She has no axes of her own to grind. The belief has been expressed that her persistent questioning has saved Colorado millions of dollars. Margaret Garner has said that she is able to ask those tough questions because she "has no law partner to embarrass."

Isabelle Sullivan, who was born in Windsor and grew up in Greeley, has been a leader on national and international levels. When she was left a widow with small children, she had to find a job. Her business activities led to membership in Quota International, an organization for professional women. Isabelle held local, state, national, and (for ten years) international offices, including the presidency from 1975 to 1976. She traveled to conferences throughout the South Pacific and Southeast Asia.

She is a board member of Freedoms Foundation at Valley Forge, a national organizaton devoted to promoting appreciation and vitality of a free society. She is also an elected member of the governing board of Northeastern Junior College in Sterling.

In 1981, Naioma Benson became the first woman ever to serve on the nine-member Colorado Agriculture Commission. She had previously won a seat, usually reserved for men, on the State Wheat Committee and had been appointed by United States Secretary of Agriculture Berglund as one of four national women advisors. During confirmation hearings for the position on the agriculture commission, a Colorado senator asked if she could harness a horse. Naioma laughed but wondered if the senator could possibly consider that antiquated skill a prerequisite for the job. She felt that the question was symptomatic of the lack of understanding of modern agriculture and of woman's role in it.

Shirley Dickinson McCune, born in 1935, grew up on a north-eastern Colorado ranch and sometimes felt that there were "certain odds against girls," especially ranch girls more interested in music and studying than horses and sheep. The feeling was intensified during her weekly piano lessons 120 miles away in Denver. Her teacher was Antonio Brico, a gifted conductor whose talents were not recognized for many years.

Shirley attended several colleges and earned degrees from three, the final one a Ph.D. at George Washington University Center for Behavioral Studies. Her interests were social change, particularly through civil rights, but she made a "conscious decision to transfer her interest" to feminism. She joined the National Education Association's Center for Human Relations as a fund raiser for the Center on Sex Roles in Education. The Center was instrumental in the passage of the Women's Educational Equity Act.

When President Jimmy Carter established the United States Office of Education, Shirley was appointed Associate Commissioner for Equal Educational Opportunities. In the subsequent Department of Education, she became deputy assistant secretary for the Equal Education Opportunity Program. She is now with the Education Commission of States with headquarters in Denver.

And so have eastern Colorado women moved into the center ring of public activities and responsibilities. Their motto could have been Missouri Propst's words: ". . . surely we are good enough to enter that world so accessible to our male students," and they had a Nannie Gunn to lead the way. But the tradition goes even further back into the history of the Colorado prairie.

The Cheyenne Indian women, for fifty years starting in the

1820s, followed the buffalo on the Colorado plains with their families and tribe. They enjoyed a unique position when compared to women in any other society of that time and for decades afterwards. Whenever decisions were made, they helped to make them. Their counsel was sought, their opinions highly respected.

Such prestige did not mean that they had easy lives. As did women who came to the plains in later years, they worked hard alongside their men. In fact, they did most of the work. Their husbands killed the buffalo. But it was the women who dragged the carcasses back to camp, skinned them, cut the meat, and dried tons of it for future use. They cooked the meals; tended children, dogs, and horses; and cared for the tipis. When time came to move, they took down the lodges, often in a matter of minutes, and lashed them to lodge poles to form a travois or "pole drag" on which the family possessions were transported. They dug hiding places near favorite camping spots, and there they stored supplies, including food, for future use. It was they who set up the new camp—in plenty of time to cook the next meal, of course.

But the Cheyenne woman's position was extremely rare, and Cheyenne girls were cherished. Their beauty and morality were a matter of pride. They were brought up in a peaceable atmosphere. Conflict was rare and violent crime almost unknown within the tribe. But a man who seduced a Cheyenne girl did so at the risk of his life. It was the one offense that could be answered however the girl's father or brothers decided. Usually the sentence for the offender was death.

Those standards evolved from the religion of the "Prairie People." It was a woman who was said to have brought the original messages from Sweet Medicine, the Messiah, son of the All Father, Maheo. His instructions concerned not only religion and ethics and morality, but government as well. The Cheyenne people believe that Sweet Medicine (or Sweet Water, as he was also called) established their system of self-rule, which was a representative council chosen every ten years. Four men were elected from each of ten bands, and they, plus four holdovers from the previous council, made the laws for the entire tribe.

When it is noted that these elected leaders were men, it can logically be asked, "Then what was so different from the whites?"

But the women were always consulted within the family and the band. Important decisions were rarely made without their participation.

Perhaps those strenuous dames, both Indian and white, left a legacy. They set the stage for a parade of fascinating women across the plains of eastern Colorado.

Above, left: Tomi Ogawa (Noguchi). *Courtesy, Kisa Noguchi Sasaki.*
Above, right: Carmen Prado on her wedding day. *Below, left:* Katsu
Shimamoto, 1943. *Courtesy, Shimamoto family. Below, right:* Rin
Inouye of Sedgwick County before coming to the United States in
1920. *Courtesy, Inouye family.*

THE SEEKERS

The plains were peopled with seekers. They came from the settled areas of eastern United States. Some had traveled across oceans and mountainous borders to reach those places. Some had headed first for Chicago or Iowa or Kansas City.

They were a strange, unsatisfied people, unlike the great masses who make do with what they have, who prefer present misery to uncertainty. And once their restless feet began to move, they were not afraid to strike out again and again.

But when they reached the prairies and stood on a quiet morning, watching the grass ripple into infinity, marveling at the huge unspoiled landscape, an unspoken message came to them: "This is home."

For some women, the plains opened a door to splendid achievements. For others, the migration was the achievement. It was the gift that they handed to their sons and daughters.

Matsu Kobayashi working onions, 1953. *Courtesy, Kobayashi family.*

Chapter VI

PICTURE BRIDES

She stood on the deck of the ship, her eyes trying to adjust to the bright light. It was a beautiful morning in this new world. The sun caught the wings of sea birds and gave poetic emphasis to the dipping, swirling patterns of their flights. It would be a good subject for a haiku poem, she thought, but not now. Not when she faced the most dramatic change in her young life.

Somewhere ahead on the piers awaited a young man. She studied his picture again. Would he look as pleasing as this photograph? Could she count on his letters to be true?

Would he be pleased with her? She looked down at her kimono and smoothed an imaginary wrinkle from the obi at her waist. She touched her hair. Weeks of traveling third class on the ship had surely damaged her looks. She felt thin and unattractive. What if he did not like her appearance?

Finally the gangplank was lowered. Finally her turn came. She made the long walk down the plank, staring at the crowd of young men, every one clutching a picture and looking from it to the face of each girl. She had never felt so alone in her life as she watched couple after couple identify each other.

And then, a young man approached her, holding out a photograph, and she saw that it was her picture.

In the late 1800s began a migration of young men from Japan to the United States. They were "seeking their fortune," and most had to work for a year or so in Hawaii before earning enough money to complete the journey to the mainland. They found a very different country from the gold mountains which they, like many immigrants in other times and places, had expected. Gold did not lie in the streets, and there was intense competition for jobs. The Japanese men took any work that they could find, and it was almost always the most difficult and menial of labor. They toiled and sweated on farms and on the docks; they picked fruit and cut wood; they even did housework. And invariably, they worked for the railroad because it provided passage to get away from the coast to less-developed areas and better opportunities.

Eventually, they arrived in Colorado, where mining and agriculture provided jobs. Many headed to the Arkansas and South Platte valleys where, they had heard, were the richest new farming lands in the world. They found their labor needed in the production of sugar beets, and they settled on farms and began to save their money.

Some day, they would return to Japan with the capital to begin a better life there. Some day, they would make marriages in their home country. That was always the plan.

But in 1905, a young woman, Matsu Kobayashi, came to the United States to join her husband, Seiichi. He had left Japan in 1901, and for four long years, Matsu had waited for him to make his fortune and return home. Finally, she could not stand the separation any longer, and even though she had to leave her little five-year-old boy behind, she crossed the ocean and joined her husband in Rock Springs, Wyoming, where he worked on the railroad.

She found Seiichi quite Americanized. He was now known as Harry, and though his hopes for becoming wealthy in America had dimmed, he had not lost his enthusiasm. In fact, the bigness of the West, the freedom that he found, had already tied him to the new country. Perhaps he still intended to return to the land of his birth some day, but Matsu discovered that he was not yet ready to go home. They moved to Merino, Colorado, and Harry joined several other young Japanese men as laborers in the beet fields.

The beet industry was just under way along the South Platte. In that year of 1905, the sugar factory was built in Sterling. There was more than enough work for all the men, for the beets had to be thinned and weeded by hand; in the fall, the green tops were hacked off by hand; and after the beets were plowed up, it was necessary to pick them up by hand, throw them in wagons, and haul them to the dump.

Matsu was frightened when she saw Harry drive a team pulling the heavy load up the narrow arch of the dump. There, chains lifted the side of the wagon and released the tons of beets into waiting boxcars below.

"What if the horses should run?" she asked him. "Or what if they should jump off that high place? You would be killed."

But Harry thought that such an arrangement was better than having to throw beets by hand onto the pile after the allotted boxcars were loaded each day. He was happy to get up long before dawn to try to be earliest in line with his team so that he might make at least one trip each day up onto the dump and get rid of his beets the easy way.

But nothing was really easy, and Matsu's life was hard as well. As the only Japanese woman in the area, she cooked enormous meals for all the young countrymen, she often washed their clothes, and she gave them advice. Her hours of work were as long as her husband's.

And the years went by. She tried to imagine her little boy as six, seven, eight. She longed to have him with her before his childhood was gone. She began to see that there would be no return to Japan, and she thought hard of how to get herself out of that endless round of work. More women! Of course. And so she began to arrange marriages, to act as a go-between for the lonesome young men and suitable girls in Japan. Later she helped to deliver the babies from those marriages.

Whenever a young woman came from her old home area, Matsu, with tears in her eyes, would ask, "And my baby? How is my baby?"

But the baby was no longer a baby. George was sixteen years old before he, too, finally made the long trip to America. A few years later, he returned to Japan and brought a bride, Miyo, to the South Platte. And the descendants of that family still live and farm — their own land — along the river.

The coming of other women gave Matsu the freedom that she had longed for. But when the family moved to the Hogg Ranch

"Have you seen my baby?" Matsu Kobayashi, left, perhaps with one of the picture brides, 1913. *Courtesy, Kobayashi family.*

Matsu began to work side by side with Harry and George, 1919. *Courtesy, Kobayashi family.*

between Sedgwick and Ovid, Matsu merely exchanged one kind of hard labor for another. She began to work side by side with Harry and George, driving a team that pulled a walking plow.

Her long years of partnership gave her a special position, however. She often drove a team of horses hitched to a buggy up and down the river to visit the other Japanese women. She shopped in Sterling whenever she wanted to. She had a freedom of movement that she could never have enjoyed in Japan.

When Hidekichi Shimamoto's wife arrived from Japan in 1914, she also undertook to help others, particularly her single brother-in-law, Hikoichi Shimamoto.

Many of the matches were "Picture Weddings," or *omiai-kekkon,* as the custom of arranging marriages was known in Japanese. Oftentimes, matching was accomplished by family members at home. They were careful to choose young women from the same area as the men were from. They took every precaution to find partners of the same general background, education, and cultural interests. When they had a nomination, they wrote the lonesome countryman in far-off America with a detailed description of the girl. The young people then corresponded and exchanged pictures. They were undoubtedly elated when the letters of agreement traveled through the miserably slow mail. But as the time came for the fateful meeting in some city on the west coast, the doubts must have mounted. One young Japanese man pleaded with his American employer: "Teach me how to woo her."

The men at least had their daily work to keep their minds off their doubts. The girls spent weeks of monotony in the bowels of a ship, one moment delighted at the prospect of the marriage and a new life, and the next, assailed with fears.

In 1912, Some Kosuge stood on the deck of the ship which had just brought her from Japan. Suddenly, the stifling air of the below-decks bunk, the crowded room where many people had slept, the seasickness that she had endured day after day did not seem so bad. She was frightened of the scene before her.

The Seattle air was brisk, the day bright. On the docks she could see swarms of people. And terror washed over her. What was she doing here, so far away from home in beautiful Japan, from her family? She was marrying a stranger, a man whom she had never seen.

Then the next terror hit. What shall I do if he doesn't come? Where will I go in this great strange world? As she moved down the plank, she listened to the foreign voices. With panic, she watched the women who had made the long trip with her, being matched with photographs carried by young men — Japanese but dressed in the garb of all those American strangers. She waved as they moved away, and the aloneness of her situation settled around her.

And then he found her. Shichirobei Nakane was only a few years older than she and was nice looking, and the years of hard labor had given him a strong, athletic body. At least he was not ugly. He had not sent some other man's picture to trap her into marriage.

Some was a graceful young woman and well educated, a graduate of a teachers' college. She had taught at a girls' school for five years. She could tell from the speech of her fiancé that he, too, had received an education, just as the go-betweens had said. She had met his family, respected people, successful farmers, and manufacturers of shoy (soy sauce).

But what did he think of her? She kept turning her head away, for she had developed an eye infection in the crowded ship. He must think she was ugly. Did she still look like that picture in his hand?

Most of all, she felt relief. At least he was here. If he did not consider her suitable, he would help her to make arrangements to return to Japan.

But to her pleasure, he attended her with courtesy and interest. He made solicitous inquiry about her eye and assured her that something would be done about it.

Some was not prepared for what was done. In the immigration office where her papers were checked, a physical examination was given and the inflamed eye noted. She was forced to take a group shower with many other young Japanese women, and she was fumigated. Some was humiliated to realize that these people did not know what a fine family she had come from; they did not care that her father was a teacher and her mother a woman of refinement.

The final blow came when she was held for a week of observation of the eye. Finally, though, when it healed, she was released

Some and Shichirobei Kosuge soon after wedding, 1912. He took her name. *Courtesy, Hisa Shimabukuro, daughter.*

to Shichirobei.

They were married June 11, 1912, at the Japanese Methodist Church in Seattle by a Reverend Yoshioka. And afterwards, they were pronounced Mr. and Mrs. Kosuge. Nokane took Some's name as had been expected of him. She was the oldest daughter of a family with no sons. He had older brothers who could carry on his name. This practice was known as *yoshi.*

On the train during the long trip to Merino, Colorado, Some learned that her new husband was now in a farming partnership with two other young men. His nine years of hard work had given him the capital to start that venture. But Some was to learn that ownership of the land often meant even longer hours of labor. Like the homesteaders, perhaps they sometimes felt that the land possessed them.

She was responsible for all household work, of course, and during planting and harvest seasons, she went out to help her husband. But on such occasions, the men did not then reciprocate. Such an idea was alien to Japanese custom. Some's only time off came at the birth of a baby, and even then she was soon back at work.

There were ten children, all delivered at home, some with the aid of a midwife—Matsu Kobayashi, no doubt; some were brought into the world by Dr. W. B. Lutes, who later told that throughout his life, all of those children, when celebrating their birthdates, would send a dollar bill to him.

Some in Japanese dress years later when there was time to write poetry and arrange flowers. *Courtesy, Hisa Shimabukuro family.*

Except for one year in Hillrose, the family lived in Merino from 1912 to 1938, then five years in the Iliff area, and later three years at Kersey. And finally, after decades of fighting the dust and drought and depresson, they decided to give up farming and move to Denver.

Throughout all the time of hard work and little leisure, Some never forgot her interest in writing, and she found spare moments to put her thoughts on paper. In Denver, her articles and poems were published in magazines and books. She also wrote a daily column, "Women's World," in *The Colorado Times,* a Japanese language newspaper. She reflected on personal experiences and philosophy, themes that touched the lives of her readers. She also included poetry and stories for special occasions and holidays.

Some was honored with membership in the Haiku and Tanka poetry societies in Denver, for her best talent lay in writing the three-line and five-line verses with an unusual beauty of expression as well as brevity. These short simple poems have been likened to photography. The Japanese people record a beautiful scene with their words, capturing it forever to share with others.

Another young woman, Tomi Ogawa, also arrived in Merino in June 1912. She was not in the least enthusiastic about coming to America to marry Minosuke Noguchi. He was fifteen years older then she; that was perhaps part of the problem. But Tomi had been attending Women's University of Japan for two years and wanted to complete her education. She had grown up in a prosperous family and had lived a most happy life. Then bad times had wiped out the fortune, and Tomi was urged to go to America and pave the way for her younger brothers to follow and rebuild the family finances.

Reluctant as she was, she did not rebel against the plan. She had had many advantages. Now it was her turn to take responsibility. In preparation for the new life, she went to live with the Noguchi family and learn their ways. Her stay was encouraging, for she found that the Noguchis were cultured people and that she had much in common with them.

Still, she met Minosuke in Tacoma, Washington, with dread. But she married him, and together they traveled to Merino. Tomi stared out at the plains and thought with despair of Japan. This

The brides arrive. Left to right, Mrs. Kitashima, Mrs. O'sato, Tomi Ogawa Noguchi, and Mrs. Motofugi. *Courtesy, SuZan Noguchi Swain Firmage.*

country looked empty and barren to her, and like most women settlers of every decade, she found her new life hard. In Japan, she had enjoyed sailing, had played tennis, and had mastered musical instruments; she had arranged flowers and followed other artistic pursuits. It was almost laughable to think about her tennis racket in a country where hard work would provide all the exercise that she would ever need.

And she knew that she would never send for her brothers.

But she was determined to make the best of her marriage, to create a good home. She would complete her part of the bargain.

Then she began to learn about her husband: that he was a man of rare grace and gentleness; that he, too, had attended college; that he approached farming as a creative, noble pursuit. He was drawn by stories of the riches of the earth. He was happy to experiment with new crops, to see the spread of lush green as a result of his labor and imagination, to farm on a magnificent scale that had been impossible on the tiny acreages of Japan. His outdoor life brought many pleasures, such as astronomy which brightened the hours of night irrigating. He was a poet who regarded the world with a philosophical eye and could find words to express his observations. And he was as determined as Tomi to have a refined home atmosphere. One of his poems read:

> *Though the house is old and dilapidated,*
> *Once I live in it, it will be my home,*
> *And I shall be happy.*

Minosuke and Tomi were happy, but they did not have an easy life. Sometimes rain did not come, but Minosuke, like other farmers, guided rivulets down the crop rows, day and night. It was hard work, and he often did not sleep except for little naps at the end of the field, with his hand resting in the furrow so that the arrival of water would alert him to go to the head of the field and move the canvas dams to the next setting. Minosuke did not complain about the drudgery. He gave thanks for the life-giving water.

Tomi and Minosuke enjoyed a lifelong love. *Courtesy, Kisa Noguchi Sasaki, a daughter.*

Nor did Tomi complain about the succession of plain little houses. Dust never piled against her door, for she always created a garden of greenery, carrying water to it during droughts.

And no matter how hard the day's work had been or how menial the tasks, the family sat down to dinner at a table laid with a white cloth. The artistic natures of both Tomi and Minosuke allowed the creation of a traditional Japanese center of beauty with whatever flowers or weeds they found in pastures or along the riverbanks.

Tomi and Minosuke enjoyed a lifelong love. No matter how tiring their work, they took time to write scraps of poems, recording (in daughter Kisa's words) "their impressions, their awe, and their emotions evoked by nature." Tomi's poems reflected her life on the prairie:

On a balmy autumn day,
I came down to the warm garden
And heard the clear song of a meadow lark.

Beyond the sky
A crane is dancing.
For its sake I pray for calm winds.

Though we don't have many possessions,
Members of my family
Are happy and satisfied.

When mealtime came, Tomi and Minosuke read their compositions to each other and so shared the beauty of their days.

It was Tomi who died first. The grief-stricken Minosuke, then ninety-two years old, wrote:

We had hoped
For a long life together
And thought that our love
Would be eternal;
So why must we part today?

After Some and Tomi, there followed a stream of brides. Shima Kamimura arrived in Seattle and married the energetic

Kaichiro Mori (called K by his American friends who found the name a tongue twister). During their lifetime, they purchased eight farms in the Atwood area. Miki Yoshida married Charlie Mabe, and they also lived at Atwood.

Mesdames Zepp, Emma Propst, and other Merino women sponsored a class to teach the Japanese ladies American language, customs, and cooking. The Noguchi daughters have said that Grace Propst, who organized new classes in the 1920s, was a near-legend in their family. But Grace, who believed fervently, "You never really give anything away in life. Good things come back many times over," was also the recipient of the Japanese generosity of spirit and beauty. Many an American mother admonished her children to be as polite as the Japanese.

Tome Kanada came in 1915 to marry one of the more prosperous Japanese immigrants. Torakichi (or T as he was known) Otsuka had paid his dues: working in Hawaii's cane fields from 1900 to 1902, laboring at whatever jobs he could find on the west coast, and finally joining the railroad crew. At Sedgwick, after several years of working beet fields, he and three other young men (Hideichi Yoshimoto and Yonejiro and Rikimatsu Inouye) pooled their resources and began farming for themselves.

That same year of 1915, Ai Wada left Hiroshima to marry Hirosaku Tomita, who in 1898 had been one of the first of the South Platte settlement to leave Japan. He was forty and she was twenty-seven. After working on a farm near Proctor for a few years, they purchased their own land near Iliff.

Another Hiroshima girl, Yukano Morita, married Karuko Shino in 1918. The two owned a farm near Merino.

Nineteen-year-old Tsuchi Tanabe Takasugi faced more than pre-wedding anxieties when she came to America in 1918. Because World War I was under way, passengers on the *Manilla Manu* were warned to be prepared for evacuation at any time.

Tsuchi was not a picture bride. Her husband had left for America soon after their wedding a year earlier. He was not able to meet her in Seattle, but she was directed to a hotel run by a Japanese man. This man arranged the train trip to Julesburg and got her safely aboard. He also gave her advice, some of which turned out to be faulty.

"All women in America wear corsets," he told her, "and if you

Tsuchi Kinoshita, soon after her miserable trip, 1918. *Courtesy, Shizue Peterson, daughter.*

want to be a part of the new country and always look nice, you must do the same." So Tsuchi wore her corset for nine painful days of traveling from Seattle to Julesburg. According to a daughter, Shizue Peterson, Tsuchi suffered severe agony.

But Tsuchi was to face more serious pain. Very shortly after her arrival, her husband died, and she was alone in America. But Matsu Kobayashi, the enthusiastic matchmaker, stepped in. Toward the end of that first year, she arranged for Tsuchi to marry Kansuke Kinoshita, twenty-three years older than she, and they moved to a farm home near Sedgwick. The couple lived together for fifty-three years before Kansuke died at age ninety-five, and they had fourteen children. Tsuchi, who died in 1980 at age eighty-one, had twenty-eight grandchildren and nineteen great-grandchildren. Her daughter, Shizue, noted humorously: "Descendants are multiplying daily."

The last year that immigration authorities allowed picture brides to enter the United States was 1920. It was in that year that Rin Inouye came over to marry her husband, Rikimatsu. Another young woman who beat the deadline, with the assistance of matchmaker Matsu, was Katsu Shimamoto. Immediately after her arrival and wedding, she and her new husband, Hikoichi Shimamoto, moved to a farm between Sedgwick and Ovid. There, for several months, they had to share a kitchen with a

Mexican housewife. Neither woman could speak English, nor (of course) could they understand each other's language. The Mexican woman earnestly pointed to objects and taught their names — in Spanish — to Katsu. No doubt, Hikoichi's bride raised some eyebrows as she began to learn English. Here was a Japanese woman speaking English with a Spanish accent.

Katsu appreciated her Mexican friend, but she never learned to like some of her other neighbors — rattlesnakes.

Hide Yoshimoto also arrived in 1920, but she was not a picture bride. She had married Hideichi Yoshimoto in 1902. The next year he had followed the Pied Piper of wealth to America. For *seventeen years,* Hide had awaited his return. Finally, her brother sent her to the United States with orders to bring her husband home, but she never did. Even after such a long separation, the two enjoyed thirty-eight years together before death parted them.

Not often, but occasionally, one of the second generation (nisei) went to Japan to live. One of those was Ruth Koshi. She remained there for many years and became proficient in the language and customs of her parents' home country. In 1930, she returned to America and married Kuichi Inouye, who had arrived in the United States in 1916, joining his father and uncle. So, although Ruth had been born in America, she was more of a newcomer than her husband, and she was eager to fit in. Visiting friends one day, she was served a piece of pie that was extremely tough, but not wanting to offend her hostess, she managed to cut the leathery dessert and to eat every bite. Only later did she discover that the particular hostess had cut the paper plate the exact size of the pie slice. Like an actor in a television commercial decades later, Ruth could moan, "I can't believe I ate the whole thing."

The Japanese women discovered, as did many other settlers, that it helped to laugh. But there were tears, too, as tragedy struck. Tome and T. Otsuka lost their little five-year-old daughter, Chitose, of complications from an injury that she received at school. No less sad was the death of their daughter, Matsumi (or Margie), at the age of forty-one from an incurable blood disease just when she was making spectacular success in her career. She was assistant director of the medical center at

Rin Inouye with her children, 1926: from left: Suma, 2; Tom, 3; Ayako, 3 months; and Tosh, 4. *Courtesy, Inouye family.*

the University of California, Los Angeles.

Katsu and Hikoichi Shimamoto's little daughter, not quite two years old, died after eating weiners that contained botulism. A son died of a ruptured appendix. He was only six.

When World War II came, Betty Urahama and her family were visiting her grandmother in Japan and were kept there. She was in Nagasaki on a ferryboat on August 9, 1945, when the world about her began to melt and crumble and the people

"I can't believe I ate the whole thing." *Ruth and Kuichi Inouye.*

to burst into flames. Betty was one of the lucky few to be sheltered by the boat structure from the direction of the blast, and so she was spared. Anyone facing the atomic explosion unprotected was instantly burned. The few survivors hurried from the boat and to an air raid shelter on a hillside. For days, they watched the city burn in a sea of fire. The stench was unbearable.

Betty afterward said, "I spent eight of my worst years in Japan." After the war, she came to Denver and lived with an uncle. She married Tadao Shimamoto of Sedgwick.

The families suffered during World War II when their adopted and native countries were at war. Though the Colorado Japanese were not relocated as were those in California, their assets were frozen and they suffered indignities. Toku Wyeno had been a picture bride of George Wyeno, who had come to Otero County in 1898 when he was only eighteen years old. When the Japanese attacked Pearl Harbor, the family was living in Crowley County. It had been forty-three years since George had come to America. Yet the sheriff confiscated their hunting rifles and shortwave radio. A family friend, he considered the government orders ridiculous but had no choice.

Governor Ralph Carr expressed his trust in the Japanese people sent into the state from California and tried to help them. Many felt that his defeat in the next election was a direct result.

Among the Japanese people who were sent to the Amache Relocation Camp in Granada, there were bitter ironies. Mary Hamano was confined there though her husband became an official interpreter for Admiral Nimitz. After the war, the Hamano family remained in southeastern Colorado. Mary operated a small flower shop in La Junta while the children attended school.

Many of the Japanese-Americans, men and women, enlisted in the armed forces of the United States, but it was not until the Naturalization and Immigration Act of 1952 opened the door to citizenship for the first generation that the hurts began to heal.

En Watada of Fort Lupton wrote a poem, "Memorial Day," which expresses the degree of commitment of immigrant families:

While I am taking down
the American National Flag today,
I sadly think that my son
should do this, but he has already died
on the battle field for his mother country.

Celebration after finally becoming United States citizens. To right of table: Katsu Shimamoto, Rin Inouye, Hide Yoshimoto.

113

The Japanese people came searching for a future. Very few of them found a fortune in the usual sense, but they received other treasures: lifelong friendship and shared experiences with a small group of compatriots who also dared to strike off into the unknown. It was not easy for the women to come to a new country, where a strange language was spoken, to marry a man whom they had never seen. But the picture brides did come, and their special courage has contributed to the fabric of American life.

En Watada has lived on the Colorado prairie for a long time. She and her husband celebrated their sixtieth wedding anniversary in late 1981. One of her picture poems (tanka) gives a special view of the prairie:

These miles and miles of ripened wheat
Need no alien moonlight glow
To brighten up the darkness;
For by themselves they yield
An inner golden incandescence.

Just so, the picture brides lent an incandescence to the prairies of eastern Colorado.

Chapter VII

MY CHILDREN, MY BLOOD

A t last the final song was sung. The last bawdy shout rang through the courtyard. A lone soldier drained his bottle, searched among those left on the tables, and stumbled off to bed. Celedonia Rebolloso watched grimly from her post, leaned wearily for a moment against one of the graceful arches, then went to her room. She must lie down for a little while to rest.

But not to sleep. She must not sleep. It had been a long day and night. But the night was not over. And so, after a few restless moments, she got up again, slipped out onto the portico, and listened. No sound came from the rooms across the way. And so she made her way to the coffins.

The day had begun like many another when the soldiers from first one side or the other swept into the city of Torreon. The people had braced themselves, hiding what they could, but knowing that before the day was over, more horses would be taken away, more food snatched out of their fields and kitchens, but pray God, no more young boys led off to fight and die.

But this day had been different. The soldiers in their ragtag uniforms had galloped straight through the streets to the heart of the city. There was an odd purposefulness to their approach. They jerked their horses to a stop in front of the banks, their weapons held high. Some thrust rifles through the front windows, sending a shattering of glass onto the portico and the floors inside. Other soldiers dismounted and strode into the banks, arrogant and sure of their plan.

"No, no!" someone shouted, and the watching townspeople came out of their sheltered doorways. They were stopped by rifles turned their way.

"You must not rob from the bank," an old man called. "We are your friends. How can we supply you if we are left with no money?"

"And how about these?" the leader answered, gesturing toward the Chinese bankers being herded out the doors. "Did not these foreigners ambush us from the galerias of these very buildings? Have you forgotten how they betrayed us?"

Then, like a scene on a stage, the drama unfolded. The Chinese men stood, uneasy but courteous as always, moving not at all, waiting, as Chinese always knew how to do, for things to calm down. But this time, they did not calm down. The townspeople saw the soldiers retreat a little and regroup themselves in orderly lines. Then the ones guarding the Chinese moved aside, and at that awful moment, as the troops raised their guns, the people realized that revenge would be taken, and they scattered to the walks and doorways. The shots rang out, and the Chinese bankers fell to the street. The soldiers swarmed into the banks, bringing out bags of money. It would help to keep the revolution going—but first there must be a celebration.

Celedonia stood in the doorway of her mortuary. It seemed like the safest place. Soldiers saw death face to face too often. They did not need reminders that the final horror could catch up with them at any moment.

Some called to her, "Where are the girls? Where are the pretty girls?"

"Gone away," she answered.

They did not believe her. They surged through the inn, looking under beds and through Celedonia's home, even searching behind hanging clothes. They roared into the restaurant and kitchen, and for a little while, they forgot the search as they grabbed food and returned to the courtyard, their arms and mouths full.

But they did not search the mortuary.

But as the drinking continued and dark came on, first one and then another moved boldly closer to the big room where the coffins sat. Remarks rang out. We'll burn this place, they decided, so that death cannot catch up with us. Like a streak from the skies, the feeling ran through the crowd, and they pressed toward the mortuary. Someone grabbed a torch and pushed to the front.

Celedonia stepped out to face them. She was seventy-six years old, but she stood straight, her eyes were strong, and she put out her arm in an imperious command. The soldiers stopped and stared. One of them called out, "Look, it is the old woman who dares to do a man's business. We'll show her a lesson." And he grabbed the torch and moved forward. Celedonia looked unafraid. The soldiers could not see what she was on the inside, and she had faced too many awful moments to give way now.

"You must not touch the coffins," she said. "They are important to Pancho Villa."

Again the dread touched the men, and they shuffled a little.

Then one called out, "Well, he will not save them for us," and soldiers ran to jerk down the remaining torches.

But Celedonia stood in the door, and she raised her arm and shouted, "It is where I hid your leader. Pancho Villa would be dead today. He may need to hide again. The government forces will look everywhere else, but they will not think to look in a coffin."

It worked. And the brains of the soldiers were too scrambled with drink to wonder if others were hiding in those coffins.

Now, after all these hours, the soldiers were asleep, and Celedonia knew that the time had come. She had worked so hard on this place. These many years since her Frenchman husband had died, she had worked, and she had found that her brain was a good one for business. When some young person needed help, she searched out his talents, and sometimes, she started a new enterprise to use those talents. But she was the businesswoman, and she did the managing. She had built her little empire here in this complex: the inn, the restaurant, the carpentry shop, the horses and carriages for rent, a little barbershop, and the mortuary and three hearses.

She moved quickly in the dark. She knew every step. She pushed coffins aside, lifted the floor, and one by one, she found the children, sleeping in those hidden coffins.

First she awoke Juan Rebolloso, her adopted grandson, and then Carmen Prado, her granddaughter. They were her fav-

Pretty Carmen Prado escaped to the
United States with her grandmother.

orites, the strong ones. Juan was the son of a German father
who had died in the fighting. His mother, too, had been killed.
It was the women who provided support forces, cooking and
washing and managing supplies, freeing all the men to fight.
And when the enemy swept over the lines, the women died with
the soldiers.

Juan was smart enough to hide like a woman and know that
he had to do it. He did not argue. He was eighteen now, ready
to take on a man's role. She had saved his life several times by
demanding that he hide when the soldiers came to town.

Pretty Carmen was only fourteen. Celedonia touched the shining hair and gently slapped the girl's cheeks until she awoke.

She had saved this beauty from the soldiers many times now. Then she awoke Carmen's little half-sisters—Juanita, twelve, and Manuela, six. They were not too young to escape the lust of the soldiers, either. Only she, an old woman, was safe.

Next, Francisca. Her parents had come to stay at the inn one night when she was only a baby. Next morning, Celedonia had found the little girl alone in the room, sleeping. There was a note from the parents: "I know you will take care of her." And so little Pancha, as they called her, became a part of the family, too.

Last of all, she aroused Dorotea, her daughter, mother of the girls. She would have the most trouble with Dorotea. Her husband had been killed years before in 1906 when he was a captain, a career officer with the government forces. Now Dorotea was married again, and this husband rode with the rebels.

But no one argued with Celedonia, not even Dorotea, who was forty-two years old. They would leave the businesses, she told them. The time had come when the businesses could not be saved. They were not important anyway.

"They will be here—or the land will be—when we come back," Celedonia said. "My children. My blood. That is what is important. I have lost enough of my family to this revolution."

When Dorotea protested that she must be there when her husband came home again, Celedonia snapped, "And do you think it will be worth it for him to find you dead?"

They packed clothes and food, each one what he could carry. "Necessities," Celedonia said. But then she herself packed all the family pictures and mementoes of other days—even the sword that had belonged to Carmen's father—and handed them to Juan for safekeeping. "They are necessities, too," she said, "to sustain us during the exile."

Last of all, from a secret place known only to herself, she brought out money. She had taken it from the bank, a little at a time, grumbling all the while about the high cost of running businesses, and had hidden it away where neither soldiers nor fire could reach it.

Silently, the family slipped to a rear door. But Celedonia stopped, and they saw her move in the shadows to look out on the sleeping courtyard. In her mind, Celedonia went through a roll call of all her family, all the ones whom she had lost through the years. Their presences were in this place where the family had lived for so long. One by one she told them goodbye.

Mariano, the handsome Frenchman who had come here and married her. He had taken a Spanish name, but his French ways had given her a new freedom.

Juan Espino, her sister's son, for whom she had set up the barbershop. He was a fine one. In the evenings, he played the guitar out in the courtyard. He was also a bullfighter, and a bull killed him one day. That had been ten years ago, but sometimes Celedonia could still hear his music drifting along the galeria.

Young Juan's parents. Carmen's father. The mysterious lost father and mother of little Pancha. All gone.

And still fighting: Dorotea's husband; Celedonia's one remaining son; Carmen's uncle, Colonel Elijio Lujan, riding with Pancho Villa as his aide. Still living, those three. But for how long?

In her mind, she told them all goodbye. Then she turned to the children. They must go north to the United States as one of her sons, Jesús, had already done. They must be saved to carry the blood to the next generations.

They hurried through the dark streets to the railway station. Thank God, both sides had saved the line, both sides looking ahead to needs when the long war would finally end. They reached the line only a short time before the train was to leave. That was the way Celedonia had planned it.

She counted out the money, peso by peso. Anyone watching would think that the old woman had spent everything she had on those tickets. Not even the family knew that a fortune was hidden on the private parts of her body.

And so began the long trip north. They had made the trip many times, first one and then another of them accompanying Celedonia to El Paso and as far away as Kansas City and St. Louis to buy supplies for the businesses. But those had been trips of pleasure. This was a journey of terror. Every time the engine slowed, they wondered if soldiers would come aboard and snatch them away.

When the train stopped at Chihuahua, the family stirred uneasily. Celedonia got up and shuffled back through the car, walking like a helpless old woman, an old woman that no one would pay any attention to, from whom no one would guard his words to keep her from hearing. And when she came back, she swept them all up and off the train. No time to ask questions. She wouldn't answer them anyway. As always, Celedonia was in command. They hurried through the streets to the home of a friend, and there they hid for two days.

No one questioned when Celedonia finally announced that they could return to the station and catch another train. This time they stayed aboard until the train passed out of Mexico and stopped in El Paso. It was 1919.

There, another friend, Trini Ontiverros, who had often entertained them and accompanied them to Kansas City, took over. She helped them get papers. She offered to move them north on her "underground railroad." But proud Celedonia said, "We are not in this country to stay. We will remain here only until we can return to our home."

And so they lived for almost a year in the Hotel Dos Banderos (Two Flags). And the money slipped away. Finally, Celedonia had to face the fact that they could not return to Mexico. Trini put them in touch with Celedonia's son in Pueblo, Colorado. He said that he could use the family in the beet fields. It was a bitter moment. Dorotea, who had cried for months, was distraught. But Celedonia, who had worked her way up from nothing, said. "We will start over."

The family left most of their possessions in the son's little house near Pueblo. They traveled first to Greeley, then near Padroni to work beets. Celedonia took a hoe and walked the fields with the children. She was still in charge, and whenever she saw one of the young ones leave a weed nestling next to a sugar beet, she sternly commanded that the job be done right.

"We did not build our businesses in Torreon by doing things halfway," she said.

Then, in 1921, came word that a terrible flood had roared down the Arkansas River, taking houses away. The little shack where they had lived was in the path, and all the cherished belongings from Mexico were washed away.

It was like a sign.

"We will never go back," said Dorotea. "I shall never see my

Celedonia Rebolloso. No one argued with her.

husband again." And she never did. Nor was that her only sorrow. Her little daughter, Manuela, only thirteen years old, died in 1926. The next year, Dorotea followed her. She was taken by hard work and, the family said, a broken heart.

Two years later, the powerful Celedonia finally was overcome by age and died in Sedgwick, Colorado. She was eighty-six. That same year, her son Jesús, who had returned to Mexico, lost his life.

Juan and Pancha, Celedonia's two adopted children, turned to each other and were married. After the revolution finally ended, they and Dorotea's other daughter, Juanita, went home to Mexico. In 1936, something happened to end Juan's life. Six months later, Pancha was gone, and the following year, Juanita. Juan was thirty-five, Pancha in her twenties, and Juanita, thirty.

Carmen was indeed strong like Celedonia. She alone survived. She hated the beet work, and she vowed that it would never be the limit of her life. Someday, she would return to Mexico and claim the inheritance that was hers. Someday, she would run the "empire." But fate intervened. In 1930, she met Daniel Torres, a strong man who had come from Mexico looking for a better opportunity. He had no intention of returning. Carmen loved him, and to share his life, she would have to remain in America.

The empire in Mexico became a lost dream, even when the revolution ended. Her uncle, Colonel Lujan, was killed along with Pancho Villa. Death stalked the family. Everything was lost.

Everything but the pride. Everything but the blood. Celedonia's blood surged in the veins of Carmen and Daniel's American children, and Carmen taught them Celedonia's pride.

Carmen's heritage was a good mix with Daniel's ambition. Their five sons served a total of sixteen years in the armed forces of the United States, and the nine children attended college. One son was accepted in the first class of the United States Air Force Academy. Several children are engaged in professions, and others are successful farmers.

The little empire may have been lost, but what was most important — the blood — was saved by Celedonia and has thrived in northeastern Colorado.

Tornado funnel, 1947. Photograph by Ellis Schmidt, who says, "Later the funnel curled back like the trunk of an elephant and dropped masses of debris on the prairie."

Remains of trees near Kelly after 1947 tornado. *Ellis Schmidt, photographer.*

Flooded house, 1965. *Dr. T. M. Rogers, photographer.*

THE TESTING

The awakening was sweet, the seeking exhilarating. But nothing would be easy.

Abandoned soddy near Orchard, Colorado. *From a painting by Jessie Scott.*

1947 tornado. *Ellis Schmidt, photographer.*

Chapter VIII

YOU CAN'T LAY YOUR HEAD
ON MOTHER NATURE'S BREAST

The woman on the plains had many fears. Daylight chased most of them away, but one enemy came again and again. Even though the woman was constantly on guard, she was never prepared for the next attack. Not even the men could provide protection.

The enemy came when one least expected her, sometimes boldly stalking across the prairie for all to see, sometimes sneaking up to a little house in the middle of the night. Sometimes she slithered across the ground. She could arrive in such a fury that her white cloak whirled about her head. Rarely — but in never-to-be-forgotten splendor — she rode on golden horses that raced across the sky, bringing death to everything struck by the sparks from their hooves.

But whatever her form, when one looked around at the destruction in her path, one realized that it was always the same enemy. Life on the plains is a never-ending drama, and the pivotal character is often that fearsome lady.

Etta Shannon first encountered the woman in 1887 soon after her family made the covered wagon trip to the promised land of Prairie Dale Settlement. Her father and the older children were away one afternoon when a fearsome electric storm prevented the mother and little ones from bringing the cows and calves to the protection of the corrals. As dark approached, coyote screams began off in the distance. The children were still not accustomed to that nightly sound which made shivers run up and down their backs. But then, they heard a second noise, a howling from a more formidable enemy, the gray wolf. And closer and closer, the sounds came.

"Children," said their mother, "we have to go out there and bring those cattle in. It's our job." The young children were frightened, but the mother said, "If we don't go, they may eat our baby calves."

The little ones had been playing barefoot around the house, and when their mother reassured them, "It won't take long. I'm sure the cows have come close," they simply slipped their feet into shoes and threw old towels over their heads to protect against sporadic showers. They went up over the hill to the west and saw nothing. And so they decided to look over the next hill, but again they saw no cattle. Another dark cloud began to gather strength in the west, and suddenly the prairie was dark. The mother decided that they must go home at once.

Etta Shannon told the story:

> A dispute arose as to which was the right direction, there being neither fences nor houses near. One of the most terrifying electric and dashing rainstorms came on us, and we wandered all night on a prairie where there were numerous open wells, snakes, coyotes, and wolves.
>
> We became so tired and sleepy that we would squat down in a circle — the ground being too wet to sleep on — and take turns imitating the bark of a dog, thinking by that means it might keep away the prowling animals. Our heads, covered with those white rags, would bob and nod at each other.

During the storm, a great ball of fire suddenly appeared as if by magic.

> We thought it possible that E. P. Morlan, who was among the last to remain in that community, had heard our cries and barkings, had gotten on a horse, and carrying a lantern, had come to look for us. We ran toward the ball crying, "Here we are! Here we are!" but it would move away from us and soon disappear.

They had seen the two sides of the woman: the terror of the storm and the false promise. And they knew from that time that you can't lay your head on Mother Nature's breast.

Those balls of fire fooled many a woman — and many a frontiersman as well. Suddenly, miles from the lights of any settlement, on a black night, the bobbing lantern would be seen in the distance. And as a woman peered nervously from her window, it moved inexorably toward her door.

"Who could be coming to my house in the middle of the night?" she would wonder. And many a time, she laid out her firearm on the bed and wondered if she dared use it.

Closer and closer came the light, veering off first one way and then another, like some lost spirit, searching a long ago path. And just when the woman was ready to scream from the tension and suspense, it would give one last bob in her direction, then quickly climb the hill behind her house and disappear.

To the early people, the light was as real as the howling of the coyotes and the moaning of the wolves. They were all supernatural forces that went together. It was only the strong-minded who could persuade themselves that the lights were a natural phenomenon, perhaps phosphorescence from marsh gas.

Another false promise occurred in the full light of day, but it was no less cruel. Families following their hopes to the country of free land could lose their way on the open prairie and wander for days without water. The weary horses or oxen took ever slower steps; the men, their skins blackened by the sun, felt that their throats were just as hard and wrinkled; and the women, faint from the midday heat, had the unpleasant task of rationing water from the barrel and trying to make little children understand the necessity.

Then suddenly, someone gives a cry. There ahead, in the distance, shimmering like a dream on the horizon, is a grove of trees. Water will be there. Another disaster is averted.

But they drive and drive, and always the trees are on the horizon. And finally, the emigrants realize that the trees are a hoax. But even after they know the truth, the mirage, like some faithless woman, continues to beckon and entice.

From those early introductions, the seekers learned that there are few places where Mother Nature can act more capriciously than on the plains of eastern Colorado. It is far enough north to be in the path of some of the most vicious winter storms, perhaps the more dangerous because they are often unexpected.

A dust storm boils over the horizon.

. . . and swallows a defenseless homestead, 1935. *From the Hazel E. Johnson Collection.*

The average rainfall of only six to fourteen inches can be reduced by drought, perhaps the most depressing of Mother Nature's unkind tricks. Both storm and drought are intensified when accompanied by wind.

The homesteaders brought on many of their woes, for much of the ground that they plowed was too unstable, and the wind set the dust to moving. Teresa Lee told of teaching during the 1930s in La Junta, a part of the dust bowl of southeastern Colorado. "A field that was green with wheat two inches high," she said, "could be bare the next day after one of those storms hit." At the schoolhouse, she and the children could see "the swirling dust and hear the sound of the sand being blown against the windows." Soon dirt began to collect on the window sills and spread across the floors. Laura E. Weaver, who also taught in southeastern Colorado, said that the day would sometimes turn to night, with dust in the room "so thick and black that we could not see each other."

Helen Sherwin Parr, who lived on a ranch near Padroni, did not expect the dust storms to reach northeastern Colorado, but one day as she worked in her garden, she noticed a haze, and about 3:00, it was suddenly almost dark. Even the chickens were fooled and went to roost. The cattle and sheep gathered at the pasture gate. They knew that something was wrong. Helen and her collie ran down the lane, the longest half mile that she ever traveled. When she opened the gate, the animals went "pell-mell — not frolicking but frightened . . . seemingly desperate to reach the safety of the barn and pens."

Regularly, Mother Nature dishes out her disasters, but her variety is astonishing. She may be cruel; she is rarely predictable. A change in weather that merely inconveniences urban dwellers can be catastrophic on a farm. A late spring freeze can force replanting — if it is not *too* late; an early fall freeze kills corn, leading to hasty cutting to salvage some for ensilage.

On two occasions, eastern Colorado beets have frozen in the ground. Men and women worked doggedly to get them out, though on some days the earth did not thaw enough to permit digging until 3:00 in the afternoon, and by 6:00, it would again be frozen. On warmer days, the fields turned to mud, and huge tractors had to pull the trucks loaded with tons of beets. Eventually, many acres were abandoned.

Sometimes, several inches of the yearly allotment of moisture can come in one pounding rain, disastrous if it falls on tiny shoots of corn or emerging beet plants. Most people think that the farmer rejoices whenever there is rain. Actually, it is a rare one that comes at the right time. It can stop planting or harvest, both crucial periods, and if it falls on heavy "gumbo" soil, the delay can run into weeks.

When one of those gully washers hit the Sorenson homestead shack in the Grover area, the water came straight through the tarpaper roof. The family had to move their table over the bed to keep it dry.

Tragedy can result from such cloudbursts, sometimes many miles away where no rain has fallen. Once, a woman, her mother-in-law, and her children waited in North Pawnee Creek while the husband, Arthur Kestler, went for help to pull the vehicle out of the sand. It was a peaceful night, and the family dozed while awaiting rescue. Then a flash flood from the Buttes area brought ten feet of water down the dry creek, and the women and little ones all drowned.

The Carl Davis family, living on little Cotton Creek, awakened

The South Platte, an insignificant winding stream, swells to fill her mile-wide bed

. . . covers roads

. . . wipes out bridges

one night when water suddenly beat against their house. They went out a second-story window and tried to reach high ground. But wave after wave hit them with such force that the wife and babies were torn from the husband's arms and swept miles away.

. . . and leaves her calling card on the Union Pacific tracks.

Chickens take refuge while, on distant hills, the cattle graze un-concerned. *All pictures of 1965 flood by Dr. T. M. Rogers.*

Northeastern Colorado is a swath of land known as Hail Alley because the area receives more hail than any other place in the United States. As a result, fearful residents can hardly enjoy any rain. The hail usually begins with a few innocent thumps on the roof, but no matter how tentative the beginning, one tenses and dreads the sudden gathering of force. Faster and faster, the ice comes, stripping leaves from trees, shredding corn and beets, pounding young plants into the earth.

And inside the house, the women and men alike walk the floor and weep.

As if playing a solitary game of Monopoly, the lady turns the cards and, with seeming indifference, sends the golden sun and brisk air which grace most days on the prairie — or one of the disasters: corn blowing down; tornadoes, rare but horrifying to the extreme; floods; prairie fires; or blizzards.

In 1947, Mildred and Marvin Felzien took a Sunday afternoon drive to see the results of a tornado that struck Julesburg.

They returned home to find that their own home had vanished.

Sometimes the storms last only hours or even minutes. Then the sun comes out; the sky is as blue as ever; the landscape glows. It is as if Mother Nature says, "Oops! My mistake." But all about lies destruction. One cannot easily forget or forgive.

Gladys Shull wore her father's buffalo coat to school on cold mornings. It scared her horse, but it kept her warm. But not even the coat was enough on December 9, 1919. The night before had been the coldest on record, and as Gladys drove her trotter and buggy to work, she froze her calves and heels.

The most deadly storm is the blizzard. The wind can drive the powdery snow so violently that a person can become lost within feet of his own house. When Etta Shannon's brother Tom went out to bring cow chips for the stove, his mother tied a rope around his waist and pulled it taut to guide him back to the house.

After the legendary blizzard of December 13, 1913, the people on Grover homesteads were snowbound for a month. The snow was packed so hard that one could walk on top of it *if* he could get out of the house. The first word from the rest of the world

Ranch enveloped by a blizzard, 1948. *Photograph by the late Sherman Sigler.*

Trying to clear the tracks. *Photograph by the late Sherman Sigler.*

came when a postal worker finally walked from Pine Bluffs, Wyoming, with a sack of mail.

The best rule, when caught in a blizzard, is to stay in the vehicle. Some people manage to reach houses, but others, even when holding hands, become separated when one stumbles, and they cannot find each other again. Two sisters had such an experience one morning when a blizzard worsened as they drove to town. The car slid into a ditch, and cold and miserable, they decided to walk to a farmhouse. One moment, they were holding onto each other; the next, one had disappeared. The screaming wind swallowed the sounds of their cries. One sister reached safety; the other's body was found when the storm ended.

Some, with even the minimum protection of a robe, have been able to survive by allowing the snow to build a fort around them. Others have smothered to death in such a situation. Even in the open snow, death often comes, not from freezing, but from the wind sucking the breath from the body.

The year 1913 brought not only a succession of such blizzards but also a great prairie fire. Winds can whip a fire to enormous heights and speed, and anything in the path may be destroyed. Fighting the fire is dangerous because of the chance of becoming trapped. Morrine Lewis Simmons, young daughter of the E. E. Lewises, helped to fight the 1913 fire when it approached their homestead in the Sligo area. She rode her horse, Old Buck, guiding and controlling him as her father plowed a fire lane.

The people on Colorado prairies are amazingly resilient and optimistic. Often when a family was hailed out, the children picked up the stones, and their mother used them to make ice cream. Clella Rieke's mother liked to say, "God gave us weeds to keep you out of mischief." Even a blizzard could be fun. When Edith Stout taught in southeastern Colorado, she found that if a storm came during school hours, children were not to be sent home. An arrangement was made with a rancher to take the students to his nearby "old, rambling rock ranch house." Since the rancher had several cowboys who also lived in the house, girl students had to be chaperoned by a woman teacher. One night, Edith stayed there with seven teenagers, four of them girls with whom she shared an enormous bedroom. She recalled:

> We slept in the host's old-fashioned nightshirts. What fun we had! When we got up the next morning, the rancher was gone, but our breakfast was in the warming oven—stacks of pancakes, ham, and fried eggs. Somehow, even the wildest weather did not frighten me. I knew that if any of the children or I were in danger, someone would search us out. We were all part of the community family.

Most of the women who came to the prairie seemed to adjust to the hardships. Sometimes they were as tough as the fearsome woman. When she threw out her challenges, there was a fight ahead.

Such an adversary was Kate Slaughterback, who lived with her three-year-old son Ernie on her farm near Ione, south of Platteville. Her legendary battle came on October 28, 1925. She and the little boy rode their horses out to a pasture for cattle work that day. Kate dismounted to open a gate and saw a rattlesnake. She matter of factly took her rifle from the saddle and shot it. Three more snakes appeared, and Kate, an excellent marksman, killed them, too.

Then the horror began. Snakes started coming from everywhere. There was no time to reload. Luckily, Kate spied a fencepost nearby. She grabbed it and beat at the coiling, striking rattlers. It was a nightmare. It seemed that every time she killed one, two more appeared. Then Ernie began to cry, and Kate, beating furiously at the snakes, had no time to comfort him. All she could do was pray that the horse did not shy and throw the child into the mass of snakes.

For two hours the battle went on. And finally when the last rattler was killed, Kate leaned against her little boy's pony, her body wracked with dry sobs.

Neighbors came and strung the rattlers on the fence for everyone to see. There were 140 of them. The story was told in papers as far away as New York and then all over the world. And ever afterwards, she was known as Rattlesnake Kate.

Many women grew to love the prairie expanse and to glory in its invincibility. Memories of muggy summers back East or down South made them appreciate Colorado's crisp, cool air — and helped them to endure the occasional violence. They tried to keep doubts to themselves.

But Anna Green, who reluctantly accompanied her husband, William, to the new Greeley Union Colony in 1870, was horrified by the "dreadful, hateful, woeful, fearful, doleful, desolate, distressed, disagreeable, dusty, detestable, homely, and lonely plains." The Green family had come as a result of N. C. Meeker's article on colonization in the "famous *New York Tribune. . . .* I remember it with many regrets," Anna wrote many years later, "and ever shall while memory lasts."

Her little book, *Sixteen Years on the Great American Desert* or *The Trials and Triumphs of a Frontier Life* recounted few triumphs. It is a dismal recital of the terrors of nature that those sixteen years brought.

For the first two weeks, the family lived in a tent which blew down almost every day. As they struggled to put it up again and to collect their belongings scattered over the ground, Anna muttered to herself that N. C. Meeker's and Horace Greeley's colony was the "greatest swindle of the age."

She was not alarmed by the wind because the "old settlers"

maintained that they had never heard of a tornado in Colorado. But one day, when dust and gravel were hitting her windows, Annie heard a roaring and looked out to see houses lifted and smashed. No one was killed, and Annie spoke of "every surviving victim of Union Colony," and she wished that she had never heard of Horace Greeley and N. C. Meeker.

Anna spent a lot of time in tears. She composed doleful songs, and if they did not bring sobs, letters from the Pennsylvania home did. Always they repeated the mournful refrain: "We never all shall meet again." And Anna cried.

One day her husband said, "Annie, do you know that you are killing me?"

Annie resolved to be cheerful, but as she fought the constant layers of dust, she pronounced the colony idea "absurd." They were told that it never rained on the aptly christened Great American Desert, and for a year it didn't. Summer came, the ugliest she could imagine, with no green, no color to break the monotony of the sun-baked prairie. Annie fumed and "wished a thousand times that N. C. Meeker, Horace Greeley, and the *New York Tribune* were at the bottom of the sea."

Then one day, she heard thunder in the distance. She was not alarmed, for her husband reminded her, "Don't you know there are no hard storms in this country?" But a few minutes later, lightning was filling the house, followed by the most terrifying claps of thunder that she had ever heard. Then rain, wonderful rain, fell in sheets. But suddenly there came a "clatter, clatter" on the tarred paper roof. Annie was so frightened that she could only think, "God be merciful to me, a poor deluded Union Colony victim." Within minutes, the roof was completely torn up, and water poured by the bucketsful into the house.

The next year was the one that Colorado old-timers always called the Terrible Winter. Anna told that on January 23, 1872, she heard a noise like the rushing of a mighty waterspout. She looked out to the west and saw a vast wall of clouds approaching with the speed of a whirlwind. The roaring grew louder as the fine snow approached, and people in the town did not have time to run the few blocks to their homes before the blinding storm hit. One man almost died a few steps from his door, and his anxious wife, peering out, could not even see him struggling in the snow.

And Annie bitterly recalled that "Father Meeker" was fond of speaking of Colorado's "Italian clime."

Only once, however, in the thirteen years that Annie's husband farmed, was it necessary to "irrigate up" the crop (water it to

"Oops! My mistake." The sun comes out and the scene glows. *Photographer, Sherman Sigler.*

bring germination). But grasshoppers seemed to come year after year, and when they finished feasting on a field, there would be little spared, though sometimes (Annie groused) they thoughtfully left enough for the rust to strike.

The Greens lived in Colorado seventeen years before saving enough money to make a return visit to Pennsylvania, and Annie hated every moment. "Oh, suffering humanity!" she would exclaim, "why did we ever come to such a place?"

Man's eternal struggle with nature is a drama; man's old story of trying to survive is a worthy subject. And perhaps Annie became more caught up in it than she knew, for after sixteen years of complaining and weeping, she wrote a song for her daughter to perform. Called "Away out in the West," it was positive enough to have been written by old Father Meeker himself. It extolled every virtue ever ascribed to Colorado: sparkling water, the snow-clad Rocky Mountains, even the pure and balmy air, and — what's this? — "the richest prairie grass!"

Perhaps Annie made her peace with that terrible lady of the plains. Perhaps Mother Nature recognized in Annie a worthy adversary.

Chapter IX

THROUGH THE VALLEY OF THE SHADOW

The mother begged for a picture of her only son. She had nothing to remember him by. Young Jacob Deabald, son of German homesteaders, had become ill out on the farm. Since there was no hospital in Sterling, the nearest town, the child was placed in the hotel where the doctor could see him frequently. But he died.

The grieving mother begged Flora Allison, county superintendent of schools and an awesome figure of power to the parents, to persuade the mortician and photographer. They were not in favor of the idea. Flora tried to reason with the mother, telling her, "What a sad picture it would be."

"Me no cry," the woman vowed.

A photographer came, and when the family was arranged, the mortician placed the boy, "standing straight and tall," beside his sister behind the seated parents and grandmother. The mother kept her promise and did not cry.

"It was a quiet, reverent group," Flora Allison said. Family strength sustained them.

But another couple lost a little boy, and it tore them apart. The marriage broke up. As with most divorces of the time, no note was made in local papers. Only when a case was sensational or involved unsavory people did the editors pull out all stops and relate every detail that they could dig out—or perhaps imagine. More often, they simply stopped mentioning the man who had faded out of the picture. When the highly respected Edna Weir and her husband Andy broke apart over his gambling, the paper began to refer to Mrs. Edna Weir. Everyone in town knew the story anyway, and readers of later generations were left to wonder about poor Andy's fate.

The people often did not divorce but simply separated. Remarriage did not happen until one or the other died.

Time after time, children did not know that a parent had had a previous marriage. There may have been gossip, but it was discreet. Entire communities entered a pact of silence. The H. B. Davis children were nearly grown before someone happened to mention that sister Ouida was not the daughter of their father but the product of Lizzie's earlier unhappy marriage. Lucius P. Cheairs learned only a couple of years before his death that his father had married twice and that there was a half sister whom he had never seen. Dallas Landrum, Jr. did not know until after his mother died that she had been married briefly before her marriage to his father.

Sometimes families actively promoted a breakup. Elizabeth Jane Weir of Julesburg married Charles Lanphere, and they had two children, but one day Charles decided he could no longer tolerate the primitive life at Julesburg and returned to Chicago. Later he was sorry and tried to make up with Elizabeth Jane, but she did not receive the letters. Her father, determined that Lanphere would never again have an opportunity to hurt his daughter, destroyed them. It was many years before Elizabeth Jane knew of the attempts at reconciliation, and by that time she had remarried.

It seemed that women's most poignant tragedies usually involved men, and sometimes circumstances forced a break between two people who cared for each other. Yellow Woman married William Bent after the death of her sister, Owl Woman. She mothered the children from the previous marriage, and she and William were also the parents of a daughter, Julia. When her nephew-stepsons, George and Charles, were badly injured in the late 1864 attack on Indians encamped at Sand Creek, they came home to Bent's Fort, full of hatred for John Chivington and his white volunteer soldiers. Yellow Woman nursed them back to health.

In early January, George and Charles joined a large force of Cheyennes, Arapahos, and Sioux who would seek revenge by a month-long—and eventually four-year-long—assault on the South Platte lifeline to Denver and the gold fields.

When they left, Yellow Woman walked out with them. She was devoted to William, and he had been a friend of the Indians. His children were half Indian. Most of her people looked on him as one of them. But now, the battle of Sand Creek had burned the word treachery into the brains of the red men. And William Bent was suddenly not the longtime friend, husband, and father of Indians, but a white man. And Yellow Woman declared that she could no longer live with a white man.

She never returned.

Much of the unhappiness of women came because of husbands with roving eyes, but some of the Indian women in trapper days were in a particulary vulnerable position. There had always been few constraints on their Indian husbands. If a Cheyenne husband wanted to be rid of his wife, he called all the band together and threw a stick into the air, calling, "There goes my wife. Whoever wants her may have her." Though the Indian women sometimes fared better with white husbands, the traders were often overwhelmed with the availability of many wives. Indian fathers were only too anxious to make presents of their daughters to influential white men.

Elbridge Gerry was one of those whites much liked by most Indians. He had lived among them as a trapper and trader since coming west from New England in 1839 when he was twenty-one years old. He was also held in respect by whites. Most believed that he was a grandson of the famous Elbridge Gerry, who had been one of the signers of the United States Constitution and had served as vice-president of the country. But, perhaps more important, he was held in gratitude as the "Paul Revere of the South Platte" for his nightlong ride to warn whites of a huge Indian attack slated to hit all the new Colorado settlements in the summer of 1864. Somehow, Gerry managed to maintain cordial relations with both whites and reds most of the time.

Elbridge Gerry had so many wives and children that it was difficult to keep his families straight. *Courtesy, Colorado Historical Society.*

He had so many wives and children that it was difficult to keep his families straight. He was good to them and provided well at his trading post near the mouth of Crow Creek on the South Platte and later at his Evans Hotel.

But the women seethed with resentment. In the 1840s, while trading in the Fort Laramie area, he married Kate Smith, a half-blood Sioux, though there were rumors that he had a white wife back in Massachusetts. He and Kate apparently had about four children, but in the 1860 census, Gerry listed his first two children (of a total of six) as having been born in Maine and Massachusetts. The marriage with Kate lasted several years, but when Gerry became involved with a young Indian woman, she returned to her Sioux mother.

Then, in 1850, Joseph Red Kettle, a subchief under Red Cloud, presented Gerry with two daughters: Mary, who was only fifteen, and her older sister Mollie. Indians often took extra wives, and it was believed that the women would get along better if they were sisters. One wonders where the men got that idea. It certainly did not work in the Gerry household.

"We fought!" Mary later told her daughter (who was born when Mary was only sixteen and Gerry, thirty-three). "She was bigger and older and stronger than I was and I didn't stand a chance against her."

One day when Mary was nineteen, she decided that she had had enough, and she took her three-year-old daughter and returned to her Indian home. Elbridge Gerry, according to a granddaughter, was so angry at the upheaval in his household that he sent Mollie away, too. Eventually, however, the Red Kettle grandparents brought the little girl, Mary, to live again with Elbridge Gerry. Her mother had remarried and was happy with her new husband. Lone Wolf was a good father to little Mary, but the child was returned to Gerry because of family concern over her safety.

The worries had begun soon after Mary had left Elbridge. Little Mary and some other Indian girls were out playing when they saw two young men riding wildly toward them on horseback. They were dragging something on the end of a rope, and when they drew near, the girls saw that they were Indians and that they were drunk. But the worst sight was what was at the end of the rope. It was the body of a little blonde white girl, barely two years old, jerking along the ground and flying up into the air. The young men bragged that they had killed the child while her captive mother looked on. Furthermore, they said, they would do the same to any other yellow-headed, blue-eyed kids that they found. And they looked directly into little Mary's blue eyes as they spoke.

The family was terrified. Moreover, Lone Wolf, a good man who tried to help anyone being mistreated, rescued the white mother, and when he intervened, radical Indians became more resentful. As the years went by, Mary and Lone Wolf worried increasingly about the daughter, especially when she approached her teen years. And so finally Mary told her daughter goodbye and sent her back to Elbridge Gerry. Her Red Kettle grandparents went along and lived at Gerry's trading post until Little Mary grew up.

The younger Mary was fortunate in her marriage. An English-

Gerry's grave near Crow Creek is on the site of his trading post where his families lived. *Courtesy, Colorado Historical Society.*

man working at the ranch watched the pretty little girl and knew that she would soon be the object of sexual pressure from both Indian and white men. He talked her into marrying him. He was only two years younger than Mary's mother. There was almost the same age span in the marriage as there had been between Gerry and the first Mary. He felt that Mary was just a little girl yet and sent her back to Gerry's house while he continued to sleep in the bunkhouse. It was a year before the two actually began their happy life together.

After the loss of the Red Kettle girls, Elbridge Gerry had taken two more sisters to wife, the twin daughters of Swift Bird, another of his good friends. And this multiple marriage did not work any better than the first one had. One day Melissa, one of the twins, went out by herself and sat on a hill on the ranch. Her sobs drew attention, and Mary followed to see what was the matter. Melissa poured out her story. She already had two children by Gerry, and now she was growing another baby. She was fed up with life in a house full of wives and offspring from several marriages plus abandoned or orphaned children that the generous Gerry regularly brought home. Most of all, she was fed up with having one baby after another.

And so Melissa left, aided by Mary and her husband and a

half-blood friend who later married Melissa and took her three children as his own.

Sometimes a woman seemed shrouded in mystery, and as the years passed, the mystery only deepened, so that three-quarters of a century later, the telling of her story is partly speculation. Adeline Estelle Sutliff came West as a mail order bride near the turn of the century, but the marriage never took place. The prospective groom's son, Irvin Monnette, wooed her away. He was no doubt an interesting man. He competed in rodeos and won the title of World Champion Steer Roper at Cheyenne. He played the fiddle.

But the marriage was not happy. Adeline was older than Irvin, and he was away from home a lot, following the rodeo circuit. She was lonely and unhappy much of the time.

Then, in 1912, he became involved in a dramatic homesteader-cattleman conflict that wound up in the courts. Irv was a friend and employee of Gene Buchanan, who had followed the custom of many people by hiring a man to prove up on a piece of land for him. He also provided money for improvements on the homestead. But though the man took the pay, he refused to turn the land over to Buchanan.

Furious, Buchanan led a raid on the place and removed the buildings to the nearby Sindt family homestead. The federal government brought suit against Buchanan, Monnette, and one of Adeline's sons from a previous marriage. The case was the first prosecution in Colorado under an old post–Civil War statute, aimed at the Ku Klux Klan, which made it illegal to deprive anyone of his rights.

The homesteader died mysteriously in Cheyenne, and the trial took on a more sinister aspect with an attempt to link Buchanan and his employees with the death. Irvin was sentenced to five years, Adeline's son to one. The case dragged on with appeals for years.

Then one day, Adeline performed the final mystery. She swallowed carbolic acid and in her agony ran into a little nearby reservoir. A water hauler found her body.

The women were a part of the history of the plains, but they did not necessarily take on the challenges out of joyous adventure. Often it was a bitter necessity. Many a child told of his mother doing the work of a man, harnessing teams, plowing, milking cows, peddling produce through the streets of a nearby town. And she and her family survived.

But long after dark, the child would hear a sound and would know only too well what it was. Night after night, he awoke to hear his mother, so cheerful by day, crying quietly, desperately, in her lonely bed.

Chapter X

WHAT ONE WOMAN CAN DO

Once, fair goers in Sterling came upon an interesting display. Mounted on a board, ten to twelve feet long, were samples of cooking, fancy work, sewing, homemade wood and leather appliances, poetry, and musical compositions. But equally prominent were evidences of other talents: carpentry, plowing, harvesting wheat, milking cows, tending chickens, peddling produce through the streets of Sterling, and even butchering animals for meat or sewing up the wound of a child. A rifle and badge attested to a career as deputy game warden. The display was titled WHAT ONE WOMAN CAN DO. It showed that the woman could and did prove up on her homestead, that she plowed it and improved it. She had made her enterprises pay.

But there was one thing that the woman could not do, and that lack brought overwhelming tragedy to her life.

Christie Payne was seventeen years old when she came to Colorado. She had worked with her father and brothers in their prosperous contracting business in Nebraska, but in the summer of 1889, she felt the need for a change. Her parents sent her out to visit homesteading relatives at Abbot.

Christie was beautiful, she was tall and slim, her long brown hair hung down her back, and her blue eyes sparkled. She was sure of herself. No young man had ever caught her fancy. But she had hardly arrived in Colorado when that situation changed.

The word spread quickly that a good-looking girl was visiting at the homestead. Soon a succession of cowboys found it

Christie and John Merrell's homestead, the only wood house between Iliff and Sterling.

necessary, for one reason or another, to visit the place and take a look. Still, Christie paid little attention.

Until the day John Merrell came to call. He was tall with dark good looks, a striking man both in appearance and speech. For John Merrell was a graduate of Yale University and came from

a wealthy Eastern family. A place in the family stockbroking firm was his for the asking. His people were distinguished in education as well.

But John was fascinated with the West, and after graduation, he had come out to explore the wide open spaces. When Christie arrived, he was working as a cowboy for Jared Brush's big JB Ranch.

They were married by the time Christie was eighteen. John was twenty-six. Their first child, a doll-like little girl, was born the following year, 1891. John was appointed foreman of Brush's main headquarters on the South Platte, and Christie became the cook for the ranch hands. For almost a year, she hardly left the place. She rarely saw another woman. But the marriage seemed like the happiest possible. A second child was born.

They made good money and saved it. They claimed a homestead and in 1894 resigned their jobs with Brush and moved to it. Christie was happy to exhibit the skills that she had learned in her father's business. Together, she and John built the first frame house on the south side of the river between Iliff and Sterling.

And four more children came during the next few years. Christie prided herself on a comfortable home. She played a little organ, sang to the children, and cooked good meals. The baby was frail and required a lot of care. But Christie also went out to help John with the hard work of breaking the sod, plowing, and planting.

Christie took pride in a comfortable home, 1899.

He had a relative send him registered Belgian breeding stock and was soon busily engaged in the horse business. Christie did more and more of the homestead work. John began to make it clear that he did not find the farming duties very exciting. Soon he was spending nights, and then days, in town. And one morning in 1903, when Hattie, the oldest child, was twelve and the baby less than one year, he came home and packed his clothes and left forever.

Christie was strong. She gathered the five oldest children about her and told them that they must all work hard to farm the homestead and keep the family together. Frank, the oldest boy at ten, would be the foreman, Christie the manager. Hattie would run the house. The other children would do their part.

Christie was strong, but tears flowed from her eyes that day. It was the only time that her children ever saw her cry, but sometimes in the night, like other abandoned women, she lay in her bed and wept.

In the daytime, she worked like a woman possessed. She had to, for soon other blows fell. First, she learned that John had sold the adjoining pasture. Then came word that he had borrowed money and mortgaged the homestead. Christie simply worked harder. Every Saturday, she hitched up the team and, with one child to help her, made an all-day trip into town. From door to door, up street after street, she would drive, selling sixty pounds of butter, fifty to sixty dozen eggs, five or six quarts of sweet cream, jars of grape jelly, a few dressed chickens, and sometimes meat from a freshly butchered hog or beef. The products did not appear magically. All week long, she and the children labored. They even managed to do the unpleasant work of butchering and dressing animals.

Yet, always before she headed home, the child with her had a treat from a Sterling store. And when the wagon pulled into the yard long after dark, the other children came running, for they knew that she had brought something special for each one. They were only children, and though they had to take on adult responsibilities, Christie tried hard to give them some of the pleasures of childhood. Every day, she saw to it that each one had some time to spend on himself, exactly as he pleased.

"We're going to make it," she told herself. "We're paying off

Five of the children, about 1900.

the mortgage, and the children seem happy."

Then one morning, she bent over to pick up the baby and to love him for a few minutes before she and the boys went out to milk the cows. He was gone. His sickly little body had failed. It was the one blow from which Christie could not seem to recover. She sat in the house alone, not crying but not talking, staring at his bed, and wondering desperately what had happened to make her life go so wrong.

Hattie continued to cook and clean house, and the boys went out as usual to milk and do chores and drive the route. Finally, when Christie became aware of the children's struggles to clean dozens of eggs, churn all that cream, and make those dozens of pounds of butter, she rallied and went back to work.

And they prospered. The debt was paid off. The farm was a little show place. All that time, the children had managed to stay in school. Christie held her head high with pride at all that they had accomplished. They were even able to hire a man now and then to help with the heavy work.

One of those men was Will Partridge. He had a reputation

for drinking, but under Christie's influence, he gave up liquor. He was a likable man, good company. She was attracted to him, and he appreciated Christie's good looks and the way that she had managed so well on the place.

And so, in 1910, they were married. At last Christie's life had turned around. With a husband on the place, she could do a woman's work and have some time for her artistic interests. Again she could play the organ and sing and write poetry. It was like being given a second chance in life.

She encouraged Will to take out a homestead, and he did—160 acres on the historic site of old Valley Station. Christie rented her farm and moved to the new homestead with Will. Once again, she and the boys helped to build a house. Once again, they broke the sod and planted crops.

But soon, Will was spending more and more time in Sterling. It was the same old story. Christie and the children were at home working hard. Will was hanging out in a saloon. Christie's money began to disappear. At first, he tried to hide what was happening, but soon he was coming home in ever worse shape. His face twisted into ugliness whenever Christie tried to talk to him. He slammed into her. Henry, though only fifteen, was the largest of the sons, and he threw himself on the man and shoved him out the door. Will stumbled to the barn and slept in the hay.

Next morning, Will was sorry and tried to make up. Then things went well for awhile. But invariably, the ugly scene was played again—and ever more frequently. Soon, life was an endless struggle of trying to do the farmwork during the day and then bracing for the every night drunken confrontation.

There came a night that none of them would ever forget. Will was drinking, enough to be mean but not enough to be unsteady on his feet. Henry was not able to shove him out the door. Will waved the whiskey bottle and cursed. He knocked Christie onto the bed. Chairs were overturned, and the young children hugged against the walls in fear. Finally, Will raised the bottle and took a long drink. Within moments, he staggered and fell to the floor. But the family did not know the usual relief after he passed out. For this time, Will Partridge did not move again. He was dead.

The sheriff came. The whiskey was analyzed and declared laced with poison. The family did not seem to know what had happened. But Henry entered a plea of guilty to first degree murder and was sentenced to life in prison. Later he was pardoned and served in World War I from 1914 until six months after the Armistice.

No one has ever heard the story of what really happened that night when Will Partridge died. But more than one man declared, "I'd say the son of a bitch needed poisoning."

For the next twelve years, Christie worked harder than ever. To repair her finances, she had taken on the job of assistant game warden. The other sons also went away to war, and the girls left to make their own lives. Christie yearned for company, for someone to love, someone to share the responsibility. She wrote a poem to her children of a dream that she had had of a strange new seed which came in the mail. She planted each seed according to directions, and lo and behold, when she awoke next morning, the plants were all fully grown, with no need of hoeing. Moreover, the vegetables and fruits were already canned, pickled, and made into jellies and pies.

But life was not destined to be so easy. Regardless of the dream, the work was still there. And she hired a new man, Harry Jones. And after a time, she married him. She wrote to the children, "I think I may have found some of the happiness I have

Christie became an assistant game warden, early 1900s.

Christie with the last load of wheat, 1917. *All pictures courtesy of Carter "Pat" Merrell, a son.*

longed for." She soon felt that she could give up the weekly egg route. She began to depend on Harry to make something of the homestead.

But Harry Jones was evidently looking for something different. Perhaps he had been attracted by Christie as a strong woman, a leader. One day he went into town and never returned.

Christie turned the homestead over to one of her sons when he returned from the war, and she moved into Sterling. She bought a small store with her savings, and very soon she married a man named Phillips. Running a store was like play after the years on the farm. Again she wrote to her children that she had at last found security and happiness.

But the store did not make much money, and one day Mr. Phillips departed.

Christie rented the store, and with income from it and again from the farms, she was well off. She was fifty-two years old and still good looking. The energy that had gone into her work now gave her some of the old sparkle of her girlhood. And she met a man who owned a large, wonderful farm on the western slope. She wrote the children that at last she had met a real man. Ralph Baird was an ardent suitor, tall and handsome, a true gentleman.

And so she married him, and they left for his home. Her letters glowed. The mountains were beautiful, people were good to her. But the farm had never been worked since Ralph Baird owned it. All of Christie's old ambitions came to life again. What they couldn't do with this rich mountain place! With work, they could make it into a showcase.

"That's what we're going to do," she wrote, "as soon as I can get Mr. Baird activated."

But Mr. Baird apparently didn't have any money or any ambition to be activated. One week, for the first time in her life, Christie failed to write letters to her children. Nor did a letter come the next week, nor the next.

Frank took time from his work and went to Baird's place. Christie was not there. She had left him, Baird said. Yet Frank found all of her clothes and belongings in the house. He called the sheriff, and Baird was jailed, still maintaining that Christie had left. Every day Frank went to the cell and badgered the man.

And one day Baird told the story. They had argued about the development of the farm and her money. Christie grabbed a gun, he claimed. Baird threw a flatiron at her, and then, in a fury, beat her to death.

All her adult life, Christie had looked for security, for someone to love her. She wanted things to be perfect, to be done right. She could not stand laziness. And what did the men in her life want? Perhaps to them, this strong woman looked like a good port in a storm. She was a wonder. She could do everything.

Everything but pick a good man. It was the only talent that had escaped her.

Frank sent a wire home: "Will bring Mother home this week. . . . Have someone clean house up good." It was the last thing they could do for a woman who wanted everything done right.

THE BITTER AND THE SWEET

In the early days, women often took the lead reins because survival dictated no alternatives. Many times, they thrived on bitter challenges, and the testing that they endured led to sweet promises and yeasty victories for women who followed them.

Annie Green. *Courtesy, Mary Alice Rice Lindblad.*

The Davis children. *Courtesy, Overland Trail Museum.*

Below, right: Jo Garner Boatright. *Below, left:* Judee McGuire consulting about pictures.

Chapter XI

GRASPING THE LEAD REINS

"**I** had determined to act for myself once in my life, regardless of the opinions of others."

The opinion was her husband's, and the act was to be a novel. The purpose: to try to pay off the increasing debt load that Annie and William Green were piling up each year of farming at Union Colony.

It was not the first time that Annie had tried to help. Frantic during the first months of living on their savings, Annie undertook to teach a school but had to quit and care for a dying friend. Then, when William was away prospecting for coal and the days stretched long and lonely, Annie began to bake and sell bread. Since the stove was hot anyway, she took in ironing, heating her aptly named sadirons and pressing away between kneading and baking.

When William objected, Annie told him: "You believe in Woman's Rights, and I claim that it is my right and also my duty to aid you when I can, without interfering in my household affairs."

But that business ended because of an event that, despite her dislike for Greeley, she would never have expected in a temperance colony. One day she ran out for an errand and did not lock her door. Why should one lock a door in a colony of saints?

She returned to a shocking sight. All the windows of their house were smashed. Bread, pies, and ironing were trampled on the floor. Neighbors found her silver forks, spools of thread, and boxes of ribbons and lace scattered down the street. Treasures from trunks were torn out and scattered, and the one mirror smashed. William's watch was broken, precious family pictures torn out of albums, and books filled with adobe mortar. Mud smeared the carpet, and syrup was poured over all.

Who were the vandals? Three children, the oldest not quite nine years old. They were "having fun."

With a wrecked house, Annie could not continue her business. And so she had plenty of time to think about her misery, to weep, and to long for Pennsylvania.

And to worry as the debts piled up. The family moved out to their homestead soon afterward, but it was 1874 before the grasshoppers and Mother Nature granted a good crop. And that year the market was no good. They lost seven horses in three years, one pair alone worth $700. Their milk cow and calf were driven away in the roundup, and they never saw them again. They had to be on guard against range cattle all the time, for their great numbers could demolish a field in a few hours. William irrigated night and day, and sometimes it was up to Annie to make usually futile attempts to drive the herds away.

Two new babies arrived. Illness complicated matters. An outbreak of typhoid left people dead in Greeley (but N. C. Meeker did not publish the news, Annie charged). Out on the ranch, William and a child were so ill that she feared for their lives. The doctor's charge was ten dollars per visit.

William took an opportunity to buy an additional eighty acres, adding to the debt load that had increased with each disaster. Annie began to have attacks of "mortgage on the brain." And no wonder. Their interest rate was a stunning 2 percent — a *month.*

In 1880, despite William's doubts, Annie determined "to act for myself." Her project of writing a novel was an unlikely one for paying off a mortgage. But she had already written a play, and she engaged P. T. Barnum's Hall in Greeley, trained actors (half of them her children), advertised, and finally presented the play with the idea that ticket sales would pay the cost of publishing the book. Then, sale of the book to theater patrons would bring money to reduce the mortgage.

The audience gave the production "prolonged cheers," and N. C. Meeker even wrote a nice review. The proceeds for two evenings amounted to over $100, but after Annie paid expenses of $60, the balance was only half enough for publication of the book. It was a slow way to pay off a debt.

But Annie was exultant over her artistic success and soon proposed taking the play and book sales to Fort Collins. Again, her "would-be dictator" objected, but she turned his own words against him when he declared that man is a "creature of circumstance . . . controlled entirely by surroundings" and therefore not accountable for his own actions. Annie did not agree, but since his argument suited her purpose, she told him that she could not help going to Fort Collins and therefore would do so.

The first performance was a success, but next day someone removed twenty dollars of "hard money" that Annie had left in her trunk because it was too heavy to carry about in her pockets. A political meeting interfered with the next production. However, the audience at the rally proposed to take up an offering for the troupe.

"By this time," said Annie, "almost every man had his hand in his pocket," and she and her daughter were on the way to collecting at least $100.

But then, one of her actors, who had taken advantage of an evening away from Greeley to partake of strong drink, stood up and made an impassioned speech that Greeleyites did not need charity from Fort Collins people. Annie still would have broken even if the same loudmouth had not rushed forward during the sale of the books, demanding that every person who had donated a dime be given a copy. Before Annie could get things under control, seventy-five or eighty books were gone.

Next she wrote her play, *Ten Years on the Great American Desert,* but her production met with similar difficulties, namely that the lawyer who rented Barnum Hall to her felt free to turn the building, at the last moment, over to a more profitable political meeting. Said Annie, "I didn't scare worth a cent," and she and her troupe took the stage and performed.

About 1886, Annie's attacks of "mortgage on the brain" were relieved. The farm at last began to break even, but it was not because of her theatrical and literary efforts, though she did occasionally sell her clever poems and songs. William should have been grateful for the writing, however, for during those enter-

Elizabeth Sarah Fraser Iliff, shortly before the death of John Wesley Iliff in 1878. The *Rocky Mountain News* noted the establishment of her Singer Sewing Machine Shop in 1868 by saying that she proposed "to set an example" worthy of her sex. *Courtesy, Alberta Iliff Shattuck, granddaughter of John Wesley Iliff.*

prises, Annie forgot to weep over life in Greeley. And as often happens, her real contribution went unnoticed until after her death. In 1980, two of her great-granddaughters, Mary Alice Rice Lindblad and Virginia M. Rice Lindblad, reissued her book, *Sixteen Years on the Great American Desert*. It is perhaps one of the best accounts of the settlers' woes and gives an entirely different view of N. C. Meeker's colony.

Other women ventured into business during Colorado's territorial and early statehood years. Elizabeth Sarah Fraser came as a seller of sewing machines and married John Wesley Iliff in 1870. A few years later, after his death, she hired managers for his cattle empire but oversaw much of the business.

Mary Ann Dickens, a native of England, lost her first husband in Canada and moved to Wisconsin, where she supported her children by farming and binding shoes. In 1848, she married Alonzo Allen, who left for Colorado in 1859. Several years later, she hired a Mr. Lowe to bring her and the children out to join him. He was lazy and slept much of the way, and the responsibilities of the trip by covered wagon fell on her.

In Colorado Territory, she managed a stage station at Burlington (present-day Longmont), feeding passengers of four coaches, each of which could carry as many as twenty-two people. One vehicle came from each direction at noon and at midnight. Many additional customers led to the building of a larger station that

Mary Ann Dickens Allen in 1881. She managed a stage station during gold rush days. *Courtesy, Lawrence Allen, a grandson.*

became a good-sized hotel. Mary Ann also provided refreshments for dances held on the upper floor of her hotel.

Josephine Meeker, daughter of Nathan and Arvilla, took a business course in Denver in 1877. The following year she accompanied her parents to the White River Ute Reservation in western Colorado. She was paid for her work, declaring, "I get paid . . . or I would not have come."

The adventure ended in tragedy with her father killed by the Indians. She and Arvilla were captives for several weeks. Josephine was treated well, however, and her captor wanted to marry the attractive girl. But Josephine never married. She was later a secretary in Washington, D.C., for Senator Edward Teller.

Lena Propst opened the first dressmaking shop in Sterling in 1881 when she was only fifteen. She no doubt had plenty of business, for a fashionable lady of the 1880s was said to have worn seventeen pounds of clothing, not even including her coat and boots. In 1938, when Lena was seventy-one, her sister Edna wrote:

> Lena is still sewing, has her sewing room piled up, and I don't see how she will ever get it all done, but she does and makes her own way. We have too much *pride* to go on any pension.

The story of eastern Colorado is full of dramatic accounts of women who realized that one must simply do what's necessary. During the Panic of 1893 and the following years, moisture on the plains dropped to only six inches per year. The people of hardy stock did not want to lose their homesteads. Mary Schmidt, near Fleming, was one of many young women who left home for any respectable job that would help to keep the families afloat. She did housework for a family down on the South Platte.

Sometimes housework was a girl's passport to life in America. Bruce Johnson, a Colorado pioneer who came west in the Gold Rush of 1859, was never a member of the Union Colony but became one of the "Garden City's" most prominent businessmen. In 1878, he built a magnificent home there and brought a succession of Swedish housemaids to staff it. Whenever one married, he sent for her next sister. Those girls and Bruce carried on a steady, undeclared war. He constantly turned down the heat on the stove, a habit guaranteed to burn the cook while spoiling the broth. Rather than have a favorite clock repaired, he would fix it himself, though it would run only when turned face down. The current maid, not seeing any sense in a clock you couldn't look at, would set it upright. Bruce would growl, "Those damn women won't let my clock alone," and would threaten to send them home. The threats never worked because each girl invariably had a line of young men waiting to court her.

Magdelina Korinek, who had come with her husband from Czechoslovakia in 1896, took a job as cook and housekeeper for beet company officials in Sugar City when the family floundered on their dryland homestead. Seven of her children accompanied her and attended school. But on weekends, Magdelina and the children returned to the homestead to work feverishly.

Barbara Budin's venture into housework was more daring because she traveled far away to the mountains. She was one of those four Czech sisters who had come to northeastern Colorado during the 1880s. She had homesteaded on Pawnee Creek, then married a fellow countryman. When the Panic of 1893 threatened loss of the only land that Barbara and James had ever owned, she kept house for a wealthy mining family in Cripple Creek while her husband stayed on the homestead to prove up and care for their three small children. He was a forerunner of the modern "house husband." Barbara came home on her one free weekend a month. Her monthly salary of ten dollars saved the land, and today Budin descendants still live on the ranch along Pawnee Creek.

Life was not easy for women on a farm even when there were men to lead the way and do the hardest work. Clara Hilderman Ehrlich was the daughter of Germans from Russia. Her father came to Leroy, Colorado, in 1890, and a year later, her mother and the first baby crossed the ocean to join him. Clara, the fourth child, was born in 1895 in the family's sod hut near Orchard on the South Platte River.

Clara reportedly became the first German from Russia to earn a doctorate in anthropology. It was interesting to her, both professionally and personally, to look back at those early days in the sugar beet fields. Her father was one of the first farmers approached by the Great Western Sugar Company in 1899 with a proposal to raise beets.

Each year when the tiny leaves appeared, the family went forth in great spirits to thin the plants. But Clara recalled that as "the hot June sun rose higher and hunger and thirst grew, that first fine elation died away." To keep pace with the family as you hoed and then stooped to pull extra plants from clusters required a remarkable dedication in a small child:

> For as the day wore on, your knees burned, and your wrist ached from leaning on it . . . you would finally give up the crawling for a time and go bent back . . . nothing seemed to help.

The family later moved to Sterling for better educational opportunities. Clara graduated from the University of Colorado in 1917 and won a scholarship to the New York School of Social Research. Her doctorate in anthropology was earned at Columbia University in 1937.

Nona Hopper Beck, within the space of a year and a half, became a bride, a mother, and a widow. Her husband and her youngest sister were killed in the Eden train wreck of 1904. Nona took a job with the telephone company to support herself and her daughter. In 1913, she became exchange manager at Sugar City in Crowley County because living quarters were provided and she could work and care for her daughter at the same time.

It was a twenty-four-hour job. Nona slept near the switchboard so that she could instantly respond to a call. The job became her life. If she took time off, the substitute had to be paid out of her seventy-dollar-a-month salary. But Nona felt such a commitment that when urgent messages could not be transmitted by phone, she did hire a replacement while she drove her Model T to deliver the messages.

"Did you think I could be your conscience all your life? I know that you know the right answer." That was the response of Mary Price when one of her daughters asked for advice. Mary Price had been through enough in her life that she could easily have felt qualified to pass judgment. She had been hurt enough that she might even have felt it her prerogative. But the answer was indicative of her character.

"I never let anyone help me," she used to say, and she had

Mary Price, newspaper editor, discovered that she was a good manager.
Courtesy, Edna Price Kellogg, a daughter.

earned the pride with which she spoke.

She came to Colorado in a covered wagon in 1895 with her husband Charles and three little children. She was twenty-eight, and life looked good. Sometimes she felt like a Cinderella. She had had a stepmother who had not cared for her, and there had been little happiness in childhood. So she delighted in her own family.

Charles was a newspaperman, and Mary helped him some of the time even while the children were small. They rented a building in Sterling, set up their press, and published the first democratic paper there, appropriately named *The Sterling Democrat.* It did well, and about 1903, the couple bought a new press. Two more babies were born during those years, and all the children were healthy and bright. Life was good.

Then one day in 1904, without warning, her husband left town with another woman, and she never saw him again. The paper was in debt, and Mary discovered that their house had been sold and the money was gone.

But Mary also discovered that she was a good manager. She

rented a small house and sublet part of it while she and the children lived in three rooms. With the children's help, she ran the newspaper, doing everything from setting type to writing editorials. Eventually, she paid off the debt and bought a comfortable house for her family and another for rental income.

And she did it almost completely by herself. She accepted no charity, no hand-me-downs. She was determined that the children would not feel disadvantaged and would not even let them wear each other's clothes. Soon they had music lessons and other extras. But their main advantage was a good mother. Long hours of work did not make her a scold. She set high standards but never blamed the children for things that they couldn't help or for her own loss.

One day, when the town of Sterling began to prosper, she went to George Henderson, who owned the building housing the newspaper, and said, "Mr. Henderson, you have never raised my rent. I would like to pay what that space is worth."

George Henderson replied, "Mrs. Price, as long as you are running that paper, the rent will never be raised."

It was the only help that she ever accepted.

Mary operated the paper for about five years, and when it was profitable, she sold it and was elected county clerk, serving several terms. In her later years, still too proud to accept help, she babysat and did hand quilting.

Perhaps her weakness was a lack of tolerance for others' mistakes. But a strong sense of right and wrong applied especially to her own life. About 1907, she bought a relinquishment of a homestead near Leroy. She went out occasionally to spend a night or weekend, for it was her understanding that since the place had been filed on previously, the residency requirements were not so strict. But when the time came to prove up, the land·agent asked her to swear that the place had been her principal residence.

"No," Mary replied, "it wasn't."

"It's all right," the agent said, "everyone does this."

Mary looked him steadily in the eye and said, "I will not swear before God to an untruth." And so she did not get her homestead, though she could easily have told herself that she was having a hard time holding her family together and deserved the help.

She was a strong woman. A daughter remembered that she never spoke one word to the children against their father. She did not make herself a heroine. But other people let the family know how much they admired Mary Price.

She was a strong woman. But three or four years after Charles left and Mary was going quietly through a divorce, she would come home and lie on the bed and not eat. One of her little daughters sat by the bed, hardly able to stand it because she knew that in the shadows, with her head turned away, her mother was fighting back the tears.

She was a remarkable woman. She accomplished miracles, everyone said. But she had lost what she most valued in life.

About that same time, another woman, a quite young one, got a job editing a newspaper, *The Merino Breeze.* Jane Weir felt a keen sense of excitement to be stepping into the world usually consigned to men. She was not alone. Several Greeley women of that time undertook unusual and successful careers. Psyche Boyd was the only woman photographer in Greeley and perhaps in eastern Colorado from 1903 to 1908. She was recognized for her portraits of children. About that same time, Bessie Smith, an architect, designed several buildings which can still be seen in Greeley. Minnie Pinneo, an expert rider, won a national title.

Edith Steiger was a new baby in 1912 when her mother and

"Playhouse" of the Steiger children.

Edith Steiger, the only girl to graduate in the college of business, Ohio State University, 1939.

the family joined Reuben Steiger on the land that he had claimed near Keota the previous year. Twelve years later, Edith, wanting an education, was on her own. While attending junior high and high school in Cheyenne, she worked in private homes, changing diapers, washing dishes, and ironing shirts in exchange for board and room. She then taught at age sixteen in a one-room school, where she enthusiastically ran out to play at recess with her pupils.

Those experiences and her early freedom on the prairie may have given Edith the confidence that led to a highly successful career. In Chicago, she worked days and attended Northwestern at night. She became the advertising manager of Revlon Corporation and later was the only woman executive at Avon. Her imaginative campaigns led to multi-million-dollar sales.

During World War II, she was a Red Cross volunteer, moving

toward the front lines behind the troops and establishing recreation centers. Afterwards, she remained with Revlon only a short time. "I could not care about lipstick," she said, "after the effects of the war."

After marriage to a General Motors executive, she earned two master's degrees and a doctorate and became an authority on marketing. While teaching for seventeen years at the University of Michigan, she was consultant to Ford Motors, Dow Chemical, Hush Puppies, Cutex, and many other national firms.

"I loved the university," she once said. "I was accepted better there. In my day, a woman executive had few friends in the business world."

Today, Edith Steiger Phillips has returned to the family homestead, where she revels in the simplicity that her mother so enjoyed. She is engaged in an attempt to stop plowing of fragile prairie grassland before the tragic dust bowl days of the 1930s are repeated.

She sums up her successful life by saying, "I just dreamed up ideas. I've been dreaming all my life. And I got paid for it."

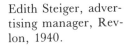
Edith Steiger, advertising manager, Revlon, 1940.

Anne Thompson was well prepared in newspaper work by the time she and her husband Ross bought the weekly *Baca County Banner* in 1951. Armed with college degrees and experience on Iowa papers, the La Junta *Tribune–Democrat,* and in free-lance work, they enthusiastically chose the *Banner*—because it was cheap.

Others were more doubtful. Their first day, a big man in over-alls, cowboy boots, and a western hat walked in. He gazed around the office and finally answered Anne's question, "Was there something you wanted?"

"Yup," he said. "I just wanted to see the darn fools that bought this paper."

And he left.

Three years later, Anne and Ross bought the Rocky Ford *Daily Gazette,* which they still publish with distinction. In 1970, the Thompsons won the University of Colorado Outstanding Journalist award, and in 1975, they were chosen Colorado's Newspaper Publisher of the Year (Colorado Press Association award). Anne was named Colorado Woman of Achievement in Journalism in 1969 and in 1981 was the first woman to be elected to the Colorado Journalism Hall of Fame, a distinction awarded by the University of Northern Colorado.

Anne has been an officer of both the Colorado Press Women's Association and of the National Federation of Press Women and has been featured speaker at a convention of the latter. Her many speeches also include an appearance before the Inland Daily Press Association in Chicago.

She has edited the *Colorado Business Woman* and is now the publisher. For the past ten years, she has also edited *Tusk Talk,* the monthly publication of the Colorado Federation of Republican Women.

Government is also a part of Anne Thompson's life. Among many positions of public service are membership on the Governor's Local Government Commission, 1963 to 1966, and the Colorado Commission on the Status of Women, 1973 to 1974. She served two terms as state representative from Crowley and Otero counties, 1957 to 1961.

In 1974, she ran unsuccessfully for the state senate. As she campaigned door to door, one woman asked, "Democrat or

Anne Thompson, award-winning editor, 1965.

Republican?" When Anne replied, "Republican," the woman grunted, "Hmph. I wouldn't vote for *any* Republican. Not after what the Republicans did to my great-grandfather."

Anne exclaimed, "Gosh! What happened to your great-grand-father?"

The woman replied, "You don't think I'm going to tell a Republican, do you?"

And she slammed the door in Anne's face.

On another occasion, Anne approached an old gentleman at the La Junta Old Settlers' Day celebration. "Excuse me, sir," she said. "I'm from the *Tribune–Democrat* and wonder if I might talk with you for a few minutes."

He glared at her.

"Never talked to no Democrat in my life and ain't going to start now."

And so it goes for women who grasp the lead reins in government and newspaper work.

Elsie Erickson, who worked for half a century (1920 to 1970) in every department at the First National Bank of Greeley, was the first woman member of the Colorado Bankers' Association

50-Year Club. She was an officer of the National Association of Bank Women.

But Lorraine Dalgleish was probably one of the earliest top officers of a lending institution. She was hired at Commercial Savings Bank in Sterling in 1922 when it was quite new and small. In fact, Lorraine, with the title of assistant cashier, was the *only* employee besides the owner, J. N. Sanders. They gained customers by staying open long hours that suited people's schedules: every day, Monday through Saturday, from 9:00 to 5:00. On Saturday night, they returned to work from 7:00 to 9:00. They got all the railroad business and survived.

In 1924 and 1925, the other banks in town had to close their doors, and by 1929, most in the area had failed. But the Commercial thrived and grew.

And Lorraine Dalgleish grew with it. She married Eliot Hays in 1933 but continued to work at the bank until 1964. As new employees were hired, some from the staffs of fallen competitors, Lorraine rose to second in command, assistant to the president.

The same year that Lorraine completed her career, Marian Peppler began her climb to the top. She joined the United Bank of LaSalle as a secretary, by 1970 had become a vice-president–cashier, and continued to move up until in 1981 she was appointed president. She is the only woman president in an eastern Colorado bank.

Women lawyers, doctors, engineers are no longer uncommon. But a woman movie producer with headquarters on the family homestead at Haxtun, Colorado?

Judee Lea McGuire's first interest was drama, and she modeled and acted in television commercials and documentary films in Denver. In 1968, she became president of the Colorado branch of the Screen Actors' Guild. She was instrumental in formation of the Colorado Film Board, the purpose of which is to entice film companies to work in the state. She "nagged the officials about the value of all that money coming into the state — as well as the opportunity for local actors and technicians."

She first met Jerry McGuire in 1965 when he was head of Barbre Productions and was filming a movie for the Disabled American Veterans. She played the wife of an amputee in the

178

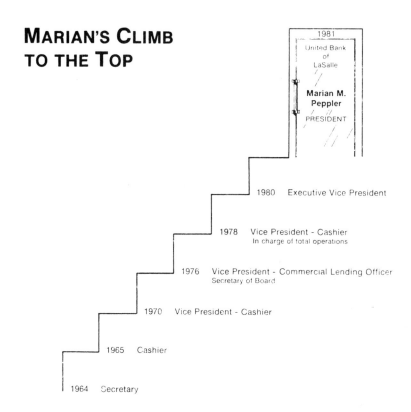

MARIAN'S CLIMB TO THE TOP

1981
United Bank
of
LaSalle

Marian M. Peppler
PRESIDENT

1980   Executive Vice President

1978   Vice President - Cashier
In charge of total operations

1976   Vice President - Commercial Lending Officer
Secretary of Board

1970   Vice President - Cashier

1965   Cashier

1964   Secretary

picture. She had become increasingly fascinated by what went on behind cameras and asked many questions of the crew. She started working as a script girl for Barbre when she was not acting, and gradually she absorbed more and more of the business. In 1969, Judee and Jerry became partners and formed Bravo! Productions. Judee worked on the first film (about cable television) as production assistant, taking care of travel arrangements and the shooting schedule. She progressed to producer, handling all business arrangements. Jerry writes and directs. In 1971, they were married.

"We make a good team," Judee says. "He's creative. I'm a stickler for details and everything running right."

But Judee is also creative. She has had several articles published, "mostly because Jerry pushed me into writing." Her first

Judee and Jerry McGuire. Once a movie is completed, Bravo personnel drop back to the two partners. *Photo by Casey Dilgarde.*

story, about inexpensive beauty aids, was based on her modeling experience, but some of her work has been about women in unusual fields. She is also an excellent photographer and does most of the publicity stills for the company. Her portrait of Harry Jackson's statue of Sacajawea, washed in a mystic blue, made a stunning cover for *Empire Magazine.*

Jerry has written over three hundred screenplays and has directed over one hundred. He is the author of seven books, including *Elijah,* which was nominated for a 1974 Book Award. Yet the two do not even have a secretary. He types his scripts, and she types hers. But she does help with the marketing of his articles, which now number over 1500 published. An agent handles the big works.

When one of their films goes into production, they may hire as many as one hundred technicians. If the free-lancers do not have the right kind of equipment, it is leased for the production. Once the show is over, Bravo! personnel drop back to the two partners.

They have done films for NASA, oil pipeline companies, John

Deere, Coors, the Solar Energy Research Institute, and many others. They try to get a name narrator. *Felicidad,* the story of a poor fisherman and his family, was narrated by Ricardo Montalban; a 1971 movie about Harry Jackson, by John Wayne. That production won the United States Film Festival Award for Creative Excellence (the third highest award in the industry) and also a special citation from the National Cowboy Hall of Fame.

Three years ago, the McGuires decided to move to the old Haxtun home of Jerry's great-grandparents, Tillie and Abner Fleming. They felt the urge to get away from crowds. They liked the idea of a place where people could make a business deal with a handshake, as his great-grandfather had done. When Abner Fleming and his partner, a Haxtun dentist, dissolved their partnership, they simpy sat down at a table with a pile of money and divided it, "one for you, one for me."

People told them, "If you move out there, you can forget about film work." To their pleasure, they almost immediately won the contract for the largest documentary that has ever been produced by a Colorado company. They were chosen above competitors all over the United States, including Hollywood, and Great Britain.

Most important to the McGuires is the unusual artistic scope of the movie. Commissioned by the Great Western Financial Corporation, headquartered in Los Angeles, it will tell the story of the horseman throughout the ages. Harry Jackson will be a part of the movie because he has also been commissioned by Great Western to create a huge statue (twenty-one feet high) of John Wayne to be placed in Los Angeles. John Wayne will be another important subject, for in the minds of most people, his acting created the best example of the American cowboy.

The hour-long documentary will show the tremendous impact that the man on horseback has had on civilization. The cowboy was simply the latest in a long line of "knights." The McGuires say that they are not making the film for a sophisticated art critic somewhere or for award-givers. They just hope that it appeals to real audiences out there in America.

As in Haxtun, Colorado. Sometimes, to get away from the typewriter and the telephone, they walk down to the coffee shop in Haxtun. Everyone is friendly. But if Judee and Jerry pull out notebooks and start to scribble ideas, the folks in Grandfather Ab's hometown let them alone.

Even today, the Judee McGuires and the Anne Thompsons are exciting models for other women, but they are the inheritors from long ago hardy dames like Annie Green and Mary Price, who made the first timid reach for the lead reins.

Chapter XII

YEAST FOR THE DAILY BREAD

"Sure, I go to concerts and the art museum in Denver. But don't tell the folks back home. I don't think they'd understand."

That remark by a rural legislator, quoted in the *Denver Post*, was enough to bring rumbling from hundreds of graves on the eastern prairies, and it certainly provoked sparks from artists still working out in the "sticks." Rural people, like others,

Lizzie Powell Davis, impresario of her day. *Courtesy, Betty Greenawalt Boyd, a granddaughter.*

appreciate the arts as a definition of life and a projection of a more meaningful future.

And it is nothing new. Settlers on the frontier used the arts to leaven a primitive existence. Sarah Elizabeth "Lizzie" Powell Davis, who arrived on the plains in 1878 at age seventeen, was the impresario of her day, staging plays, dance programs, and musicales in "Th' Rink," the Sterling all-purpose community center, or the "Opera House," atop the county courthouse. Her most successful performers were her three children, who traveled throughout the United States on the Orpheum Circuit. Little Madeleine with her long curls was an especial favorite. Composers sent her their songs, and her picture was used on sheet music. In later years, a promoter said that the little girl had been the Shirley Temple of her time.

Lizzie taught painting and held competitions. Many of her students were adults who led busy lives of developing the "new

"Th' Rink" in Sterling, where performances were staged. It was built in 1885 in a town of 150 people. *Courtesy, Overland Trail Museum.*

Madeleine Davis (Greenawalt), the Shirley Temple of her day, age three in 1895. *Courtesy, Betty Greenawalt Boyd, her daughter.*

country." Cattle businesses and others commissioned her paintings. One, a covered wagon, originally created for the W. C. Harris Company, now hangs in the Overland Trail Museum. But Lizzie's greatest contribution was that she involved scores of other people in the arts.

Mary Stanley, stranded in a Keota hotel during the 1913 blizzard, used the time to quilt. *Courtesy, Auriel Sandstead, a granddaughter.*

Rozene Meeker, oldest daughter of Nathan and Arvilla, exhibited her lace work at the 1893 Columbian Exposition in Chicago and won a prize. Her childhood in the East and later at Greeley Colony had been plagued with misfortune and illness. She had nearly drowned in a well when she was five years old. Perhaps her parents were over protective of her, and it has been suggested that she suffered brain damage in the accident.

Yet she helped to bring up her sisters and the children of one of them, and she cared for her mother in the years following Nathan's death in the White River Massacre. Moreover, she was a nationally known lecturer about the Greeley Colony and Indian problems, with particular emphasis on her family's tragedy. Back in 1876, during the drive for Colorado women's suffrage, she wrote an article for the Greeley *Tribune,* declaring: "What a woman needs is education of more than fingering the piano keys. . . . Woman needs salvation from incompetency."

Other women contributed to beauty in an often unique way. Mary Stanley, who homesteaded at the lonely high plains community of Keota in 1910, made at least fifty quilts and eighteen rugs over the next fifty years. They are family treasures, known as "scrap bags" because they were made from bits of material left over from Mary's dressmaking business. All those efforts were

Mary Stanley and her husband created an oasis on the plains. *Hightower Homestead.*

probably worked into her busy daily schedule because she could do little of her meticulous stitching at night without electricity. Moreover, she left nothing unfinished. When she died, there was not one extra square to be found. It was quite a record for a woman who came west to save her health.

In June 1977, Mary's granddaughter, Auriel Sandstead, presented the Mary Stanley and Succeeding Generations Quilt Exhibit in Keota, which today is almost a ghost town. The 200 visitors so enjoyed the trip into yesterday that second and third shows were staged in 1979 and 1981. They included Mary's rugs and the works of others, many of them persons to whom she had taught the folk art. To these shows, again held in Keota, accessible only by a gravel road, thronged 350 and 660 people respectively. Many were long-ago residents who took the occasion to see each other and remember the old days.

Two raffle quilts were of special interest, for they were a veritable history of the Keota and New Raymer communities. Homesteaders had paid twenty-five cents each to have their names em-

Keota at its peak during the early 1930s. *Courtesy, Auriel Sandstead.*

broidered on them. Then a winner's name was drawn from a
hat. The Methodist women of Keota worked for months to create
their elaborate squares of embroidered red roses surrounded by
names. For all that labor, they probably netted no more than
twenty dollars.

The Colorado Quilting Council, which is spearheading a new
birth of interest in the old art, has held meetings in Keota. It
must have been a unique experience to walk the deserted streets
where only one house is now occupied, to cross the ghostly and
abandoned road bed of the *Prairie Dog Special* that once chugged
through the middle of the town, and to meet in the Farmers and
Merchants Building, where long ago homesteaders gathered. It
was an appropriate setting for people reviving an almost lost art.

Isabelle Hamilton was successful in a popular event of early
Colorado days. She had crossed the ocean from Scotland when
she was two and, according to her weary mother, cried all the
way. The family came to Phillips County in a covered wagon,
and Isabelle grew to be more appealing. In 1902, she was run-
ner-up in the queen contest for the Mountain and Plains Festival held in Denver.

Women have been active in preserving history. For one historical play in Merino, Elsie Morlan noted that some of the old-timers always had a story to tell, and feeling that it was unnecessary to write their speeches, she simply told them that, at a certain point, each was to tell one of his yarns. The play went well until that moment. The old men, usually ready to talk, had nothing to say.

Emma Burke Conklin and her sponsor, the Daughters of the American Revolution, made a rare contribution in 1928 when they published *A History of Logan County,* a fascinating collection of letters and memories of early experiences, many of which might otherwise have been lost.

Sarah Barber Claypool, who with her parents homesteaded in 1909 in the Golden Prairie area east of Hereford, wrote a novel based on her early experiences. In 1971, she began to write a column, "It Ain't Like It Used to Be," for the *Town and Country* newspaper, comparing the Greeley area today with "way back when." In 1979, selections from the column were published in a booklet. Through her essays and light poetry, she recaptured the feel of early days on the prairie.

Ruth Dunn, historian of Julesburg, wrote articles and several booklets about the dramatic stories of that area.

Hazel Johnson is an "amateur" historian who is recognized as an authority on Weld County. It hardly seems possible that this vibrant, modern-day woman could have gone by covered wagon to Oklahoma, where her parents homesteaded. Later she lived through the Dust Bowl days in Baca County, Colorado. Perhaps those experiences explain her fascination with the history of Weld County, where she has lived since 1938.

Hazel says that she is totally undomesticated, that it "makes my back ache to think of threading a needle," and though untrained as a journalist, writing and speaking about western history is what she loves to do. And she has had remarkable success even while holding a full-time job. Her second career began accidentally when, having difficulty lining up a program, she decided to do it herself. She was soon in such demand that First National Bank of Greeley became her sponsor in 1958 and underwrote expenses of presentations for public gatherings in Weld County.

Hazel has given at least 1200 programs, some of which have

Hazel E. Johnson, authority on Weld County history. *Photograph by Walt Clark.*

been taped by local schools and the University of Northern Colorado for future use. She has taped seventy-five one-minute historical spots for national release by a local radio station, and she has assisted with the nationally recognized Outdoor Education Program at UNC. She has a unique collection of old photographs, books, diaries, and other historical materials. She helped to mark four historic sites in the Greeley area.

Her very first article "hit the big time" with *Christian Science Monitor.* Since then, she has written for *Monitor, Empire, Ford Times, Carousel,* and other publications. One of her photographs was among fifty chosen to appear in the *Professional Photographers of America's Great Nostalgic Review, 1880–1980.* She has won writing contests, including several sponsored by the local branch of the American Pen Women. Starting in 1958, Hazel wrote a column, "Out of the Past," for *The Greeley Journal.* During the next twenty years, that interesting page appeared over one thousand times, and her name became a part of local history.

Hazel's contributions have been recognized by membership on the Greeley Museum Board and the regional vice-presidency since 1960 of the Colorado Historical Society (representing Adams, Weld, and Morgan counties). She was declared an "Outstanding Centennial Citizen" in 1960 by Governor Steven A. McNichols and is quite proud of having been the Parade Grand Marshal of the Greeley Independence Stampede in 1975. Her most valued award was a national Certificate of Commendation from the American Association for State and Local History in recognition of her contributions to research and preservation of the history of Weld County. Because her greatest concern is to stimulate interest in the heritage of the area, she has established the Hazel E. Johnson Annual Colorado History Award at the University of Northern Colorado.

Hazel Johnson has said that she is sincerely grateful to have been led into such an absorbing work, that it has "added new dimensions to my life."

Anna C. Petteys was a modern-day Lizzie Davis. Governor John A. Love had no sooner appointed her to the first Colorado Council of the Arts and Humanities in 1967 than she enlisted Sterling friends to organize the first local council in the state. The new society began life with a flourish — a regional art show featuring the works of Dick Brown, art instructor at Northeastern Junior College, and Jessie Whitney Scott, who painted in a studio on her family's ranch in Phillips County. It was only the first of a long line of arts events of every kind.

Under the leadership of Anna and son Bob, the *Journal–Advocate* newspaper exhibited a remarkable degree of community responsibility. If something was good for eastern Colorado, the paper backed it. In 1975, the paper and its Woman's Page editor, Margaret Martin, then also president of the Sterling Arts Council, received an annual Governor's Award for excellence in journalism for the arts and humanities. It was the first time that journalism had been so honored.

Mrs. Martin is now arts editor of the paper and writes a column, "Potpourri." She has won awards from the Colorado Press Women's Association (of which she has been president) and the National Federation of Press Women (in which she has served as secretary and as convention chairman). She is a member of the Society of Professional Journalists and is listed in the 1982 *Who's Who in America*. In 1958, she conducted a seminar for Colorado Business and Professional Women at United Nations Headquarters in New York City. She is executive director of the Miss Colorado Pageant, a division of the Miss America Scholarship Pageant.

Celena Smith of Julesburg, another area representative of the Colorado Council of the Arts and Humanities, had been one of the people who stumped the state to build support for the council and to get the bill establishing it passed by the state legislature. In 1973, she received a Governor's Award. Celena is a dynamo who is involved with everything promoting the arts and increasing people's pleasure in them. She is in demand statewide. In 1976, she was a member of the Centennial–Bicentennial Commission and served for a time as chairman of the Festival Council, helping to plan and encourage celebrations all over the state.

But she works continually on local projects such as the tongue-in-cheek historical musical, *The Trapper's Story,* which she helped to write and produce in Julesburg. Under her leadership, the town enjoyed the first artist-in-residence in a Colorado town, Loretta Slota, whose two weeks of classes led to an annual spring arts festival for which students make and sell commemorative medallions as admittance "tickets."

In 1969, Mildred Quinn and the Southeast Council of the Arts at Lamar were also winners of a Governor's Award.

No doubt the first woman artist working actively in eastern Colorado was Mary O'Farrell. She had been trained in Philadelphia but arrived in Colorado during the early territorial days and married Henry C. Fursman, whose ranch was in the Colorado Springs area. One of her best known portraits (of Mary McCook, wife of a territorial governor) is now in the Colorado Heritage Center.

Barbara Smith Guerrero, descendant of prominent Colorado and Wyoming ranch families, was an artist who specialized in illustrating children's books. Her first, *Hannah's Sod House,* was written by Helen Littler Howard and concerned the prairies of Colorado, where both women grew up, and specifically the Littler family homestead. Later, when Mrs. Guerrero lived in New

Helen Littler Howard, author of *Hannah's Sod House*. *Courtesy, Robert Littler, a brother.*

England, she exhibited her watercolors throughout that part of the country. She was on the board of Rangemark, a watercolor master class.

Wanda Beal has a lively curiosity that manifests itself in all of her life. While living in Limon, she painted and taught others to paint. She fashioned clothes which were sold as specialties to good stores in Denver. Wanda believes that art should be used in everyday life, that it should be reflected in one's home, clothing, table settings, and in the appearance of food served.

Jessie Whitney Scott is often called the "prairie painter," and she has been painting since the third grade near Haxtun when she won a prize for the best artwork. Soon afterwards, her rancher parents bought oil paints for the child. Her study at the University of Colorado from 1929 to 1930 was cut short by the depression. For years afterwards, Jessie was busy with marriage

Jessie Scott at work.
Photograph by Schure's.

(1931), family, and ranching. There was little time for painting, but during those years, she soaked up the "dramatic moods of weather . . . the color in the great expanses of sky and plains . . . the untold stories lurking in old buildings and windmills."

Finally, in 1953, she enrolled in the Famous Artists' School. It provided the impetus that she needed. Jessie began to paint seriously. She studied with William Sanderson at the University of Denver and traveled over the country for workshops with other well-known artists. A member of the Foothills Art Center of Golden, she now lives and paints in Fort Collins.

Her paintings are in homes and public buildings across the United States, as well as in western collections of Tennant Art Gallery at Northeastern Junior College and the Wyoming State Art Gallery, Cheyenne. She has exhibited in group and one-man shows in the Rocky Mountain states. Her largest work is a twenty-five-by-five-foot panorama of her home area located in the First National Bank of Fleming. One of her paintings was included in a 1966 exhibit of Colorado artists in the Washington office of Senator Gordon Allott. In 1968, she was represented in a National Farmers' Art Exhibit in the agriculture building of the nation's capital and later at the Agriculture Hall of Fame in Kansas City. She was the artist for the book jacket of *The Logan County Ledger* by Dale Wells.

Jessie Scott is listed in Peggy and Harold Samuels' 1976 *The Illustrated Biographical Encyclopedia of Artists of the American West* as a landscape painter, watercolorist, and muralist. A new interest is clay, but she prefers watercolor.

One of the most enduring artists is Laura Gilpin, a pioneer photographer recognized internationally as among the finest of the Southwest. She was born in 1892 on her parents' ranch near Ramah, sixty-five miles east of Colorado Springs. Her fascination with the camera began at age twelve, when someone gave her a Brownie. And from that moment, Laura Gilpin knew what she had to do with her life.

It was a life too busy for marriage. In 1917, she graduated from the excellent Clarence White School of Photography in New York. For a long time, she earned her living in commercial photography: as a publicist for the Central City Opera Festival during the 1930s productions by Robert Edmond Jones and as chief photographer for Boeing Corporation during the war years.

The only sex discrimination that she ever experienced was at Boeing. But when someone tried to give her credit for breaking down barriers for other women, she responded, "Oh, fiddlesticks! It gives me a pain in the neck."

Laura Gilpin's rare artistry brought recognition. Her photographs taken throughout the United States, South America, and Europe have been exhibited in numerous one-woman shows. Her book, *Temples in Yucatan,* received the annual Award of Merit from the Photographers' Society of America. She won the first Fine Arts Award bestowed by the Industrial Photographers of the Southwest.

But her books about the Southwest (for which she also wrote the texts) have brought the greatest honors. In 1946, she moved to Santa Fe and began to photograph American Indians. She invariably wore a battered old Stetson hat to shade the lens, and it became a mark of her personality. She produced *The Enduring*

195

Navaho, which won the Western Heritage Award, "because I wanted to." In 1977, she was a winner of the Colorado Governor's Award for the Arts and Humanities. She was elected to membership in Women of the West. Santa Fe was the 1975 site of a major showing of her work spanning sixty-four years. In 1979, when she was eighty-eight, major shows were held at the Fine Arts Center of Colorado Springs and the International Center of Photography in New York.

Her works are in permanent collections at the Fine Arts Center; the Print Division of the Congressional Library; and at the Amon Carter Museum in Fort Worth, where 21,000 negatives and 10,000 prints comprise the most extensive collection.

Laura Gilpin's response to all the attention focused on her work was amusement and wonder that suddenly she was discovered: "I've earned a living at photography ever since I can remember."

She died in 1979 at age eighty-eight, and until the very last, she was still being honored. But more important, she was still taking her pictures of remarkable clarity, drama, and humanity.

Two sisters from Greeley and later Sterling have excelled in the performing arts. Jo Garner Boatright continued her piano studies (begun with her mother Margaret Garner) at Colorado College and the New England Conservatory of Music. She won the prestigious Lavan Award at Boston's Tanglewood Festival and soloed with the Boston Pops Orchestra. She often appears in concert and on radio and television. Raymond Erickson, critic for *The New York Times,* wrote that she is a ". . . beautiful, outstanding pianist." Another reviewer described her style as "superb, hypnotic."

Since 1968, Jo Boatright has been associate professor of music at Texas Christian University, where she is special assistant to her former teacher, internationally famed Madame Lili Kraus. She and her husband, Dallas Symphony flutist Harvey Boatright, helped to found Voices of Change, a small group of singers and instrumentalists who specialize in performing new works from both acclaimed and unknown composers. They have appeared in major United States cities, as well as London, Edinburgh, Paris, West Berlin, and The Hague. The New York debut in 1980 was acclaimed in *High Fidelity* magazine: "New music is

Jo Garner Boatright is congratulated
by Ingmar Bergman, internationally
acclaimed film director, 1981.

alive and well in the Southwest, thanks to VOICES OF
CHANGE." *The New York Times* hailed a Messiaen quartet as
"extremely well performed, its many unison passages beautifully
in tune." One reviewer stated that a concert by Voices of Change
was "an experience that only a few people will be fortunate
enough to sample in their concert-going lives." The group
received a Meadows Award Presentation for Excellence in the
Arts, Southern Methodist University, in 1981. The occasion was
noted by *Ovation* (a magazine for classical music listeners) in its
March 1982 issue.

Jo Boatright consistently draws enthusiastic notices. Olin
Chism of *The Dallas Times Herald* has written that her playing
is captivating and "abrim with musical life . . . the kind of
polished performance that has come to be associated with her."

Jerri Garner Lines is a dancer who lives with her singer-stage
manager husband in a Greenwich Village loft that is large enough
to house her studio as well. For ten years, she was principal
dancer and assistant choreographer with Lotte Goslar's *Pantomime*

Circus. She also appeared on Broadway as a principal dancer in *Dance Marathon* and on network television in *Patchwork Family* and *Jacob's Pillow Summer Dance Festival.* She has worked in dozens of Off-Broadway, Off-Off-Broadway, touring, and summer stock shows as a dancer, singer, actress, or choreographer.

Under a National Endowment for the Arts touring program with Lotte Goslar, she has taught dance and mime at colleges and universities, including Bryn Mawr, University of California, and Stanford. She has also toured with the American National Theatre Association in the United States, Canada, and Europe. Now a free-lancer, she was called to London to choreograph a New York show, *Discoella,* which opened in London to favorable reviews.

Eastern Colorado has produced several women who have succeeded as writers. Faye Tanner Cool, formerly a ranch wife of Kirk, began by winning school essay contests. The prizes were usually ribbons, but she soon graduated to money. Her children's stories appear regularly in top national publications, including *Jack and Jill, Wee Wisdom,* and *Highlights for Children.*

Jerri Garner Lines, New York dancer and choreographer.

One has been reprinted several times and picked up in Europe. She also publishes poetry and articles in a dozen magazines. She even submitted a story — about a babysitter — to a confession magazine contest and won first place. A science fiction story won grand prize over several hundred other entries in *Farm Wife News'* first creative writing competition in 1981.

Faye Cool wrote a weekly column, "Cool Comments," in *The High Plains Farmer* for three years and a monthly column, "From the Far Forty," from 1966 to 1969 for *Colorado Country Life.* All of this work was turned out from her ranch home, then near Fleming.

The poetry editor of *Saturday Review,* John Frederick Nims, taught Faye a valuable lesson at a workshop. He said that the ending of one of her poems reminded him of a Maidenform Bra advertisement. At first, she was insulted but then determined to "show him I could improve it." And he included the resulting poem in the workshop magazine. Faye learned that "criticism isn't a putdown, it's a dare."

Sue Baker Josties, a retired journalist and former director of information for Hastings College, Nebraska, and Northeastern Junior College in Sterling, has published poetry and articles in newspapers of several states, national publications of the Presbyterian Church, *The National Parent-Teacher* magazine, and books. Her very first byline came at age eighteen on page one of the *Omaha Bee News* under an eight-column streamer. *Gleanings* consists of selected writings from 1927 to 1979. One little verse, written long before "Women's Lib," whimsically expresses what writing has meant to many a woman.

Bound by spouse and children three,
I have no identity.
But a measure may be found
Just by pushing words around.

One author from northeastern Colorado has influenced women writers from throughout the whole country. Maxine Firestack Lampshire was born on a farm near Orchard and says that she owes much to her Fort Morgan teacher, Norma S. Cochran, who encouraged her to use a scholarship to the University of Colorado and then helped her find a school to teach. Maxine taught in one-room schools north of Orchard and Snyder and then first grade at Hillrose.

Her writing career began at the *Fort Morgan Times* and continued in papers from the east coast to Japan. She has sold articles, some of them prize winning, to various newspapers and anthologies and has helped to conduct creative writing workshops. She is author of *One Giant Step for the Handicapped* and *Not By Bread Alone* (the story of psychic Dorothy Moore). She has been listed in various editions of *Who's Who of American Women, Two Thousand Women of Achievement,* and *Personalities of the South.*

She is now president of the National League of American Pen Women, an eighty-three-year-old organization of 6,000 professional writers, artists, and musicians. In 1978, the League won the Literary Hall of Fame Award for distinguished service to the craft of writing. Other winners that year were noteworthy: Alexander Solzhenitsyn, Ariel and Will Durant, and Charles Schulz.

Though Maxine's writing has taken her among the famous, including interviews with First Ladies at the White House, she considers a 1953 article in *The Nippon Times* as her most worthwhile. Two doctors, American and Japanese, were performing surgery on young people with congenital cataracts. Blindness would result if the growths were not removed at an early age. Though cost for surgery was only $15.50, many families could not afford even that amount. As a result of Maxine's article, more than $1,000 was contributed, and several dozen young people were saved from a life of blindness.

Chris Petteys is working on her first book, a dictionary of epic proportions. It is an unlikely project for someone whose original interest was music, for it is a biographical listing of women artists born before 1900. The development no doubt bemuses Chris as much as it does professional art historians. It all began when she and her husband Robert decided to collect the work of early women artists. Assuming that only a handful of such paintings were to be found, she began a search. To her astonishment— and perhaps second thoughts by Bob—every discovery led to another. She has uncovered 15,000 names from all over the world. The search is the climax of her involvement in the world of art. Her slide presentation about women artists is one of four

Chris Petteys with Armand Hammer at Hammer Exhibit, Denver
Art Museum, 1978.

Chris Petteys presenting national award to Helen Lundeberg,
1981 conference of Women's Caucus for National Art Awards,
San Francisco. *Photographer, Linda Anderson, formerly of Sterling.*

selected for the Denver Art Museum symposiums for volunteers and is presented regularly in schools and colleges. She is a trustee of the museum. She has written articles for *Women Artist News, Empire Magazine,* and *The Washington Print Club Newsletter.*

In 1980, Chris was appointed to the Committee for the Women's Caucus for National Art Awards and has helped to choose women artists for recognition at the annual ceremonies. At the 1981 conference, she was a panel speaker on Women Collectors, and as a part of her presentation of the 1981 award to Helen Lundeberg "for outstanding achievement in the visual arts," she gave a slide talk about the artist and her career.

The International Dictionary of Women Artists Born Before 1900, which has been contracted for publication by G. K. Hall, has grown far beyond its original purpose. It is now international in scope with a network of researchers and translators assisting Chris. She speaks on such occasions as the convention of the National Association of Art Librarians and a panel presentation on women in the arts at Stanford University. From these contacts come further information and offers of assistance.

The book lists amateur, professional, and primitive artists. Chris Petteys says that she cannot make a judgment as to whether a woman was a "talented artist since only a few pieces of her work may be known . . . nor can I make a decision based on exhibition record, as this is often unknown." Sometimes a woman worked secretly because of family objections or showed her art under the name of her father or brother. Chris Petteys' aim is to be as inclusive as possible to provide clues for future researchers. She hopes that the dictionary will be "a lasting memorial to those forgotten women artists of the past . . . and will be a source of pride to women throughout the world."

And all of this monumental work is being directed from Sterling, Colorado. Someone should tell that legislator.

Several poets have come from the Iliff–Proctor–Padroni area. Grace Smith of Padroni edited what was said to be the only poetry magazine in Colorado during the 1940s. It grew from a period when she was bedfast and became club poet and edited a small publication for 400 women all over the United States. This led to the women's club editorship of *National Pen Pal.* In 1944, she began publishing her own magazine, *The Living Quill.*

Sister Michael Marie was born in 1923, daughter of Ralph and Veronica Schell Kaiser, German-Russian immigrants who had come with their parents to the United States in 1905. They were drawn to the South Platte because of the sugar beet industry. Young Pauline had to work long hours in the beet fields at Proctor. And she hated it. But she loved books and school. And she particularly loved poetry. One day her fifth grade teacher discovered that behind the geography book, Pauline had hidden something else to read—not a comic book, as one would have suspected—but the poems of Shakespeare. Emily Dickinson was another favorite.

From age ten, Pauline wrote her own poems. And she was not a bookworm but a tomboy who loved to race her horse along the South Platte River. Those moments of joy colored her poetry, but so did the tragedies that she observed. Sometimes she could be seen off in the distance watching when a burial took place.

When Pauline was seventeen, she entered the Incarnate Word Convent in Texas, and soon she was teaching while completing her degree. And always she wrote poetry, vivid poetry with images that come to life before the eyes of the reader. Her rain wore a "startling, streaming gown." Without beauty, she said:

My soul would fling its anguish
To a godless night.

Her thoughts often returned to childhood on the prairie. Somewhere, she wrote, there are ". . . hills shimmering in silver and

Pauline Kaiser was not a bookworm.

The tomboy grew up to become a nun and a "poet's poet." *Pictures courtesy of Veronica Schell Kaiser, mother of Sister Michael Marie.*

gold," and somewhere "there is a lonely little river." She remembered growing up "hungering for a sign" of love from her mother and thought that she would be glad to escape her "gruff peasant ways."

"But I lengthened in years and thought," she wrote, and she found that she kept remembering the beauty of her mother's hands

> *Whose stains and scars are stories*
> *Seared in deep with love.*

Sister Michael Marie's mother recalls her as a loving girl who, when food was sometimes short, would not fill her own plate until her mother had taken a serving.

Sister Michael Marie, once called a "Poet's Poet," saw her works published in an anthology, in *The New York Times, Land and Home, The Catholic World,* and other Catholic publications. Her first book, *You Have Filled the Days,* published when she was twenty-six, was the only one that she would see in print. Before too long, in her body "a monster claws. . . . And the night swims in pain." But she continued to write, and sometimes her words bled anguish. Her mind went back to those girlhood days as if she had thrown them away too fast and longed to step into the old scene once more. In "For Remembering" she wrote:

There will always be a dusk
For remembering —
A first star at night to bring
A little girl, running and laughing
Down the hills of my heart.

She comes in blue, a vision
That catches my throat with pain.
She comes, a white dream drifting
Over memory's plain.

Sister Michael Marie's convent friends sifted through 600 of her poems for another slim volume, *Songs For a Journey,* published in 1980 on the twentieth anniversary of the death of the girl who became a nun and, when she was only thirty-six, left the world of beauty.

Lora M. Conant was the daughter of homesteaders who took their children to picnic at Chimney Canyons. Years later, Lora remembered the occasion. The parents, looking at the pitiful drip that passed for a spring,

Recalled the Ohio River's rolling flow,
And felt it was a bitter sorry thing
This was the land their children were to know.
But we who knew no softer, greener place
Found joy in nature's harsh, distorted face.

Lora proved up on land while she taught at a one-room school northwest of Padroni. In later years, she lived in Denver and published poetry in periodicals and several books. The latter include *Willie Magee of the Ranch Sandee,* lighthearted verses about an appealing little boy. Poems in *Things As We See Them* hark back to her prairie days. She remembers "Prairie grass lies like a bed" with cactus blossoms a quiltlike pattern on the green. She remembers the blizzard and its

sudden savagery. It gnawed
Grown men between its monstrous jaws
To cripple them. It smothered small
Lost children with its huge white paws.

Some poems in *As the Wheel Turns* are bitter cries from desperate women, achieved in a few stark words, as in "Lament":

> My husband snores in drunken sleep,
> My babies moan with cold,
> And restless in my body lies
> The child I dread to hold.

"Transmutation" tells of a family whose home was on a dryland farm, bleak and bare, where the wind and sand blew.

> Their neighbor on the right
> Went starkly mad;
> She killed herself one night
> When winds were bad.

Perhaps the people who lasted were like her "Grim Philosopher," who wanted an easy life but inexplicably came West.

> George later developed philosophies,
> Simplicities tough and hard and grim.
> Now faith or fallacy who can say?
> They made his desert bloom for him.

Another writer lived at Iliff as a child, and even then she wrote poetry that would one day bring her a Pulitzer Prize. Even then, she felt frustration — other children thought that writing poetry was "odd" — and after her verses had made her famous, she once lamented that in America "not reading poetry amounts to a national pastime."

The poet was Phyllis McGinley. She wrote almost compulsively, according to classmates and teachers. Verona Foy McKenzie lived on a nearby homestead in 1914 when she and Phyllis were in the fifth and sixth grades. They rode their horses three miles to a country school. Phyllis was pretty and smart and had a slight lisp that was appealing. But Verona never felt close to the older girl. "Her head always seemed to be up in the clouds, and she didn't play with us much."

When Verona studied piano with Mrs. McGinley, she would watch Phyllis gazing out the window, her thoughts far away, while she ate cocoa and sugar and occasionally wrote deliberate passages on a tablet.

Frances Swedensky (Garfield) did not teach Phyllis at the Iliff school, but the child often came to her room to talk. Mrs. Garfield, now in her nineties, remembers that ten-to-twelve-year-old Phyllis was a joy, lovable, but "peculiar. She stayed by herself. She made up poems and sang them to herself." Once she excitedly reported that she had seen a fairy at the top of a tall tree. On another occasion, it was an angel.

Laurence Ramey was in the eighth grade in 1917 when Phyllis was a high school freshman. He says that it was apparent even then that she was "far ahead of most people when it came to stringing words together. She was always writing little four-line ditties about people and about what should or shouldn't be done." He felt that "she had ability to spare" but, interestingly, that "she was very forward."

The McGinley clan—two brothers and their families and an unmarried sister—homesteaded and hoped to establish a real estate business. Though Mrs. McGinley's fine furniture and dishes, brought from the family home in Oregon, helped to transform the simple prairie house, it was evidently never really home to the young girl. The real estate efforts were not successful, and when the father's health began to fail, he bought the Ramey hardware store in Iliff. One pleasure was visiting the Fred Lutin family in Sterling. Dorothy Lutin Curlee recalls that the children, devout Catholics, refused meat on Friday but that afterwards her mother found chicken bones stashed away in their room.

Perhaps such childhood transgressions helped Phyllis write her many books for children. Ten of her total output of eighteen volumes are verse, and two are lightly philosophical and rather autobiographical. She wrote numerous articles for major periodicals, ranging from top women's magazines to *The New Yorker*. One of her children's works about Santa Claus was a television special.

Her career was rewarded with numerous honors. *Love Letters* won the prestigious Edna St. Vincent Millay Memorial Award in 1954. Next year she was elected to the National Institute of Arts and Letters. In 1964, she won the Laetere Medal, given by the University of Notre Dame to a man or woman who has "enriched the heritage of humanity."

Phyllis McGinley said, "I wrote out of a fairly passionate concern for tradition or morality."

She received a dozen honorary degrees, including one from all-male Dartmouth College. In 1965, she was invited to read some of her poetry at Lyndon Johnson's White House and was subsequently the feature of a *Time* magazine cover story (18 June 1965). But her greatest honor was the Pulitzer Prize for Poetry bestowed upon her *Times Three: Selected Verse from Three Decades* in 1961. It was the first time that light verse had been awarded a Pulitzer. But to say that Phyllis McGinley's poetry is light is not to do it justice. It is clear and witty and touches a common chord in readers, but it is also literate, and the words flow with refreshing originality.

Most references to her childhood seem strangely out of kilter with life on the prairie. She speaks of pleated skirts and middy blouses when she was eleven, "Indistinguishable from my friends." Perhaps, but not on the prairie. She says that "it was a rare middle-class household without a maid." One wonders if this urbane poet ever could have lived on the plains during homestead days. Her childhood in Colorado seems obliterated by the happy life that Phyllis McGinley created in the East, a place she said that she would hate to visit but where she loved to live. There she gloried in her work, her husband, and her two daughters.

There are vague statements that she was "badly educated," despite studies at two universities. She speaks of the "odd advantages of a bad education. . . . To the length and breadth of classic English writing, I came as an astonished stranger." Finally, one finds a specific reference to Colorado:

> As a child I lived on a ranch in Colorado with the nearest one-room schoolhouse four miles away and the roads nearly impassable in winter. Sometimes there was no teacher. Sometimes my brother and I were the only pupils. In my teens, the public high school of a very small western town did little to mend the damage.

It may have been that the hardships on the prairie were too painful to remember. The family's real estate dreams did not materialize, and the store did not prosper. The father's condition worsened when Phyllis was about twelve, and he died. The mother, a cripple, was stranded and managed to get the post office job. She and her son and daughter lived in rooms behind the office. Several years later, they returned to Mrs. McGinley's home after selling the fine possessions to people who could not pay the real value.

It would be understandable that Phyllis McGinley would want to forget. But one hopes that she knew of the other talents that sprang from that prairie, or at least from the genes of the kind of people who tackled it. Did she ever hear of the Hamil brothers who attended the McGinley School with her boy cousins? Like Phyllis, Harold is a writer. One of his books, *Colorado Without Mountains,* waters his genius from the well of boyhood memories on the Blue Ranch. Dave Hamil made distinguished contributions to government as Speaker of the Colorado House of Representatives, head of the state Department of Institutions, and administrator, under four presidents, of the national Rural Electric Association.

Did Phyllis ever cross paths with the Noguchi sisters who also lived near Iliff? Their fame as writers and artists has been on a national scale.

One hopes that she saw the grandeur, the scope of the prairies. In one poem, written as usual about suburban New York life, she mourned the loss of a meadow with trees, the view wiped out when someone built a house on the only vacant lot of her block. Did she at those moments treasure the old limitless vistas in Colorado? It does not show in her poetry. She sings of the green of the golf course; the joy of her husband coming home on the commuter train; the blackbird-like migrations of children from seashore to bicycle pedaling to kite flying.

The shadows of antelope may not stray into Phyllis McGinley's poetry, nor the ghosts of buffalo roam. But seldom is heard a discouraging word in her verse, and her skies are never cloudy.

And she won a Pulitzer Prize.

Above, left: Bertha Kaepernik Blancett competing at Endicott. *M. O. Dunn Collection, Overland Trail Museum. Above, right:* Marvel Crosson. *Courtesy, Overland Trail Museum. Below, left:* Dr. Sugi Noguchi operating at army hospital in Yokohama during the Korean War. *Photograph by army photographer. Below, right:* Major Helen F. Brecht. *U.S. Army photograph by Corporal Kondreck.*

THE DAUGHTERS

The daughters were born into a world that stretched to an unending horizon. Their lives knew a freedom that few ever find, a security in their place in the big world. Their eyes were accustomed to looking far distances; their minds used to the discipline that loneliness and a limitless landscape demand.

And like their parents, they were seekers. Their forebears' gift of migration to the plains had given them a dual confidence. They had roots, but like the family behind them, they could strike off into the unknown. They were hungry to make their mark on the prairie and eventually on the big unseen world somewhere beyond that horizon.

Lou Piel awaits her turn at bat at the National Sports Festival in Colorado Springs, 1979. *Photograph by Ivo, Colorado Springs.*

Chapter XIII

CHAMPION LADY RIDER OF THE WORLD

"Unladylike!" That's what they said in 1894 when Nannie Gunn and her campaigners abandoned the side saddle. But only ten years later, Colorado and Wyoming were buzzing about the exploits of a young woman who went far beyond the small freedom of riding "clothespin style."

Bertha Kaepernik had come with her family to homestead in Colorado in 1886 when she was only three years old. But even the baby of a family was needed in the tough business of breaking the prairie sod and trying to make a living on 160 acres. One day, Bertha's father put her on the back of a horse and commanded her to stay aboard and do some chore for him. She was then five years old.

Bertha did stay aboard—endlessly. Anytime that she could not be found, the family looked for her horse. She was fearless and began to ride other horses. As time passed, the Kaeperniks noted that there did not seem to be one that Bertha couldn't gentle.

Then, in 1904, the officials of Cheyenne Frontier Days issued an announcement that surely must have caught the attention of everyone: Women would be allowed to compete in the upcoming annual event. Whether they expected a response is not known. But the announcement must have made good publicity for Frontier Days, which was then in only its eighth year and faced stiff competition from many small-town events.

There was nothing easy about rodeo in those days. Each contestant had to bring along his own bucking horse. It might not be too simple for a woman to acquire a horse or to get him to Cheyenne. There surely was a lot of speculation among the men, and perhaps curiosity did lead to increased interest in Frontier Days. As the big event approached, a woman was indeed on her way to Cheyenne, traveling across country on horseback and leading her bronc.

It was Bertha. Her family was probably doubtful about her going off to compete against men, but Bertha had been doing a man's work on the homestead. To the twenty-one-year-old, going to Cheyenne was the answer to a prayer. She loved showing her skill, and she felt that she could ride a wildly bucking animal just as well as any man. She took pride in the number of horses that she had tamed.

Cheyenne opened a whole new world to Bertha — Wild West shows, exhibitions, movies — but her great love remained rodeo. And she made her mark. For that first competition at Cheyenne, Bertha borrowed a green bronc from Len Sherwin, a trader who was as crazy about horses as she was. "You can take Tombstone," Len said. "He's my best. You'll get a hell of a ride on him."

There was no road from Atwood, Colorado, to Cheyenne, but Bertha followed the tracks of the little *Prairie Dog Special* across the high open country. She rode her horse and led Tombstone. She carried her food, oats for the horses, and a bedroll, and when the first night came, she picketed the horses on the prairie and curled up on a bench at a little depot alongside the tracks.

The next day rain began to fall. The prairies of eastern Colorado don't get a lot of rain, but sometimes it comes in big batches. Bertha was caught out on the open plains, but luckily she came to a homestead where the people allowed her to turn the horses into the corral and welcomed her into their home.

Out in that big open country, Bertha may have found encouragement for her daring project. Many women had come alone to homestead out there, and some, like Sarah Ayars, had been following some pretty independent activities of their own, like driving teams across the prairie in all kinds of weather to deliver mail.

Bertha arrived in Cheyenne and learned that she was the only woman who would compete. The Frontier Days crowd may have laughed at the pretty girl mounting her bronc in the chute and undoubtedly made some dire predictions, but when she catapulted into the arena on the back of Len Sherwin's white horse, the grins faded. A *Denver Post* reporter wrote that Tombstone was a bronc that "few would have mounted in fun." The horse put on quite a show. The reporter declared that throughout the ride Bertha "sat straight in her saddle while she rode him to a standstill." Failing to buck her off, Tombstone reared on his hind legs. Once he fell backwards, but Bertha simply slid to one side as the horse went down and was "aboard" again as he exploded to his feet.

The crowd jumped on the benches, yelling in admiration, and, according to the newspaper, "cheered themselves weak at the sight of a woman riding as they had not conceived that a woman could ride." Bertha left the arena in triumph "without a glance at the howling mob."

Afterwards, as she returned home, she thought, "Why should I be leading this horse?", and she rode Tombstone the hundred miles, delivering him, broken, to the astonished Len Sherwin. One of the men criticized her, "You've spoilt him. Now he'll never be any good for bucking."

Bertha realized that if she intended to continue rodeoing, she would have to forget her pride in breaking horses and would have to concentrate on simply making a good ride. And she certainly intended to continue. She rode in shows at Loveland and Fort Collins that year. Len Sherwin gave her the first big opportunity in 1905 when he, his brother Claude, and a friend, Joe Baker, organized the Sherwin Wild West Show. He lined up an impressive array of talent who pitted their skills against local challengers wherever the show played. The Sherwin crew included three who later won world championships: Sam Brownell, World Champion Rodeo Rider; Irvin Monnette, World Champion Steer Roper; and Bertha, Champion Lady Rider of the World. Bertha was the only woman.

In 1911, when women were first allowed to compete officially at the Pendleton, Oregon, rodeo, Bertha won her title and a saddle for the women's bucking horse championship. Next year she was again champion, and in 1914, she came within twelve points

"I was always a lady," Bertha said, and she looked it as she rode to Cheyenne. *Courtesy, Overland Trail Museum.*

of capturing the men's title. The following season, women competitors were placed in a separate category.

Bertha also participated in relay races. One of her most exciting events was the Roman race. Stunned audiences must have felt that she had each foot in a separate world. She would stand upright, urging her horses forward, her left leg braced on the back of one, her right leg bending with the movements of the other. The crowds did not believe that this daring competitor was a girl, but they admitted that she was good — so good that she finally accepted a handicap of turning her horses backward at the starting line — and she still won!

Bertha also rode with the Pawnee Bill Show, and in 1906, she joined the Miller Brothers' famous 101 outfit. There were probably occasions when it was necessary to put a man in his place. But the cowboys in the show learned very quickly that though Bertha followed an unconventional dream for a woman, she was nevertheless a good girl. "I was always a lady," she said many years afterwards, "and they always treated me as such." Still, when the show pulled into a new town, men on the lookout for girls figured that a woman riding with a Wild West outfit was no doubt appropriately wild. Bertha wasn't wild, but she was strong. Most of the time, though, she didn't even need to protect herself. Her teammates on the rodeo circuit saw to it that no local Romeo bothered Bertha.

Everyone liked Bertha. Billy Armour, who traveled with Len Sherwin's show and who was a real-life cowboy as well, liked to look back at those early days. Once, when he was ninety-two years old, he commented that during those long years, one girl had stood out as a dancer. It was Bertha, "the best dance partner I ever had. She was very much a girl, a lot of fun."

But Bertha had fallen in love, and her eyes were on only one man. He, too, was a member of the 101 outfit, and in 1909, when the show played Detroit, the two decided to get married. He was Dell Blancett, a topnotch cowboy and a World Champion bulldogger. Bertha was then twenty-six.

Bertha and Dell pooled their considerable talents. In a ball park at Endicott, Washington, they regularly staged trick riding, roping, and bulldogging, with Bertha hazing for the latter. Bulldogging was Dell's big event — he was the first to introduce it at Pendleton — and he wasn't about to have his performance ruined by an inept hazer. Bertha was as good as any man at controlling the steer so that Dell could plunge from his horse and wrestle the animal off its feet in record time.

In 1910, they first worked for the old Bison Movie Company with Tom Mix, Bebe Daniels, and Hoot Gibson, a former World Champion cowboy.

Then came World War I. Both Dell and Bertha had strong feelings about the country that had given them a life that they loved. Dell helped to organize a volunteer cowboy cavalry troop at Pendleton. He was full of excitement and patriotism, and

Bertha was proud of him and of his leadership. On the morning that the cowboys were to take their physicals, he kissed her goodbye and announced, "When you see me next, I'll be a soldier in the U.S. Cavalry."

Dell was strong and vigorous. A man who rode bucking horses, who could wrestle an eight-hundred-pound steer onto its back, who spent most of his time in the outdoors, had a lot to give his country. It never occurred to him that he might not pass the physical.

Bertha loved Dell completely. She knew how he wanted to go with his buddies and fight "old Kaiser Bill." But she loved him. He was her life. Perhaps she felt a secret relief for a moment when he was not accepted. But she had faced danger to do what was most important to her. She knew what that meant to a person. And so she kissed Dell goodbye again. He went to Canada and enlisted in the Canadian Cavalry and served with the Lord Strathmore unit. Bertha took the quietest job of her career, in a print shop, while Dell was away. It was as if she put a hold on things until he came home.

But he never came back. The man who could face all the open dangers of bucking horses, flailing hooves, and horns of wild bulls and steers in the arena was as vulnerable as any other to the unseen menace on the Western Front. Dell was killed by a German sniper.

Bertha never married again, and she never competed after that year. She continued in the rodeo world, however, until near sixty, as a pickup rider. That the cowboys would trust her to rescue them at the end of a ride was further proof of the horsemanship of Bertha Kaepernik Blancett.

During another of her riding jobs, tour conducting at Yosemite, Dwight Eisenhower, then an army colonel, told her, "I have never seen anyone else, man or woman, who could ride like you."

Bertha's final years brought many satisfactions. She traveled freely, driving her old 1958 Plymouth around Portersville, California. Her eyesight and hearing were excellent, and she remained "very much a girl," having her hair set once a week. She came for a heroine's welcome to Logan County, where she had first been put aboard that horse. She gave advice on care of horses to admiring 4-H girls. She was then in her mid-nineties.

Bertha's final years also brought significant honors: at the age of seventy-five, riding as Grand Marshal of the Portersville Roundup Parade; that same year, charter membership in the National Cowboy Hall of Fame; at ninety-two, induction into the Rodeo Hall of Fame, an honor accorded to only a handful of women. She traveled to Oklahoma City and attended all the events with relish. The saddle that she won at Pendleton is on display in the Hall of Fame.

She lived to be ninety-five, and she always felt pain when she remembered the message that her Dell would not be coming back to her.

But there were good memories, too, of her unusual accomplishments, and perhaps the most exciting remained that revolutionary ride at Cheyenne before the "howling mob." From that moment, Bertha indeed had her feet firmly planted in two worlds—worlds that stretched far beyond the Roman race. She was a part of the high drama of rodeo. But she always kept one foot firmly rooted in the traditions and standards that her family had taught.

She was a good girl.

Chapter XIV

COLORADO'S MARVEL OF A BIRD GIRL

"Why don't you do like the rest of us?" Other women were always asking that question. Sometimes it concerned a trivial matter, like not following fashion by having her hair bobbed. More often, the query was about her extraordinary choice of a career. But she loved her chosen field so much that she gave up her life for it.

It all began on a summer day in 1913 when two young children stared through a hole in a board fence at the wonders of the Logan County Fair. What so entranced them was not cattle or crop displays from the high plains, and it was even more exciting than the customary rodeo and Wild West show. Behind that five-foot fence was an airplane, the first that they had ever seen. A "pusher" with the propeller in back, it was shipped by rail from one town to the next and piloted, barely off the ground, by a gypsy flyer who introduced the wonders of the new Aviation Age to rural America.

The girl was Marvel Crosson. She and her younger brother Joe glimpsed their future through that hole. If they could have seen it clearly—not only fame, smashed records, adventure in Alaska where Eskimos looked to "Gods in the sky," friendships and work with famous people, but ultimately tragedy as well—perhaps the scene would have been even more awesome.

Marvel was thirteen, and though three years older than Joe,

she admired all that he did. And so when he began to dance up and down, shouting, "I want to be an aviator," Marvel yelled along with him, "I want to be an aviator, too!"

Thus began an ambition that made Marvel and Joe Crosson well-known members of that vanguard of young Americans who with Charles Lindbergh were intoxicated by the Air Age. Though they would never match Lindbergh's dramatic solo flight to Paris, they would set records and chalk up some impressive accomplishments of their own. Their names and faces would appear on magazine covers and the front pages of the nation's newspapers.

Joe was to become one of the early Alaskan bush pilots, flying mercy missions that caught the imagination of the world. It was he who found the bodies of his friends, the revered Ben Eielson, and four years later, Will Rogers and Wiley Post. He was the first manager of Alaskan Pan-Am when it replaced the pioneering companies in the Territory, and he helped to make the first air exploration of the Antarctic.

Marvel was a symbol of the new freedom of the air. Perhaps because she was a woman, she drew particular attention. Joe had more faith in her flying ability than in that of any of his bush pilot friends, and he showed it in a daring stunt.

But the two children had a long wait after the excitement of seeing that first plane. They passed their growing up years on their father's farm near Merino, contenting themselves with rides on their balky Shetland pony and listening to the stories of old-timers who had pioneered in the area back in the 1870s. Who could have guessed that they soon would be pioneers in their own right?

Both children were excellent students and curious. School friends said that Marvel was aptly named: her vibrant personality made her a marvel. She was an honor student in high school. Joe was considered a natural mechanic, but both he and Marvel used to say that she was an even better one. In later years, Joe told that she could "smell out" a weak spot in a plane and repair it faster than he could.

When their father, E. E. Crosson, bought a new car, Joe and Marvel took it apart to see how it worked. Just when they had all the pieces spread out on the ground, their father unexpectedly appeared, and when he saw what had happened to his new automobile, ". . . his face was a picture," according to Marvel. "When he recovered from his shock, he told us exactly what he thought of us." He then ordered his strange children to put the car back together. They did.

In 1917, the father proposed, "Shall I keep saving money and maybe have you fight over it when I'm gone, or shall we start traveling and have some fun?"

The young mechanics chose fun and did the driving for the 20,000-mile trips. They were already experienced, having learned when Marvel was thirteen and Joe ten. When the family reached California, the young people maneuvered their parents to San Diego, the aviation center of western United States. The first thing that they saw was a flying formation of army pursuit planes going at the fabulous speed of 125 miles per hour. Marvel saw her feeling mirrored in Joe's face — as if they were "coming into the promised land."

Next they reminded their parents how they had always wanted to see Mexico and managed to get them to take the bus trip alone, leaving the two young people "with nothing to do and a car to do it in."

"All aboard for Dutch Flats!" they shouted, and within thirty minutes they were at Lindbergh's flying field, staring at all the planes and watching the heroic figures who owned them. One pilot was charging five dollars a ride. When he strolled over to ask the two if they'd like to go up, they fervently declared yes but added that they had only $2.50. Perhaps the pilot sympathized with their symptoms, for he said, "Hop in." He zoomed off the field so fast that "our chins hit our chests," Marvel said. And their ambition to own a plane was born. She was nineteen and Joe sixteen.

They realized that Sterling, at 4,000 feet altitude and with no airfield, could not fulfill their ambitions. It would be like "trying to drive a car on a burro trail," Joe said. And though they did not tell their parents what those ambitions were, they began a subtle campaign of influencing them to move to the west coast. Several months of their "California treatment" finally led to the permanent move to San Diego.

Both got jobs and saved almost every penny that they earned.

Their parents must have wondered about the sudden conservatism of the young people. The beautiful Marvel no longer bought new dresses or jewelry. And when other girls asked why she still wore her hair long, she never told the truth — that a haircut cost at least a dollar and that she was saving her dollars for an airplane.

"In those days," Marvel said, "flying was regarded as dangerous for men and impossible for women (except for the few wild ones who did circus work)."

The search for a plane was not a simple matter. Only obsolete army craft seemed to be available, and those they couldn't afford. Finally, one day a man came into the garage where Joe was a mechanic and told of a ship on sale for $150. This they could afford, and no wonder. It was an old N-9 seaplane with pontoons, had no engine, had been wrecked, and was in pieces.

Marvel and Joe brought the plane to the family backyard. It was the first that the parents knew of their ambition, and they were understandably upset at seeing their lawn littered with boxes of parts. The reconstruction soon began to assume enormous proportions. The Crossons at first were horrified about the dangers in such a venture — Marvel said that there was "quite a revolution" — but as the weeks went by, their parents began to understand.

One day their father said, "Well, if anything is going to happen to those kids, it'll happen anyhow. Let them alone — they're happy!"

Night after night, Marvel and Joe worked on the plane. The pontoons were replaced with wheels and the depth controls removed. Whenever they were stumped, they drove to Dutch Flats and asked for advice. They studied and measured planes. Marvel made cloth covers for the wings and fuselage; Joe put in stick controls, landing gear, and struts in the wings. They worked from fall 1920 to February 1921, spending no time or money on shows or dances, and finally they showed off the ship — finished but lacking a motor. Friends and neighbors laughed at the project.

The search for a motor seemed hopeless. Joe asked everyone who came into the garage, and Marvel said, "I used to make people think I was crazy by telling them that their films would be done at such and such a time and then asking, 'Do you know anyone who wants to sell a good airplane motor?' "

Then one day a man brought Joe the news that some Curtiss OX-5 ninety-horsepower motors were for sale. They were for boats, but when Marvel and Joe learned that the price was only $125, they mortgaged their Ford "Lizzie" to buy one. Again they struggled in the backyard each evening, and every night the weary pair went to supper covered with grease and dirt. One day a week later, Marvel hurried home from the film store to find Joe excitedly waiting.

"Get in the ship, Marvel," he said. "I'm going to start her, and I want you to be the first to do it." Later Marvel said:

> I know now that it was a selfish thing to do, but I could not resist the temptation. I got into the cockpit and a minute later Joe cranked the propeller. I felt the motor catch and a split second later, the propeller began to whir. Then I did something that I would never do again. I "gave her the gun" or opened the throttle wide and the result was glorious. The motor came to life with all its ninety horses bucking and the propeller whirled into invisibility. But Joe suddenly shouted to cut it off. . . . He was waving his arms and seemed very excited.

Then Marvel saw what had happened. The propeller had blown the neighbors' unsuspecting chickens against the fence and had sent a cloud of feathers sailing down the street.

All night long, they kept going out to look in wonderment at the plane, saying over and over, "It's ours and it's paid for."

They took the craft apart again for the trip to Dutch Flats, towing the fuselage behind the little Ford and loading the wings on a tow truck borrowed from the garage. Two weeks later, a former army instructor took the plane up while the ecstatic young builders watched from below. The little one-time seaplane with the boat motor worked perfectly. Marvel watched her brother leap about with the same abandon of the ten-year-old who had seen his first aircraft back in Sterling, Colorado. He was still only eighteen, and she was twenty-one.

Joe hollered, "It flies, Marvel, and it's ours," and Marvel proclaimed it "the swellest ship on the field."

By this time, Joe had been taking lessons and had about three hours of solo time to his credit. Marvel, of course, was his first

"A smile was as much a part of her costume as her leather coat and helmet." *Courtesy, Edward Bryan Davis and Mary Davis Weidner, cousins of Marvel Crosson.*

passenger, and soon she was recruiting business. They charged $2.50 for fifteen minutes. When they began to get cross-country jobs, Joe decided that it was no good flying alone and started teaching Marvel in the evenings after work (when there was money for gas).

The two were so hard up that at first they owned only one pair of goggles. They had no instruments. They wet their hands to check wind drift. Every penny went to gasoline, which was twenty-six cents a gallon. Ten gallons kept them aloft for an hour. Sometimes Marvel was tempted to spend a dollar for beads or other pretty things, but she would stop herself with the thought, "Four gallons of gas."

But she was never tempted to cut off her long hair, for she found that the braid looped around her head made a pad so that the helmet was more comfortable.

Marvel was as natural a pilot as Joe, but no one considered flying a serious business for women. Despite her progress, the men at the airfield treated her with a shade of condescension that "used to get under my skin," Marvel said. "I could feel the sex line drawn against me. . . . Joe was not long in sensing the way the gang regarded me, and I later found out that it got his goat, too."

One day he said, "You're getting good, Marvel, and it won't be long now before we show this gang something they'll not forget in a hurry."

Two nights later, at about 1,000 feet, Joe turned the controls over to Marvel for the first time. Just as she followed his instructions to head the ship over Dutch Flats Field, Joe got out of his seat and climbed outside. They shot over the hangars at 100 miles an hour with Joe out on the wing. But when they landed in triumph, they discovered that no one had seen the stunt.

Back up they went, and that time when the little plane passed over the field, much lower, everybody was out looking. And there was "Joe on the wing waving like all possessed." Marvel reported with satisfaction, "There was a very different tone to their good fellowship from then on."

Joe was not just a foolhardy kid. Though he repeated the stunt with Marvel—a picture was made when she soloed in May 1922—he never ventured out of the cockpit with any other flyer.

In 1926, Joe went to Alaska for a wonderful job of flying passengers and mail. The brother and sister could not believe his luck in actually being *paid* to fly. Moreover, he had the satisfaction of making the first commercial flights to much of Alaska.

Marvel remained in San Diego, working but spending all her spare time flying. Soon she had logged 250 solo hours. She was also purchasing agent for the Alaska company, buying everything from nuts and bolts to motors and wings—even complete airplanes. A press dispatch of the time reported that she could "dismantle and put an airplane together again with the best mechanic."

But she longed for the excitement of Alaska, and she worried about Joe. Stories kept coming out about his daring flights, most of them at night and without a compass, though up in the plane, at 3,000 feet, he could see the sun shining in every direction.

Joe and Marvel Crosson, aviation pioneers in Alaska, 1927. *Courtesy, Overland Trail Museum.*

Once his plane crashed on a river of ice, but he saved the passengers. A week later, when he and a mechanic returned to the site, their second plane caught fire, and they were saved only because the mechanic shielded them from the flames with a piece of burlap while Joe sideslipped the plane to make the flames go the other way. Another time he was forced to take off where there was no field. He headed the plane down a 1,200-foot incline and zoomed over the precipice at the bottom out into space.

In 1927, when Joe came home to the air races, they sold the homemade plane for a profit, and Marvel accompanied him to the North to "look after him." She was immediately popular. Someone said, "A smile was as much a part of her costume as her leather coat and helmet." She kept house for herself and her brother in a little log cabin at Fairbanks and amused herself by playing basketball on a team organized by Klondike "Klondy" Nelson, author of "I Was a Bride in the Arctic."

She accompanied Joe whenever possible and also made her first long passenger trips with their new aviation friends. She was thrilled to fly alongside Mount McKinley at 10,000 feet elevation. She helped to run tractors to keep airfields open during blizzards. Joe and Marvel were proud to be "doing something that must be done."

She entertained their friends in the cabin. Ben Eielson, the first bush pilot to fly out of Fairbanks and Joe's boss and later partner, was a frequent visitor. Hubert Wilkins often came to talk. Marvel listened with delight to his stories of polar exploration. He had been on a sea and dog sled trip through the Canadian Arctic Islands from 1913 to 1916, and in 1920 and 1921, he had gone to the Antarctic. He and Ben Eielson had been the first to fly to Point Barrow, northernmost point of Alaska, and had continued 600 miles beyond across the Arctic Ocean. His ambition was to explore the poles by air.

Marvel could not believe her fortune at being a part of such an adventurous world. She also learned that Joe had established some firsts. He had flown medicine to far distant villages and saved lives. When the dirigible the *Norge* had made its record-breaking trip from Norway across the Arctic and had gone down on the ice at Teller, it was Joe who found the famous crew (Roald Amundsen, General Umberto Nobile, and Lincoln Ellsworth) and took the first pictures.

But not everyone in Alaska liked the changes that the airplane had brought. The dog drivers hated the bush pilots for taking their business. Not only were the planes carrying more and more passengers but also furs and mail. When a float plane got stuck on a sandbar one day, not one boatman or dog musher offered to help. They stood on the bank, yelling insults. The roadhouse proprietors were also unfriendly because they, too, lost business as the planes replaced the dog sled trips. Klondy Nelson told that some roadhouses had signs reading: NO DOGS OR PILOTS ALLOWED INSIDE.

Such stories did not spoil the adventure for Marvel. Ben Eielson, who was also an inspector for the Department of Commerce, gave Marvel her pilot's examination. She was the first woman to receive a flying license from the Territory of Alaska. The miners began to request her for a pilot, and they declared a public holiday in her honor. She was called "Pollyanna of the North" because she spread good cheer as well as delivered mail, medicine, machinery, gold dust, needles and thread, vegetables and fruit — even watermelons — which led to another nickname, "The Watermelon Girl." On a 200-mile flight, there could be two dozen stops.

The country was practically one big swamp, and what wasn't swamp was mountainous. There were few airfields, most of them hundreds of miles apart. Frequently, the landing field was a sandbar in a river, and more often than not, it was under water.

Nevertheless, the airplane transformed Alaska. Klondy Nelson said that as she and her husband Frank traveled up the Yukon, they often saw the bush pilots flying overhead. "There's Joe now," Frank would say, "on his way to Nome." And after Marvel got her license, there she would be, too, making flights over the great wild country. Before Klondy and Frank had proceeded very far upriver, they would see the plane again, already making its return.

Alaska was a wonderful liberation for Marvel. Her choice of a career no longer brought comments of "How extraordinary!" from other women. She had absolute confidence in her knowledge of airplanes, and she was proving that a woman "can do a man's work in the air."

Joe went to New York to raise money for the airmail company that he, Ben, and Marvel planned to start in Alaska. While he was away, he received a wire from Hubert Wilkins. The success of Wilkins' recent flight from Point Barrow to Norway had brought him an English title and backing for his ambition to be the first to fly over the Antarctic. He wanted Joe to go with him.

Joe was dispatched to California to pick up a Lockheed-Vega. He wired Marvel to meet him. Not even knowing the reason, Marvel was in such a hurry that when she got off the boat at Seattle, she caught a plane and reached Los Angeles two days ahead of schedule. Joe wanted her to help him ferry Wilkins' new monoplane to New York. There it would be loaded on a ship, the *Southern Cross,* for the first lap of the trip toward the South Pole.

Marvel had been in Alaska for a year, and on this first trip out, she saw her mother for only thirty minutes. But Mrs. Crosson had learned the demands on her "bird children's" lives. When they took off, the last person that they saw was their mother, far below, waving and waving.

Their flying time was only twenty-five hours and five minutes. They took turns sleeping and piloting at 10,000 feet, and with a compass, they had no difficulty finding the way. Marvel said:

> It was one of the happiest times of my life. You know, there is something cozy and wonderful about being 10,000 feet up in the air, above the clouds, with the motor humming sweetly and the ship making 130 to 140 miles an hour and the best friend in the world there with you.

Despite nights on the ground at El Paso and St. Louis, they surprised Wilkins by arriving at the Waldorf-Astoria, expedition headquarters, twenty-four hours ahead of schedule.

On September 22, 1928, as Marvel stood on the deck of the *Southern Cross,* seeing Joe off on his great opportunity, he showed her a dollar bill owned by his good friend, Dan Burnett. It was the famous Lindbergh dollar carried by the Lone Eagle on his landmark flight to Paris, as well as his flight to South America. Burnett had refused $3,000 for the lucky bill, but now he lent it to Joe. Marvel looked at the bill with amusement, and she said something that afterwards seemed painfully ironic: "Those things do work with men, I believe, but we women . . . do not have to have toys for luck. We make sure of our luck before we start, and that means that we do not start until we are sure we can come through with success."

Perhaps the lucky bill should have been given to Marvel. At first she was lucky. She entered races and became well known. The beautiful young aviatrix caught the fancy of an American public in love with the Air Age. In late May 1929, she set a new altitude record for women, 23,996 feet. Her picture appeared in national magazines. It was on the cover of the *Mid-Week Pictorial Magazine of the New York Times*. NEW STAR OF THE CLOUDS, announced the headline, and the caption read:

> Miss Marvel Crosson, Pretty Twenty-five-year-old Los Angeles Flier, Who Recently Ascended 24,000 feet, Breaking All Previous Records Held by Her Sex. Miss Crosson and Her Brother In-augurated the First Air Mail Service From Alaska.

Marvel was actually twenty-nine. Shortly afterward, she returned to her old home in Colorado, enjoying a heroine's welcome. She spoke to the admiring students at her Merino and Sterling schools.

Three months later, she entered the Women's Air Derby of the National Air Races, so eager for the competition that she was first to file an official entry. The past ten years of her life had been devoted to aviation. Recognition had come to her as well as her increasingly famous brother. Perhaps, even as she flew, Marvel's head was spinning with plans for new challenges.

Despite her confidence in her mechanical ability—despite her statement that women "do not start until we are sure that we can come through with real success"—something went wrong with the plane. Lieutenant Colonel Dan Hofmann, long-time member of the Colorado Civil Air Patrol, a pilot who has flown countless rescue missions, and an inductee in the Colorado Aviation Hall of Fame, says that something was wrong with Marvel's plane at the final stop. But she brushed off suggestions that she wait for a check. She was so eager to win, so sure of herself. After all, she had flown over the vast wastelands of Alaska under far more difficult conditions.

She zoomed into the air, headed for glory, up into that wonderful world above the clouds.

But she did not arrive at the next checkpoint. Did she in those last moments feel betrayed when the "sweetly humming" motor began to falter? Did she cry out for Joe, that best friend in the world, who was far away in Alaska and could not help? Did she remember the strangely prophetic final words of an article that she had recently written for *The Country Gentleman:* "I have given up my life to prove that women are the best pilots in the world."

Search parties found her plane, crashed on the Arizona desert. Nearby was Marvel's body, shrouded in her silk parachute. She had tried to bail out but did not have enough altitude for the chute to open.

Marvel's grieving family remembered the young girl dancing about the Sterling fairgrounds, crying, "I want to be an aviator!" They remembered the day that she and Joe dragged the wrecked plane into the backyard. They had told themselves, "Something could happen to them in a motor car. They might as well do as they like."

Marvel had done as she liked—as she loved—and at twenty-nine she was dead.

The National Exchange Club, which sponsored the 1929 races, held memorial services for her at all clubs. A thirty-second period of silence was observed at the Cleveland Airport ceremonies following the races, and a vacant seat marked Marvel's place at the awards banquet. Back in Sterling, Colorado, a memorial plaque was presented to her high school by the alumni association in memory of the gallant schoolmate, the "marvel" who had followed her dreams to death.

Perhaps she would have been most surprised at another recognition in Colorado. Today when a pilot drops down to the airport at Sterling, where Marvel and Joe long ago saw their first thrilling plane, he discovers he has landed on Crosson Airfield, named for aviation's unique brother–sister team.

It was Joe Crosson's fate to search for the bodies of several of his friends. He would become almost legendary for his mercy and rescue flights. Marvel's quest for adventure and recognition were cut off at the very time that she seemed on the brink of spectacular success. Had she lived, she would have had three years before Amelia Earhart surprised the world by being the first woman to fly the Atlantic alone. And who knows—perhaps the name of Marvel Crosson might have been celebrated for that feat.

Joe and Marvel were representative of the best of the adventurous twenties. They dared to live on the edge, risking everything to expand a new frontier. They were pioneers, just as surely as the old-timers back on the Colorado plains had been. And like the pioneers, they have not been forgotten.

The earthbound among us may consider Marvel's story a tragedy. If she had chosen to stay in the camera store, if she had found the pleasures of marriage and children, she could have lived a long, contented life.

But she did not. She joined the select group, who throughout the history of man, have been willing to take a step over the edge onto a new frontier. The tragedy will come when we run out of those people.

Chapter XV

MABEL'S CHILDREN

"There's just one moment when you get your impression," Mabel Landrum once said, "and then you work it out, for little children don't stay still long."

Even as a child herself, Mabel amused her playmates with drawings. Her observation of their faces led to a unique ability to portray the charm of little children. Her sculpture captures moments of wonder and joy so fleeting that one would expect them only from the work of a skilled photographer.

Mabel was born in a sod house near Sterling in 1886, granddaughter of one of the earliest settlers along the South Platte. All she could talk about or think about was art, but she did not always receive encouragement. One woman stared at a still life entered by Mabel in a local show and commented, "Hmmm. Chickens, pears, and grapes." Then looking pointedly at the young girl, she asked, "Mabel, do you paint?" The words became a family expression. Always afterwards when Mabel created a new work, even after she had gained recognition, someone in the family would murmur, "Hmmm. Mabel, do you paint?"

When she began to carve in marble, the noise drove her parents from the house. Her mother said, "Pa, we'll have to send her away to college, or she'll drive us crazy." At Colorado State Teacher's College, Mabel's study was primarily painting, but she tasted the wonders of sculpture, and when an instructor studied her bust of Wagner and proclaimed, "You are a sculptor," she decided that she must go to the Chicago Art Institute

Mabel Landrum Torrey, creator of "Wynken, Blynken, and Nod, Washington Park, Denver. *Courtesy, the late Lorena McKay, a niece.*

for further study. But her father reminded her, "I've had to hustle to put you through college. Now you'll have to hustle to go any further."

Mabel "hustled" by teaching school, and just as soon as she had saved enough money—in 1912 when she was twenty-six years old—off she went to Chicago, where she taught to help pay her expenses. It was heaven. She could work at sculpture all day and into the night. Absorption in her work led to eccentricities that amused her family. She sometimes wrote letters on toilet paper. In later years, she would dig out stationery on which at some time she had begun a letter. She would write a letter, seemingly oblivious that the page was dated way back in the early 1900s. She never carried a purse but would tuck a dollar in whatever book she carried. After her death, the family found money and uncashed checks in books all over the house.

At Chicago, she was surrounded by sculptors, others who shared her fascination with the art. She was attracted to Fred Torrey, then completing his study at the institute. Four years later, they were married, and Mabel joined Fred as an associate at the Midway Studios of Lorado Taft, one of the foremost sculptors of the time. They lived at the complex in a little room with a sink on one side and a stove on the other. It was inconvenient, but Mabel often spoke of it as "the happiest time of my life."

Not only could the artists engage in independent work at the studios, but they enjoyed the company of other associates. Each noon, everyone gathered for lunch, cooked by the Italian janitor on a blacksmith forge and presided over by Lorado Taft. Happy discussions of works in progress were spiced by visits from well-known artists, writers, and other achievers.

Later, the University of Chicago, which owned the buildings, reclaimed them for their own art department, but in 1966, plaques bearing the names of the original occupants were placed on the doors. By that time, there were only three survivors of those early, heady days, and Mabel and Fred alone were able to attend the ceremonies. She was then eighty.

Mabel's children and mother-and-child themes became her favorites. Her "clay children" included: "Joy," "The Little Cowboy," "Whoa" (a small boy playing horse with his shoelaces), and "I Spy" (a baby playing peek-a-boo). Her groups, "On the Beach, In the Field, and In the Street," were inspired by Winston Churchill's famous rallying speech when Great Britain faced extinction by Germany in World War II. Mabel remarked with emotion, "We shall hear laughter on the beaches, in the fields, and in the streets when peace comes," and she depicted that joy in three groups of small children.

"Creep Mousie," a baby girl playing a finger game, was exhibited at the first Woman's World Fair, Chicago. Portraits of young Stanley Matthews brought the First Prize in Sculpture at the Chicago Galleries. Mabel and Fred had seven pieces accepted in the Horticulture building at the Century of Progress Exhibition. Her "Fountain Group" was shown at the Chicago World's Fair, 1933 to 1934 and is now located on the front of the administration building at Chautauqua, New York.

Mabel Landrum Torrey was listed in *Who's Who in Art* and *Who's Who Among American Women.* A picture-story of the Torreys and their little daughter Betty, all three at work in their own studio-home near the old Lorado Taft complex, appeared in *The New York Times* rotogravure section on Sunday, April 8, 1928.

A later move to Des Moines, Iowa, led to association with craftsmen in porcelain, and many of Mabel's works became available to a wider public in that medium. "Robin's Song," the most

"The Little Cowboy," created for a children's cemetery.

popular, sold 4,000 copies. But more fellow artists have bought the devilish little boy "Jerry" than any other of Mabel's sculptures.

Some of Mabel's works are to be seen in Colorado. The First Presbyterian Church of Sterling commissioned two urns with reliefs of Jesus and the children. In the church foyer is a large representation of Sterling's first Presbyterian Church. Porcelain and clay versions of many of her works are in private Colorado collections, at the Sterling Public Library, and at the Overland Trail Museum.

But the largest and best known is "Wynken, Blynken, and Nod," which represents the figures of Eugene Field's famous poem of the same name. In 1915, Field's daughter Mary approved Mabel's small model of the statue. When the nineteen-ton block of marble arrived in Chicago, eight horses were needed to haul it to Mabel's studio, where she transformed it. It was given to the City of Denver in 1918 by Frank L. Woodward, a Denver pioneer, and his wife as a memorial to Field, who was a reporter for the *Denver Tribune* from 1881 to 1883.

The "wooden shoe," in which sail the three little children of Field's and Mabel's imaginations, was placed in Denver's Washington Park in a small cement pool, equipped with sprays to create a fountain. It has delighted several generations of children.

Until recently. The modern phenomenon of vandalism has not spared the three little figures. The fountain was allowed to fall into disrepair, and a new breed of children have tossed mud at "Wynken, Blynken, and Nod," and worse, have chipped away parts of a hand and foot.

Jeanne Walter, head librarian of the Eugene Field Library in Denver, said several years ago, "It is surprising the number of people who come from out of state and who make a point of coming here to ask about Eugene Field and the statue." Russell J. Ellenhaas, who served for fifty years as Denver's superintendent of parks, once said that the statue is "one of the most valuable pieces that Denver has. You can't get a replica anywhere." Fortunately, it has been moved near the library.

In Des Moines, Mabel and Fred collaborated on one of their final great works, a one-and-a-half-times-life statue of Abraham Lincoln and his son Tad. Fred had made a specialty of sculpting Lincoln, and Mabel, of course, created the son. The Iowa State Legislature voted to place the statue on the state capitol grounds, and on November 19, 1961, the dedication service was held. The highly human representation brought acclaim. Carl Sandburg, primary biographer of Abraham Lincoln, sent his congratulations.

Mabel Landrum Torrey earned much appreciation during her

long career. But one story about her work seemed most meaningful. A little girl who grew up in Denver loved "Wynken, Blynken, and Nod" and would often coax her mother to take her to see them. Then, in her twenties, she met a tragic death. Afterwards, the mother was often observed going to the park alone, sitting for long periods in the company of the three little figures who had been her daughter's playmates.

Chapter XVI

THE NOGUCHI SISTERS

A superior mind finds the austerity of the prairie not a handicap but a fertile ground for intellect and curiosity. The very absence of easy entertainment makes imagination a necessity.

The five daughters of Tomi and Minosuke Noguchi were taught early to respect their surroundings. When the youngest ones leafed through the wonders of the art books from Tate Gallery in far-off London, an older child or parent sat with them, not only to teach care of the treasures but also to help the little girls' minds transport them to that far-off place that neither parent had visited but that each knew well through reading and thought.

Tomi was a gifted storyteller. In the kitchen as she ironed, the children gathered and listened spellbound. Often she relived her childhood days in Japan or told Japanese legends. But her repertoire also included European stories that she had read in college. The parents, like most Japanese, nurtured the love of learning in their children.

Kisa, the youngest daughter, has commented, "A pupil in the Japan of our parents' time was to honor his teacher even to the point of never stepping on his shadow."

Tomi sometimes played the koto, a long stringed instrument, but her years of studying piano could not bear fruit because the family had no money for a piano. But one day Minosuke surprised her with a cottage organ. She would forget to pump the pedals, however, and so whenever she filled the house with music,

The little Noguchi girls, about 1924. Left to right: Yoshi, Sugi, Tsune, SuZan. In front: Kisa. *Courtesy, Kisa and Hideo Sasaki.*

whichever girl ran to do the pumping deserved some of the credit.

The girls were also taught to work. They fed chickens, gathered eggs, pumped water for the house, and even assisted their father in unhitching the team. Then they helped Tomi to prepare her meal of French and American, as well as Japanese, dishes and to set the table just so. They helped their mother make beautiful clothes that she designed. After dinner, they reported about their day and then gathered around the table to study homework. They also learned by hearing their father read the newspaper and discuss world events with their mother.

Minosuke had definite ideas on the rearing of children. He once moved within walking distance of a school solely to prevent his daughters from riding the bus in too much ease. If he was ever disappointed to have had only daughters, he never said so. In fact, he once remarked that even though sons are important to the heritage and traditions of the Japanese, his daughters had given him "threefold what any male descendant could have done." He took an active interest in the development of the girls' talents. As soon as each was big enough to hold a pencil, she took her place at the kitchen table on Saturday afternoons for sessions of artwork. It was soon evident that all the daughters possessed unusual talent. Perhaps Minosuke's exacting requirements led to their success in the art world.

The children learned not to pine for a distant world of ease and beauty but to incorporate beauty into their own lives. Kisa told how the "night sky kept Father company" during his long hours of irrigating:

> Once I remember taking a midnight snack to him and sitting on the ditch bank visiting with him. From his explanation that evening, illustrated by a sketch scratched onto the ground with a twig and illuminated by lantern light, I understood for the first time why the planet Venus sometimes appears in the morning sky and at other times in the evening.

The girls learned to make their own fun. They went on picnics even when picnic weather was months away. Kisa remembers tagging along with her older sisters and a friend, Agnes Bishop, on a day so cold that they huddled next to a sand bank where the sun but not the wind could reach them. The little girls soaked up impressions of sunshine on the waters of the South Platte River. Their parents would have recorded the scene in poetry. The girls did so with their paints.

Clella Rieke, whose father owned one of the farms on which the Noguchis lived, accompanied her father at every opportunity when he traveled to talk business with Minosuke. She was attracted by the delights of Tomi's "goodie drawer" (a custom that she persuaded her mother to adopt) and by the latest creations of the girls. She was entranced by the tiny teacups which they had made of mud and painted. The doll-size teapot looked as if it actually worked, and the "refreshments" served on little plates were so realistic that Clella delighted in the mud pie parties as much as the real refreshments served from the goodie drawer.

As the daughters approached high school, they began to earn money for school expenses and college. Tomi had made it clear from the time that they could talk that they would be expected to complete college, "even though we had no money," Kisa said, "and would have to work while we attended." Three of the sisters were twenty-five, twenty-six, and twenty-seven years old before earning a bachelor's degree. Tomi offered sympathy over the constant grind. "Yet," said Kisa, "when we finished talking to her, we realized it was best to go on."

In later years, SuZan reflected, "In tragic crises or overwhelming good experiences, I was able to keep a more even keel because of things my mother used to say—or better, how she met all kinds of happenings, good or bad."

Tsune graduated from high school in 1932. Eight years passed before she earned her bachelor of arts at Colorado State College of Education in Greeley. The next year, she received her master's and stayed at the college as instructor of fine arts. From 1943 to 1945, she taught at the one-teacher school of Rockland in Phillips County.

But in 1945, Tsune decided to leave the security of teaching and try her luck in New York City. Her paintings had attracted attention during college, but in New York, she concentrated on leather work and learned business skills as well by working in several leather craft establishments. Soon she opened her own business, the Seasoned Leather Shop, where she made and sold fine purses and other accessories for women.

"I felt the growing need for women to express themselves in activities outside the home," Tsune has said. "The shop was dedicated to 'women on the go.' "

Sugi, the second daughter, also graduated from high school in 1932, and it was seven years before she had worked and studied enough to earn the bachelor of science degree at the University of Colorado. Four years later, she was granted her medical degree. After internships and residencies in several eastern and southern cities, she was a physician for four years in the health service of Carleton College in Minnesota. Sugi became an officer in the U.S. Army Medical Corps, working in orthopedic and pulmonary disease services. Later, she worked with the blind in New York. Though Sugi did not pursue an active career in art, she became an excellent photographer. She died in 1982.

Yoshi Lorincz, daughter number four, completed high school in 1936 and worked at the Overland Trail Museum, helping to create a diorama representing the town of Sterling in its early days. The tiny houses and figures still bring pleasure to thousands of annual visitors. Yoshi's degree in industrial arts at CSCE came seven years later. She has done graduate work and has used her art in occupational therapy, adult education, jewelry making, ceramics, and public school education. After World War II, she was a personal draftsman for General Robert M. Lee.

Kisa Sasaki, the youngest, graduated in 1942 at age twenty-three from the University of Colorado with a bachelor of fine arts degree. She later studied painting at the Museum School in Boston. Kisa illustrated South American archaeological studies for Carnegie Institution. After marriage and the birth of her daughters, she worked at home, illustrating children's books dealing with early tribes, primarily of South America. She also illustrated Japanese stories for *Child Life Magazine.* Her paintings were included in the Japanese Show of the Museum of Fine Arts, Boston, and the U.S. Pavilion of the New York World's Fair. She had a one-woman show in 1977 at the Penthouse Gallery of Boston. Today she lives and paints in California. She calls her abstract landscapes "Moodscapes."

Best known is the third daughter, SuZan Swain Firmage, who graduated in 1938 at age twenty-two from the University of Colorado with many honors and a bachelor of fine arts degree plus a minor in biology. She continued her studies at Pennsylvania State College, Brooklyn Botanical Gardens, American Museum of Natural History, and Audubon Nature Camp. She earned college expenses by illustrating publications of biology professors. That led to a rather specialized and dramatically successful career, first as staff artist for the School Nature League at the American Museum in New York City. She married Dr. Ralph B. Swain, entymologist, also a graduate of the University of Colorado. Together they published a comprehensive study, *The Insect Guide*, which has sold over 100,000 copies. Dr. Swain also wrote and SuZan illustrated the insect section for *Compton's Encyclopedia.*

Over a period of thirty years, SuZan, recognized in *Who's Who Among American Women* since 1968, illustrated more than forty books for Doubleday, Putnam, Random House, and Golden Press; four major encyclopedias; and numerous magazines ranging from *Jack and Jill* to *Audubon* and *National Geographic.* She is the author and illustrator of Doubleday's *First Guide to Insects* and two charming little books, *Insects in Their World* and *Plants of Woodland and Wayside.* She has had numerous one-woman shows, notably at the American Museum of Natural History in New York and at the Science Museum, University of Colorado. The latter is one of ten with permanent collections of her work.

SuZan once said, "If there is one merit to my work, it is accuracy." But others see far more. In 1981, she was cited in *Contemporary Authors,* not only for accuracy but for encouraging children to become curious and observe nature.

In 1951, SuZan and her sons, Ralph and Tom, accompanied Dr. Swain to Managua, Nicaragua, for the U.S. State Department Point Four program to improve crop production by controlling insects and training students. In 1953, the family met the tragedy that was to call forth all the resources that SuZan had gained from her parents. Driving through Mexico after home leave, they were ambushed by bandits, and Dr. Swain was killed. SuZan and her sons, only twelve and ten, returned to the United States to, as she expressed it, "put together our shattered lives."

Yoshi found support on December 7, 1941, when the ringing of a dormitory phone broke her Sunday morning sleep with reassurances from classmates, professors, and even the college president—before she fully realized what had happened. "Until the war began on that day," said Yoshi, "I had never thought of myself as different. Though we were taught to appreciate our Japanese heritage, we were Americans."

Tomi and Minosuke had long considered America their home,

though, according to law, they could not be naturalized. Minosuke had volunteered to serve in World War I but had been turned down because he was "too old." Now Yoshi joined the air force as an occupational therapist and later as a draftsman. Kisa enlisted in the army as a Japanese linguist and eventually worked in allied military research. Sugi was a medical officer, serving eight and one-half years with two tours of duty in the Far East.

When Tsune began to teach at Rockland School, families who objected to teachers of Japanese ancestry were allowed to enroll their children in another school. Some did so, but after they realized that Tsune was not an enemy and that her pupils were getting a good education, some returned. By the end of the year, she was recognized as a valued addition to the community.

According to Kisa, "For our parents, a war between the nation of their birth and the country they had chosen must have been heart-breaking."

It was traumatic to be classified as "enemy aliens" with bank assets frozen. However, friends and neighbors came to their aid. When C. F. Poole, principal of Sterling High School, commiserated with Mr. Noguchi about the experience, Minosuke replied, "I believe in the familiar metaphor: the tree growing on the mountainside, exposed to the burning sun and the freezing winters, to the buffeting wind, develops the deepest roots."

On Sunday, April 29, 1979, all five Noguchi daughters, accompanied and assisted by Hideo Sasaki, Kisa's husband, and William K. Firmage, SuZan's second husband, returned to Sterling to participate in the Noguchi Sisters' Art Exhibit. The show, sponsored by the Sterling Arts Council, featured paintings by all the sisters; Tsune's leather designs; a humorous puppet and photographs by Sugi; Yoshi's crafts and a large photograph of the Sterling diorama; SuZan's original paintings for *The Insect Guide* and her books; and Kisa's "moodscapes." Also on display were large reproductions of historic photographs of Japanese people along the South Platte; Minosuke's calligraphy; and the poetry book in which he had collected his and Tomi's compositions.

Bill Hosokawa, editor of the Editorial Page of the *Denver Post,* wrote that the event was a "well-deserved honor for a remark-

At the Sterling Exhibit, 1979. Left to right: Kisa, Yoshi, SuZan, Sugi, Tsune. *Photograph by Edwin Shimabukuro.*

able family" and for all the Japanese-American families "which have played such an important role in the development of Northeastern Colorado."

It was a glorious day. Over six hundred people viewed the opening of the exhibit and attended the program honoring the early Japanese settlers. Traditional sweets and tea, served from Japanese cups, plus costumes and dances contributed by families still living on the South Platte, added to the occasion. Old friends came from throughout Colorado and neighboring states. The Nakamura family traveled from Texas and California. For some people, it was the first visit to the South Platte in fifty years.

Sometimes one can indeed go home again.

One likes to think that invisible presences also attended the show. One could almost see Minosuke, carefully scrutinizing each work, nodding in pride at the gallery displays—but occasionally pausing to make a judicious suggestion. And Tomi—

was that her lovely figure applauding and encouraging in the background? Did she shed a few tears of pride at what her daughters had accomplished?

It was a rare fortune that she and Minosuke built in America.

Chapter XVII

ONE YEAR OF MY LIFE

"Welcome to the army—GET IN!" Helen Brecht picked up her suitcase and teetered on high heels through the snow, climbed a stepladder into a two-and-one-half-ton truck, held on for dear life as it bounced and slid down the road, and wondered what had possessed her to wear her best clothes, complete with hat, gloves, and a coat with a fake fur collar.

But she looked hardly more ridiculous than the women soldiers, lost in male army combat boots, overalls, and enormous overcoats. Soon Helen was issued a similar uniform, all male except for olive drab bras and girdles. Her coat, too, was so large that it struck her ankles, and the sleeves had to be rolled back to the elbows.

And so, on January 13, 1943, did eastern Colorado's first volunteer join the Women's Army Auxiliary Corps. Basic training was at Fort des Moines, Iowa, a post that had once been used as stables. It was a forecast of things to come.

Because of the depression, Helen Brecht had not been able to attend college. She studied cosmetology and operated beauty shops in Crook and Sterling. But she wanted more. When the Women's Army Auxiliary Corps (later the WAC) was created in 1942, twenty-seven-year-old Helen decided, "I'll join. I can give one year of my life for my country."

On that first day, the year loomed bleakly before her. All women shared a community bath. Because Helen was one of the youngest recruits, she was assigned to the top bunk of a three-decker bed. She carefully wriggled under the tight blankets (an important rule was that a quarter dropped on them must bounce) and tried not to turn all night for fear of falling out of bed. A move to single cots at another base was an improvement, but the women could sit on them only on Sundays.

The recruits were needed as clerk typists, cooks and bakers, and truck drivers. Helen did not want to drive a truck, and she was sure that would not be her assignment because she was too short, and besides, she had requested office work for which she had had training. But like many a male recruit, she discovered that the army moves in mysterious ways. She became a truck driver. And, indeed, her legs were too short for double clutching. And, of course, it was against army rules to prop herself forward with a pillow. That didn't look proper with a uniform.

It was not an encouraging beginning for a woman who would eventually become chief of all recruiting and in second level command of WAC forces.

Somehow she escaped the truck and went to Officers' Candidate School. Her one year stretched to twenty-three. And Helen stretched. She attended college wherever she was stationed throughout the United States, in Paris, in Tokyo. It was an education far beyond the confines of one campus. The Women's Army Corps was a part of that education, for it developed that Helen had unusual qualities of leadership. Moreover, she had human attributes of friendliness and humor.

As a new second lieutenant, she was sent to England during the worst siege of the terrifying V-bombs over London. There she had her own little room and bath — but no heat — on the third floor of quarters. Fur-lined toilet seats helped very little.

Helen was haunted by a story that a bomb blew a male American officer out of his third-floor room while he was taking a bath. The thought of sailing naked to her doom was horrifying, and so for six weeks, she never completely undressed. She bathed one area, covered it, and then moved on to the next.

Every night, she heard buzz bombs and raced down three flights of stairs to the basement air raid shelter. But she was the only person to do so. Finally, she learned that her nightly bombs were the subway rumbling under the building.

Soon she began her climb up the ranks. She was made commander of fifty women and assigned to lead them to Paris, where they were to be a part of the first all-female Signal Corps Battalion.

But nothing was destined to be easy. The train which took them to the coast was an old "40 & 8," used in World War I to transport forty horses and eight men. The trip across the mine-filled English Channel, which ordinarily took six to eight hours, lasted *seven days* in total blackout. Then, on the truck ride to Paris, the roads had not been cleared of mines, and again the women were not allowed to get out. Helen described the difficulties: "We had to use our helmets to go to the bathroom and then throw it out of the back of the trucks."

While the Battle of the Bulge was being fought, Helen was a company commander in Paris, as well as officer in charge of special services for the entire battalion. Eighteen months later, after the liberation of Germany, she became a major, regular army, and WAC battalion commander in Germany.

The women felt proud of their service to America and were given official recognition many times in army ceremonies. But at least one combat unit in Europe had mixed emotions. About the time that the first WACs were sent overseas, the men ordered B-cups (beverage cups) from the quartermaster. When the case was opened, they knew with a certainty that the United States Army had changed. For they had received a full case of brassieres, all B-cup, of course.

When the war ended, Helen became commander of WAC troops at Fort Lee, Virginia. During the Korean War, she was WAC battalion commander in Tokyo. In 1953, she was chosen for advanced WAC officers' training at Fort Lee and later was one of two women and seventy-five men selected to attend the top-level staff and command college. Afterwards, she became senior WAC in charge of all women personnel in the Third Army Area (seven Southern states). By this time, she was a lieutenant colonel.

And there at Atlanta, she met Colonel Homer Drissel and married him in a dress blues ceremony in December 1962. Then she became chief WAC army recruiter, speaking all over the United States. She won orders to spend six months completing her college degree and was in line to be promoted to director

General Matthew B. Ridgway, Mrs. Ridgway, and Helen Brecht (WAC staff advisor) present arms while national anthem is played, Tokyo, 1951. *U.S. Army photograph by Sgt. R. Turnbull.*

of the WAC, the top job. But by this time, her husband was ready to retire, and Helen wanted to retire with him.

After twenty-three years, she returned, in 1965, to civilian life. It had been a good "year" of service for her country. It had been quite a record for eastern Colorado's first WAAC recruit.

Chapter XVIII

GOOD GIRL, LOU!

M odern, competitive sports for girls did not begin in
Colorado schools until 1974 and 1975. Lou Piel was then
a junior at Prairie School, which was literally on the prairie midway between Stoneham and New Raymer and had only sixty-
five students, boys and girls. The girls played in volleyball and
basketball tournaments that year and won both. They could
hardly wait for the next season when the first state tournaments
would be held.

It was worth waiting for. Suddenly, everyone knew where little
Prairie School was. In volleyball, they won league, subdistrict,
district, and state. In basketball, they won league, subdistrict,
district and — not state but second place.

Lou Piel, who thought basketball was the most wonderful sport
of all, was crushed not to win that final game in the state tournament. But her personal record was astounding. In both volleyball and basketball, she was voted everything from All Conference to All State, Most Valuable Player of both state tournaments, and Player of the Year in Class A schools for both sports.
In addition, she captured the state records in all classes for the
most points in a single basketball game and the most points in
the tournaments.

The team tasted the heady delights of being heroines to the
home folks. After the final volleyball game, everyone came
rushing onto the court to greet the first state champions that
Prairie had ever produced. And what made it most exciting was

Lou Piel while playing for Prairie High School Mustangs.

that it was accomplished in the first state tournaments for Colorado girls.

Lou said, "I'll never forget the 'high' of that first state championship."

Then why did she return to school after the basketball tournament "nearly devastated"? She had a feeling of having missed the train. After so many years of longing, she had finally been able to compete, and now it was all over.

But not quite. The coach came up to her with an astounding request. Would she be willing to play on the boys' baseball team? In that small school, they were short of players. "I'm sure my eyes answered the question," Lou said, and next day, she reported for practice. She played in the outfield. The boys accepted her, gave her no problems at all. But not even the occasional cutting remarks, which are inevitable from some spectators, had prepared her for the catcalls by opponents and their fans for daring to play on a boys' team. Worst of all was the "ever present echo of 'Good *boy,* Lou!' "

The six-foot Lou, eyes of blue, was pretty and all girl. She was hurt and shed tears. But she had already learned a valuable lesson: "If the belittlement stands in your way, you've let *someone else* write the end of *your* story."

Lou had had dreams about athletics ever since she was seven years old and served as bat girl for the women's softball team coached by her dad. Arnold Piel knew how to establish esprit de corps, right down to the bat girl, for Lou had a uniform just like those worn by the big girls. And when they won a couple of championships, she felt a part of it. At nine, she was third base player for the championship team in the Sterling Summer Youth League. She learned then that "a winning attitude is very contagious to those around you and it's carried over into every-day life."

Sports was a wonderful part of life to a girl who lived far out on the prairie, miles from other children and entertainment. Her father spent much time playing with his children:

> Dad was always the neutral member of both teams. . . . In football he was the quarterback. In basketball he would only pass and we did the rest. It all seems so simple now. I'd be clobbered one minute and the next staging a comeback. At the time, I never thought anything peculiar about intercepting passes or stealing the ball away. Now all those "coincidental" bad passes or double dribbles of Dad's seem to have come at a very convenient time.

But the father did not encourage Lou at the expense of her brother. The "mistakes" kept her in the game and her spirits up. She had to accomplish actual wins by herself. The spirit of competition would take her far, for Lou, who was so afraid that her chance at sports was gone after high school graduation, began to receive scholarship bids from colleges. Incidentally, she was also the valedictorian of her class and had more than athletic ability to offer.

But the greatest moment of her high school career came with the Freddie Steinmark Memorial Award in 1976 as the most outstanding girl athlete in the state of Colorado. Freddie Steinmark's words inscribed on the trophy have stayed with Lou (especially during the inevitable "not so good" moments): "Surely one cannot always be successful but one should certainly not admit it."

Lou chose to attend the University of Northern Colorado. In basketball, she was the all-time leading scorer and rebounder of the university; was named All American by the Women's Pro

Lou beams as teammate Venus Jennings slams out a home run for the University of Northern Colorado, 1977.

Basketball Scouts in 1979; and in 1980 was chosen All Conference and All Tournament at the National Invitational Tournament.

In softball, she was All Conference pitcher for four years and was named All American twice by both the Association for Intercollegiate Athletics for Women and the American Softball Association. She was nominated in 1979 for the Broderick Award, which honors the nation's most valuable pitcher, and won the Colorado Sportswoman Award for all four years of her college career. As a senior, she was chosen Colorado Woman Athlete of the Year by the Colorado Sports Hall of Fame; won the YWCA Colorado Sportswoman Award; and received a "Faces in the Crowd" recognition cup from *Sports Illustrated* magazine.

As a high school sophomore in 1974, Lou had played on a state championship summer softball team that had progressed to regional championship and played in the national tournament. Playing for Colorado's Law Team, she pitched three innings of their final game. She was only sixteen years old. Over the next few years, she pitched in nine ASA national tournaments, three times reaching the championship games. One of those (in 1978)

Lou grimaces with the effort of the "rise" ball which has helped her to win the title of "Nation's Most Valuable Pitcher" and an appearance on television's *60 Minutes*. *University of Northern Colorado photo by Lyn Eisminger.*

was against the legendary Raybestos Brakettes of Stratford, Connecticut. Lou's team lost, but that was nothing to be ashamed of, for the Stratford team was seldom defeated.

But the next summer, in the National Sports Festival, a sort of Olympics within the United States, Lou played with the USA West team and again faced Stratford, and that time, her team won. The score was only 1–0, but it led to a silver medal, and to Lou Piel, the pitcher, it was the turning point of her life. Until then, she could attribute her wins to luck, determination, being in the right place, or being pretty good, like many athletes. But after that memorable evening, she felt the marvelous confidence of knowing that she was among the very best, that she could hold her own. It was one of the big moments of her life.

If anyone had doubts about the win over Stratford, there was very soon an opportunity to resolve them. Lou told about her second big moment.

As that same 1979 season drew to a close at the National Tournament, we faced Stratford in a "do or die" situation. The losers would end at 18th in the country. The winners would continue on toward the championship.

Lou spent two nights lying wide awake while her mind went over and over strategy to keep Stratford off balance. And it worked. Her team was the victor, 2–1. More impressive, it was the first time since 1933 — almost fifty years — that the Stratford Brakettes had finished below third place in the national finals.

Lou throws a knuckle ball.

That summer, Lou was a candidate for the Pan American games, but she still had not attained her goal of pitching a winning team straight through the national championship. That came two years later in 1981, when she pitched for the Orlando Florida Rebels. "It was the most special feeling I've ever experienced in sports," Lou said. "No words can describe it and second place will never be good enough again."

She won the Bertha Tickey Pitching Award, honoring the nation's most valuable pitcher. That should have been the high point. It was what she had dreamed of since she was a small girl. Moreover, she was then on the coaching staff of the University of Utah. Her career was under way.

But there was more to come. She was chosen a member of the USA team in the 1981 Tri-Nation Championship Tournament. That would be her third *big* moment in sports. The games took place in several different cities in Japan. Lou will never forget:

> The feeling of pride became overwhelming . . . old Glory rose against the sky and the National Anthem boomed in the background. We brought home the Gold Medal from Japan, and I left there at least a million different cases of PROUD AMERICAN CHILL BUMPS!

That climactic moment might not have come to Lou Piel if she had not been a daughter of the prairie. Days of solitude gave her much time to practice and to dream. Only in a very small school would she have been invited to play on the boys' team. The prairies made her a seeker.

Good *girl,* Lou!

THE CHRYSALID WOMEN

Two women in eastern Colorado were notable because their lives and accomplishments spanned separate ages. They emerged from quiet cocoons of the past to become dynamic forces in modern Colorado.

Dr. Portia shows one of her babies to nurse Mary Jones.

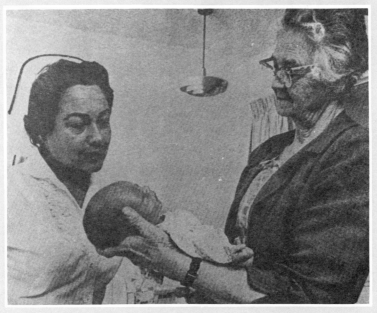

Above, left: On the face of three-year-old Portia McKnight may be seen the determination that led to her becoming one of the earliest women doctors, 1890. *Above, right:* Anna Petteys with her family at Bear Lake, Colorado, 1923. *Below:* Mrs. Petteys at her *Journal-Advocate* desk. *Photographs courtesy of Robert Petteys.*

Chapter XIX

THE GIANT STEPS
OF DOCTOR PORTIA

The patient lay on an examination table and looked up into the reassuring eyes of the doctor. The table was regulation, and the doctor was real. But all were crammed into a closet in a Denver apartment. It was the latest unpredictable step of Doctor Portia McKnight Lubchenco, one of the most noted physicians in Colorado history.

It is a long way to Moscow from the South Carolina plantation where Portia McKnight was born August 6, 1887. Once it was a giant step to the treeless plains of northeastern Colorado. But perhaps the biggest step that Portia McKnight ever made was to neighboring North Carolina.

A graduate of South Carolina Co-Educational College, twenty-year-old Portia was a teacher in 1907 but was eager to become a doctor. However, South Carolina Medical College had never admitted a woman. Moreover, Portia's family disapproved. But a Russian agronomist, visiting the plantation to study cotton production, saw nothing odd in her dreams. Russia, he told her, had many women doctors. "Don't give up your dreams," he said, and then Alexis Lubchenko added a Russian proverb: "When you hunt for bears, don't shoot at rabbits."

South Carolina did not admit Portia, though the president dangled hope for another year. But she could not wait. She applied at North Carolina State Medical College and was ac-

Portia McKnight at graduation. *Courtesy, Lois Tolleson, Greenville, South Carolina.*

cepted. It was the first of several giant steps that the serene young southern gentlewoman would take.

Portia found most of her young men classmates congenial and courteous — ". . . but never too much noticeably so!" The professors soon shelved their doubts. When one asked what he should do if she fainted in the dissecting room, Miss McKnight replied, "What do you do with the fellows?"

"We stack them all together on a pile outside the door."

"Well, if I should faint," Portia calmly answered, "would you please make a separate pile for me?"

After that spirited exchange, she was on her way. One of the doctors even gave her a microscope, the key to which ". . . opened doors . . . which could have been opened in no other way." Portia had studied typing and shorthand, and she paid her way through medical school by working as secretary to the president.

Throughout the four years of medical school, letters came regularly from the Russian agronomist, and finally Alexis wrote that he was coming on the famed *Titanic* for her graduation. As the day approached, Portia looked forward to his arrival. One day, she realized that she was as excited about the arrival of the fascinating Russian as she was about the forthcoming triumph of finishing medical school. But she told herself that what she felt was gratitude for his encouragement.

And then came news of the sinking of the *Titanic*. That largest ship in the world, so often proclaimed unsinkable, had struck an iceberg in April of that year of 1912 and, within three hours, had gone down. Over 1500 people were lost at sea. When the lists came out in the paper, Portia studied them frantically, searching for Alexis' name, praying that it would not be there. And it wasn't. But when Portia read the list of the fortunate ones who were saved, she did not find his name there either. Now the excitement about her unusual accomplishment was clouded by anguish and fear over the fate of Alexis.

Graduation day finally arrived, and the new Doctor Portia was singled out for special honor. She was the first woman graduate, was second in her class, and was offered a position as assistant to the president.

But the high point came when Portia spotted all the McKnight family in the audience. Her eyes traveled from one loving, proud face to another: her father and mother, her brothers and sisters, husbands and wives of some of them, nieces and nephews. And then she caught her breath and for a few moments did not hear anything that was said. For there with her family sat Alexis Lubchenco, his eyes, too, shining with pride — and perhaps more. As Portia soon learned, he had been delayed for twenty-four hours and had providentially missed the sailing of the *Titanic*.

She married Alexis and sailed for Russia. He was forty-one and she was twenty-five. She learned the customs of his country, practiced medicine, and especially enjoyed delivering babies. She began to have her own babies.

She found Alexis' family prominent and interesting, quietly working to end the tsarist government. But life became increasingly somber. Alexis had once been imprisoned for three months, and a brother, Phyllip, served time for writing a revolutionary poem. They were friends of Alexander Kerensky, head of the "White" Revolution and president of the new republic. But this victory soon ended with the counterrevolution of the Bolsheviks or "Reds." Anyone suspected of loyalty to the old regime — or the new republic — was shot as the Communists took over. Alexis was in double danger because of his government position as agronomist and because of a resemblance to Kerensky.

The country was not only wracked by two revolutions but by war with Germany at the same time. Food was increasingly scarce; milk, almost nonexistent. Once Portia paid a high price for some, only to discover that it was water mixed with flour.

Buildings burned. Bullets rang through the streets. Women were shot along with men. The Lubchencos knew that they had to get out or face death, but Portia's passport did not come. One day a bullet slammed into the apartment, hitting the piano. They moved into the cold interior hall and spent seven days there, huddled in the dark, telling the children stories to pass the time, crawling when it was necessary to enter the more exposed rooms, seeing their scant supply of food give out. Finally, they lived on birdseed.

Repeatedly, Portia made the dangerous trip to the passport office, where the friendly manager tried to reassure her. One morning, after particularly bad fighting, she found him shot to death. The office had been ransacked. In despair, afraid that their last chance to escape was gone, she searched through the disorder—and found her passport.

Then she made the perilous trip home on bloodstained sidewalks, ducking into gaping windows and doors whenever she heard the whine of a bullet. A midnight visit by "inspectors" left no doubt that they must get out of Russia, and perhaps because of a dream that Portia had, they planned a roundabout route—east across Siberia and China. In the dream, a sister's voice warned her to get out but urged, "Don't come this way."

The sister suddenly screamed, "Run!" and Portia sat up, wide awake, terrified, and knowing that if she and Alexis and the children did not escape now, they never would.

They rode a sled to the railroad. Somehow they got aboard a train. Somehow, at the various stops, Alexis found bread. They saw people killed by soldiers or simply thrown off the train. They watched their three children fearfully. If they cried, they would be killed, too. And so, hour after hour, day after day, they played games and told their babies stories to keep them quiet.

Then Portia was able to use her medicine to help the soldiers, and that factor kept them on the train and ultimately saved their lives. Eighteen days later, they finally passed out of Russia. Eighteen days of hunger and without a change of clothes or a bath.

In South Carolina, the family settled on a farm that Alexis operated. Portia again began to practice. She was just in time for the great flu epidemic of 1918. Many times she drove her horse and buggy all night along country roads on her way to treat emergencies or deliver babies. To bolster her courage, she sang hymns to the horse. Once, when a train blocked the road, she crawled under it in order to reach her patient.

Alexis was a good farmer, but eventually the boll weevil infestation of cotton drove them out. They joined Portia's brother Jim, a doctor, in his Haxtun, Colorado, practice. Alexis became the laboratory technician for the two doctors. In Colorado, Doctor Portia became a near legend. She cared deeply about people, sharing their thrill over a new baby, their sorrow in the loss of a loved one. People came to her for reassurance, for her hand on a shoulder, her warm kind eyes, and her words, "You're going to be all right."

After treating several generations of the same family in Haxtun and later in Sterling, she knew what to expect from them. She couldn't always remember a name, but she never forgot an ailment and might murmur, "Gall bladder, 1936."

Laughter followed in her wake. Hers was not always subtle humor; maybe because she was a physician, there wasn't time to beat around the bush. But her soft southern accent took the sting out of her words. When a young druggist, Nick Townsend, brought his wife for an emergency appendectomy, Doctor Portia handed him an impossibly long list of prescriptions to fill. Only later did he realize that it was a strategy to keep him occupied. But he filled the prescriptions because no one questioned her.

When a woman delivered a fifteen-pound baby and afterwards sighed, "That was pretty bad," Doctor Portia retorted, "Well, do you want me to put it back?"

She had a repertoire of stories from her long practice. On one occasion, she delivered two babies almost simultaneously. One was quite dark, and the nurse by mistake showed him to the wrong father. The blond young man studied the baby for a time, then grinned and said, "Well, she's burned everything else in our marriage so far."

The giant steps were remarkable, but even more admirable was the success of Portia and Alexis' family. The warmth and love of the South Carolina cotton farm and the Moscow home were transplanted to their Colorado home. With no household help available on the prairie, everyone shared chores and cooking. In the evenings, while Portia studied medical journals, Alexis helped the children with science and math. Coming from Russia where people had to go hungry for an education, he was insistent on serious study by the children. The parents often quoted a poem to their five young people:

I do not think all failure undeserved
And all success is someone's luck. . . .
Some men are down because they chose to shirk,
And some men high because they did their work.

The parents set the example. Alexis, until his death in 1941, did research on fungus diseases and contributed his findings in articles published in medical journals. Doctor Portia took many postgraduate courses in medicine at top universities. According to her daughter, Portia, "Her bedside table was always stacked with medical journals which she seemed to devour every night. She used to say she didn't want her doctor children to think they knew more than she."

After the modern Logan County Hospital replaced the old Good Samaritan in Sterling, she became the first chief of staff. Forty years after receiving her medical degree, she studied to become anesthetist at the hospital.

Honors came her way. She was chosen 1963 Business and Professional Woman of the Year and during World War II was an honorary member of the 29th Hospital Unit, son Luby's outfit. Colorado Woman's College cited her for distinguished service in 1965. But she considered a 1954 honor — Colorado Mother of the Year — among her most valued.

When the Colorado Medical Society sponsored her for membership in the 50-Year Club of American Medicine, Doctor Portia was still not ready to quit. A 1964 book, coauthored with Colorado journalist Anna C. Petteys, told of her early revolutionary adventures. It seemed the last step. In 1967, at age eighty, she moved to Denver and retired.

A son said, "Now, Mother, the first time you examine someone there, you'll be back in business."

He spoke in warning, but Doctor Portia's eyes brightened. The next thing the children knew, she had an examining table set up in a large closet and was indeed back in business. She defended herself, "Well, I was never much for baking cookies. This is something I can do for my neighbors."

Even that was not enough. She joined the Denver Clinic, working for Doctors George Curfman and Frank McGlone, providing the same service that she had been giving her new neighbors. Still driving her car (until age eighty-five), she made the rounds of thirteen nursing homes, examining people and determining who needed further attention. She was enormously popular with the elderly patients and boasted that she took many away from their clinic doctors.

Of one she said, "I'd feel his pulse and he'd feel mine. We talked about the Mason–Dixon line, dogwood blossoms, and fishing

267

Dr. Portia autographs her book. *Courtesy, Robert Petteys.*

in the ocean. I told him the proverb, 'Feed a man a fish and he'll live a day. Teach a man how to fish and he'll live forever.' "

Eying the elderly doctor, the old man said, "Doctor Portia, that's what's wrong with us. We both know how to fish."

She said that the most flattering request came from a ninety-nine-year-old charmer: "Doctor Portia, why don't you crawl in bed with me and keep me warm?"

When the clinic doctors presented the eighty-three-year-old Portia with an award for her work with the aged through the Medical Care and Research Foundation, she followed the example of government heads and submitted a "State of My Nation (Health)" to them. "I'm living on borrowed time," she wrote, "but maybe because I know this, life is even more interesting."

Somewhat tongue-in-cheek, she recited a list of ailments:

I do not see as well as previously, so I have eye corrections. I do not hear as well as I once did, so I have a hearing aid. . . . I have a polyp in my nose, a bunion on my right foot, and arthritis in my knees. I still have a malady which developed many years ago in Moscow. I thought then I was continually pregnant but finally found I was allergic to mushrooms. . . .

I have so many of the ailments that my patients have, I'm sort of a specialist — or at least I'm experienced. We discuss together the things we have in common and the things for which to give thanks.

The clinic doctors gave Doctor Portia a vote of confidence, and she continued her rounds. It was not until 1975, when she was eighty-eight years old, that she finally quit practicing. She did not resent growing old. "Remember," she used to say, "many are denied that privilege."

During the last years of her life, Doctor Portia looked back

Enduring recognition came to Dr. Portia for her giant steps. *Photograph courtesy of Dorothy Curlee.*

on the giant steps and felt that it had been a magnificent time. And so did her admirers. In 1976, the American Mothers Committee chose her as a Mother of Achievement in American History, 1776 to 1976.

Her philosophy was contained in one of those lines that she and Alexis had often quoted to their children: "Most men themselves have shaped the things they are." The life that Portia shaped was a credit to Colorado and her birth state of South Carolina — and to North Carolina, where she took that first giant step of becoming a doctor.

The honors continued, even after her death at the age of ninety-one. At the University of Colorado health services commencement, the Distinguished Service Award for 1979 went to Portia McKnight Lubchenco, who had died six months previously. In 1982, she became the first woman ever inducted into the South Carolina Hall of Science and Technology, and the Le Conte Medallion was presented in her honor. The awards were like a final "Amen," the enduring recognition that healing the sick was her life, her dedication.

Chapter XX

ANNA C. PETTEYS — CATALYST FOR THE PLAINS

She was born Anna Columbine Fedderman on an Iowa farm. Her serene expression reflected the grace of her home. The wide blue eyes looked out at a good world. She graduated, Phi Beta Kappa, from Grinnell College in 1912 and taught school for a year. After becoming engaged to a fellow Grinnell graduate, Alonzo Petteys, she returned to her parents' farm for a year of instruction in how to run a home.

The young Petteys' first home was in Weldon Valley of northeastern Colorado, where Alonzo and a partner had established a small bank. Six years later, they moved to Brush, from where Petteys ran his growing chain of banks, farms, and other businesses. For twenty-eight years, Anna employed the skills and graces that she had learned from her mother to create a good home. To her four children, she was the "best mother a child could have," vitally interested in their schooling and projects. When ten-year-old son Bob lay ill with polio for several months and published a small neighborhood newspaper to pass the time, Anna listened and encouraged — and learned. Perhaps those days were a chrysalis for the career that would eventually mark her as one of Colorado's most dynamic women.

For after twenty-eight years centered on her home, Anna Columbine emerged. Out of the pain of loneliness and death was born a new Anna C. Petteys.

Anna hikes in the Rocky Mountains.

Perhaps Bob's fight with polio was the turning point. Determined that he would not be a cripple, she took him to California, where doctors were performing pioneer surgery to correct the aftereffects of the disease. The mother and son spent three years there, from 1935 to 1937, engaged in the war for his health. And they won.

"It must have been a painful experience for her to be separated from family and friends for such a long period," Bob Petteys has said, "but there was never the slightest hint that it was any kind of sacrifice for her."

That struggle may have opened the world for Anna. Perhaps she saw needs that had never before touched her comfortable life. Perhaps a new awareness of the fragility of one's days on earth led to a different course for her. With her children in college and her job with them well done, she began to commute a hundred miles every day to Colorado State College of Education in Greeley, and in 1943, she earned a master's degree.

She had just enrolled at the University of Chicago for further study when word came that her oldest son Jack, an air force cadet, had been killed in a training flight crash. The tragedy seemed to intensify Anna's concern with the world beyond. She and her husband established three four-year Jack Petteys college scholarships to be given annually to talented young men from the Brush, Fort Morgan, and Sterling areas. Ten other scholarships in Jack's name provided for young people to attend Northeastern Junior College in Sterling each year.

And Anna moved out into the world. There followed an extraordinary thirty-year career.

In 1945, she was invited by the United States Department of State to attend the United Nations Charter Convention. She was appointed an original member of the Speakers' Research Committee for the United Nations and in 1948 attended the General Assembly held in Paris.

Anna Petteys confers with son Bob about the newspaper. *Photographer, John Rees, from* Black Star, *New York.*

The family purchased a farm weekly, and she and Bob transformed it into *The High Plains Daily Journal,* one of the most creative and readable papers of eastern Colorado. In 1953, it was merged with *The Sterling Advocate* to become the *Journal–Advocate,* an eloquent voice for rural concerns. Anna Petteys wrote a daily column, "Post Scripts," in which she expressed her view of the world, her hopes for the community and nation, and her delight with accomplishments of fellow plainsmen.

To say that she opened a window to the world is no exaggeration. She traveled all over the globe and brought home a personal view of current hotspots in the news. Some of her trips were in conjunction with meetings of Country Women of the World. She became, as Max Price of the *Denver Post* once wrote, "an articulate spokesman for rural women."

Her journeys took her to Europe, Ceylon, Japan, South America, and the Middle East; and very often, she met with leaders of nations. When she was serving the second of three six-year terms on the Colorado State Board of Education, she toured the Soviet Union to study the Russian system of education, which had produced the startling space victory of *Sputnik.* Her trips were always for a purpose far beyond a tourist's diversion. Of her journey to Africa in 1960, she once remarked:

> A trip near the equator isn't ever a pleasure jaunt. Water may not be safe, and you share your room with lizards. So people want to know why I went — alone and at my own expense. Well, I'm curious, and I like to know people who make news. Besides, I can pass along what I see to readers of my column.

Anna Petteys also did a daily radio commentary for two years, and her articles were published in state and national magazines. She was increasingly in demand as a public speaker, and she rarely turned any group down. She gave as generously of her time to the smallest 4-H or home demonstration club as to large audiences across the nation.

She introduced the awesome figures of world news as people of human dimensions. After the trip to Africa, she delightedly recounted that when she had injured her leg there, the great humanitarian, Albert Schweitzer, gave her an umbrella to use for a cane.

Anna leaves an editor's office using her Albert Schweitzer "cane."

She brought writers, artists, and performers to share their creations with northeastern Colorado audiences. Some were well known; others, beginners who needed the exposure. Always, she shared with local people. When Doctor Portia Lubchenco was host to Alexander Kerensky, who had led Russia's White Revolution, she and Anna Petteys arranged a meeting to give others an opportunity to meet the man who served briefly as president of Russia's only experience with self-government.

Her primary concern was education. For the At Large seat on the State Board of Education, she campaigned all over Colorado with handshakes and a genuine smile. She was a leader on the board; she became a member of state, national, and international councils; and she served as a delegate to a White House Conference on Education.

Dozens of professional and service honors came her way. The Colorado Press Association chose her as Woman of Achievement in 1965, and she was twice the speaker for conventions of National Press Women. The *Denver Post* elected her to their Gallery of Fame; she was chosen Woman of the Year by the Denver Business and Professional Women; and Governor John A. Love gave her a 1969 Colorado Governor's Award for the Arts and Humanities. Half a dozen *Who's Whos* (*of the West, American Women,* among them) elected her to membership. She

Her primary concern was the education of children. *Photographer, John Rees,* Black Star, *New York.*

received honorary degrees from her alma maters and two other colleges; and schools and a library are named for her.

A master of ceremonies once introduced Anna Petteys as: ". . . an artist who works through the media of governmental arrangements to create better schools and colleges. She expresses artistry in the newspapers she publishes; the books she writes; and in the speaking she does."

But most of all, Anna Petteys expressed artistry through other people. It was not only the honors and accomplishments that set her apart. Her unique contribution was the ability to stimulate others, whether to work together raising funds for a rehabilitation center in northeastern Colorado or to pursue individual dreams. All over Colorado were countless people who responded to her welcoming smile and looked on her as a personal friend. They told her their hopes, and she gave them encouragement with more than words. Local artists were invited to show their works in a gallery at the family's Sterling bank. Every year, the bank and the paper sponsored a free series of book reviews, lectures, and readers' theater. When someone organized meetings to better the community or gave a play or opened an art exhibit, she was there. Very often she wrote about the event in her column, and always she sent a note of congratulation.

She educated others, but she also listened. As one friend, Dorothy Corsberg, chairman of the humanities division of Northeastern Junior College, once noted, "She never betrayed a confidence." Her trust in others was returned by thousands of people. Even small children recognized the unique goodness of Anna Petteys. Her own son Jack made an unusual gesture for an eight-year-old by presenting his mother with a bouquet of flowers on *his* birthday. Voters sensed the same genuine qualities. At every election, she was the biggest vote-getter on the ballot. Bob Petteys has said, "Even demolished opponents became admirers, and a couple of them became lifelong friends."

She was delightfully human. When working on a project, she submerged her office with piles of papers. Once, attending a special course at Colorado University, she got in the wrong line for a luncheon meeting and ate with a gathering of lawyers. She wondered why there were no familiar faces but reported afterwards that the lawyers were extremely nice to her.

She could ask a small girl to luncheon, all by herself, and give that child her undivided attention.

How could one person do so much? She had unfailing determination. When she decided to write the dramatic story of Doctor Portia Lubchenco's life, the two had difficulty meshing their busy schedules. Anna Petteys was determined that the book should be written. Her solution was unique. She persuaded Doctor Portia to take a trip to Egypt and Africa with her. For several weeks, they traveled and talked and made notes. Afterwards, when pressures made the actual writing difficult, the two rented an apartment in Denver away from people and the telephone. There they hid out and worked until the book *Doctor Portia* was a reality.

She could not have completed her chrysalis from a shy Iowa farm girl without that quality of determination. It also saved her life. In 1947, when she was coming home from a speaking engagement, her car upset on the lonely road between Limon and Brush. For several hours before the wreck was discovered,

Anna travels in Egypt.

she lay unable to move. Only determination kept her alive. Her leg was permanently injured, but Anna Petteys refused to let it sideline her.

Her expressive face occasionally gave glimpses of the inner self: distress when she had to "abandon" a young companion upon learning that she was expected to sit at the head table of a dinner meeting; delight when someone exceeded his own expectations; genuine pleasure at an expression of appreciation for her simple goodness rather than her prestige; shock when introduced as elderly. She was not the only one who was shocked. How could such a vital person with so many ideas teeming in her head be described as merely elderly?

Still so much to do. Still the full exhilarating schedule when death came suddenly in 1973 in another automobile accident. Incredulously, one realized that this timeless woman was eighty-one years old.

One mourned the stilling of the catalyst who had been such a stimulus to her family and friends in northeastern Colorado.

With that influence gone, how could the area retain the fermentation necessary for excellence? And then one realized that her influence would not be lost. Her rare appreciation and faith in others had led them to glimpses of mirages that they turned into reality.

Mrs. Petteys would have approved her children's decision to establish the Anna C. Petteys scholarships for girls of northeastern Colorado. And the last honor, which came after her death, was perhaps the one that would have pleased her most, because it recognized not only the remarkable career but also the twenty-eight dedicated years as a full-time mother.

That honor was designation as one of ten Colorado Mothers of Achievement in American History, 1776–1976.

Anna C. Petteys, Mother of Achievement in American History, 1776–1976.

THE HARVEST

The Strenuous Dames pitted their nerve against the prairies. They evolved against that implacable background. What were their rewards?

Back in 1887, Lizzie Gordon noted that some people looked upon the lone women as "undesirable citizens." Something must have driven those women to risk that kind of ridicule. Lizzie wrote a poem that explained her drive.

It's wanting keeps us young and fit,
It's wanting something just ahead
And striving hard to come to it,
That brightens every road we tread.

Lizzie's road stayed bright, and she got what she wanted: teaching in Sterling once her homesteading venture was completed, and marriage at age forty-two to Kossuth Buchanan, who thought that Lizzie was highly desirable. And she stayed fit. On her eightieth birthday, to prove it, she turned a somerset for visitors.

Most of the strenuous dames got what they wanted, and if they didn't, they seemed to make the best of things. They were

Lizzie Gordon and Kossuth Buchanan in their happy later years. *Courtesy, Marguerite Sherwin Donovan.*

searchers — some for land, some for fame — and a surprising number harvested rewards: the pleasant discovery that they could do the unusual and do it well; and recognition — if not fame — for their accomplishments.

The list of women adventurers is a long one. One has to ask: what did their daring do to their lives? One measure is longevity. Only a few died young, and some of them were taken by accidents. The very pioneering of a Marvel Crosson brought her death. But a significant percentage of the others lived into their eighties and nineties. And death, when it came, had to run to catch them.

Etta Shannon Monroe was still speaking and organizing. Anna Petteys, snatched away at eighty-one, was traveling somewhere to speak. Nadine McCormack, who spent her life caring for other women's children, lived to age eighty-eight. The outspoken and witty Vesta Keen Mollohan remarked at her eighty-eighth birth-

Etta Shannon, still speaking and organizing. *Courtesy, Ellen Knudson Patten, niece.*

day party (when someone asked her age), "I don't always tell my age when single men are around." Laura Gilpin made her stunning photographs, had major showings of her work, and nonchalantly accepted fame and interviews to the very end of her eighty-eight years.

Doctor Portia lived to be ninety-one; Alice Mosser Propst and Isabelle Landrum, two of the nightingales, to ninety-three and ninety-four. Ethel Spoor Johnson, long after her service on the battlefields of France in World War I, was a lone woman member of the American Legion. She lived until near ninety, and her influence is felt yet, for she bequeathed a substantial sum of money to the Logan County Hospital, the Logan County Historical Society, and the Overland Trail Museum, all of which are carrying on the work that she considered vital.

Bertha Kaepernik Blancett caught attention for her unique rodeo career until the very end of her ninety-five years.

Many are still living: Effie Brown, in her mid-eighties, organizes entertainments, not with school children now but the elderly in her retirement home; Lillian Schulz and Frances Swedensky Garfield, in their nineties, delight friends with memories of the past; Amy Dickinson Worthley, over ninety, is researching and writing. Doctor Ruth Bennett may have re-

Amy Dickinson Worthley, who was first principal of Sterling Junior High, 1918 to 1925, spoke at cornerstone ceremonies for a new building in 1982 when she was ninety-one years old. *Photographer, J. Howard Crooks, Sterling* Journal-Advocate.

Dr. Ruth Bennett, eighty-two, on cruise to Alaska in 1978.

tired, but she still has "itchy feet." Just a year or so ago, at age eighty-five, she made a medical tour of China.

Willa Clanton, who at 105 has lived all but one year of Colorado's statehood, occupies a unique position. Still living alone, still vibrant and beautiful, she reads, she thinks, she is an intellectual. Her voice comes over the phone cheerful and lilting. She sometimes berates herself for retiring at age eighty-five and "wasting all those years." Her conversation is bright and knowledgeable — and humorous. In 1980, when she and friends celebrated her 103rd birthday in a restaurant, a small boy saw her cake blazing with all those candles and asked in awe, "How old are you?"

"Three," said Willa. "I'm starting over."

Perhaps the women lived so long because a vital stake in life spurred them into activity every day.

A valid way to judge them is to look at the lives of their children. Were they harmed? Even that newspaper editor in 1893 conceded that the "strenuous dames" were good mothers. Some of the most gifted delayed their careers to devote to their children — or swept them along with them.

The Japanese are a good example. Almost all descendants of those first immigrants have attended college, many at the most

Willa Clanton, ninety-nine, rides in a round-up.

Willa starting over at 100. She has probably lived more of Colorado's history than any other person.

prestigious universities. They have been named Phi Beta Kappans, valedictorians — and beauty queens. They are presidents of companies, professors, doctors, engineers, artists, researchers, and splendid farmers.

Sometimes a family faced such hardships that the children were not able even to complete high school. Mary Price's son dropped out of school in the ninth grade to help her publish the *Sterling Democrat*. But he became owner of three newspapers, and he was head of the West Texas Newspaper Editors' Association.

Frank Merrell, because of the discipline that he and the other children had to learn while helping Christie hold the family together, advanced to an executive position with the Chrysler Corporation. His sister Hattie studied fashion design in New York and became head designer for a large chain. Carter shared his mother's passionate individualism and love of the outdoors. He often spent long, winter-bound months in a tent alone in the Rocky Mountains, trapping like some frontiersman from

Christie Merrell with her children: Dot, Hattie, Frank, Henry, and Pat. Despite tragedy, the family had a triumphant harvest. *Photograph courtesy of Carter "Pat" Merrell.*

Colorado's past. Even though Christie's life was horrendously tragic, there was a triumphant harvest, for she did keep her family together, and they grew up to be self-reliant people. Even today, her surviving children, in their eighties and nineties, speak of her with awe and reverence.

Catherine Lingelbach brought those twelve children west to wrestle a living from a homestead and to capture wild horses. Today, her fifth-generation descendants still live on the high plains.

Some women, like Doctor Portia, had the energy and temperament — and often the cooperative husbands — to make work and home life a mix of fun and stimulation for parents and children alike. The Lubchenco children are all accomplished. Portia was a teacher, Peter an engineer, and three (Alexis, Lula, and Michael) became distinguished doctors in Denver. As their father would say, "The apple never falls far from the apple tree."

The record of the strenuous dames is astounding. They had the nerve to take steps, not tentative and testing, but bold, seemingly never looking back, never doubting. They set records that are amazing even today. There cannot be two Bertha Kaeperniks or another Lieutenant Colonel Helen Drissel. They were products of their own times. They carved their own handholds.

Most would probably say "Fiddlesticks!" with Laura Gilpin if someone suggested that they had paved the way for future women. They might suggest, "Carve your own handholds." But their spirit is contagious, their example like a light out on the dark prairie, showing the way. And there will be further lights in the years ahead.

What could have produced such women? Something in the water comes a suggestion, half serious. Something in the genes. Did a longing inside make them — or their forebears — seek the West? Or did a mystic spirit of the plains take hold of them? Things could have not been easy. A poem by Minosuke Noguchi hints that it was people with far-reaching thoughts who survived on the prairie:

To my desolate home
No caller comes
But a cosmos taps gently at my gate.

Perhaps one reason for the often spectacular success of prairie women is that the solitude and vastness of the plains can best be tolerated — if not appreciated — by people with special resources of mind and imagination. No woman is ever lonely when the universe taps gently at her gate.

SOURCES

Those Strenuous Dames of the Colorado Prairie is the result of years of fascination with the people of eastern Colorado and the events and surroundings that shaped their lives. Some of these women I was fortunate to meet while doing research for my master's thesis, "Where the Buffalo Roamed," a drama about the history of Logan County, Colorado. Many I have known and observed for years. Some have been so widely admired that it would be impossible to list all sources of their stories. Still others came to light only recently, adding to the special rewards that research brings.

I.   THAT AIN'T NO HOMESTEADER — THAT'S A LADY

Among the homesteaders whom I have known personally are Amy Dickinson Worthley and Ida Watkins Ladd. The latter's story was amplified by interviews with her sons, Lloyd and Lowell "Bob" Ladd, and her daughter-in-law, Birdie Ladd. Ninety-year-old Amy Worthley not only told her own story but helped with research of homestead laws and other women's stories.

Marguerite Sherwin Donovan, one of northeastern Colorado's most enthusiastic amateur historians, provided the unpublished autobiography of Lizzie Gordon Buchanan. Opal Lingelbach Houghton told of her grandmother, Catherine Lingelbach, and made available her collection of family records and newspaper articles about the northeastern Weld County area. Velma Biddle, a Delta Kappa Gamma member of Holyoke, told of ninety-one-year-old Lillian Schulz, ex-homesteader and prairie teacher, and Mrs. Schulz wrote an account of her early adventures. Lawrence Ramey is responsible for Mrs. Elmer Sheaffer's story.

Pat and Jim Merrell's book, *The Merrells* (Sterling, Co.: Royal Printing Co., 1979) was the source of the account of Mrs. Townsend. Other helpful books were: Sarah Claypool, *It Ain't Like It Used To Be* (self-published, 1977); Franklin M. Jones, *The History of New Raymer* (1943), reissued in 1960 by the Prairie High School classes of 1959, 1960, 1961, under the direction of Everett Thorpe, principal; Dale Wells, *The Logan County Ledger,* ed. Nell Brown Propst (Lincoln: The Nebraska State Press for the Logan County Historical Society, 1976) for the Minnie Palmer story.

The story of Hattie Belle Graves Rothwell was found in a magazine article, "Charles Rothwell, Homesteader, Cowboy, and Pullman Porter," as told to Margaret Passoth Picher, *Empire Magazine,* March 9, 1978.

Another helpful article was "Grover, Colorado, Pioneer Recalls Seventy-five Years of Friendship" by Martha Thompson, the Cheyenne, Wyoming *Eagle,* February 27, 1969.

II. WINNING THE WEST WITH A MCGUFFEY READER

Personal knowledge of and interviews with the following were the basis for their stories: Grace Benson; Gladys Shull Brewer, who provided use of her extensive collection of newspaper articles, correspondence, and awards; Effie Brown; Willa Clanton, who also gave access to her 100-plus years' collection of family and Colorado history; and Catherine Byrne Hume, who assisted with research of other teachers as well.

Interviews with the following added knowledge of several teachers: Alice Dawson, story about her mother; Frances Swedensky Reed Garfield; Ellen Knudsen Patton (Etta Shannon Monroe); Clella Rieke Best; and Kay Russell, story of Esther Stogsdill. Research materials were contributed by: Jean C. Balderston of Yuma, great-grand niece of Mary Pratt, the Pratt family genealogical records; Helen and Paul Budin and Frances Garfield, Madeline Veverka information; Auriel Oram Sandstead, material about her mother, Fae Stanley Oram; Mrs. Don Shipley, "The Shannons," unpublished account by Etta Shannon Monroe, "the youngest female 'rivulet' of the river 'Shannon.' "

Some information about Al Cochran came from Jones, *The History of New Raymer*. Other local or autobiographical books that proved helpful were: *Action on the Plains* (Yuma County Historical Society, 1971); Flora Allison, *My Autobiography* (privately published); Emma Burke Conklin, assisted by members of Elbridge Gerry Chapter, Daughters of the American Revolution, *A Brief History of Logan County, Colorado, With Reminiscences by Pioneers* (Denver: Welch-Haffner Printing Co., 1928); Ernestine Koenig, assisted by the Pawnee Historical Society, *Pawnee Country* (1979); Pat and Jim Merrell, *The Merrells;* and Gwen Schroeder, editor, *The Crowley County History* (Dallas: Taylor Publishing Co. for the Crowley County Heritage Society, 1980).

I am especially indebted to the Colorado chapters of the Delta Kappa Gamma Society International for their book about 100 years of classroom experiences in Colorado: Margaret J. Lehrer, editor, *Up the Hemline* (Colorado Springs: Williams and Field, Inc., 1975), with specific stories from Neva Bright, Edith Brummer, Grace Dawson, Grace Fitzgerald, Beryl Foster, Maude Linstrom Frandsen, Helen Fuller, Dorothy Gardiner, Catherine Byrne Hume, and Edith L. Stout.

III.   PRAIRIE NIGHTINGALES

This chapter is based on interviews with Maxine Wright Hughes, Ordway, granddaughter of Laura M. Wright; Dr. Jack Naugle, Sterling; the late Alice Mosser Propst and study of her records; and Alice Landrum Reynolds, daughter of Isabelle Landrum. Another of Isabelle's daughters, Virginia Landrum Garfield, Emmett, Idaho, wrote her memories of her mother's hospital. Many details of early Sterling came from almost a century of letters by Edna Weir Westlake, courtesy of Norene Hyde, Florence, Alabama.

Koenig's *Pawnee Country* and *The Crowley County History* provided additional material.

IV.   VOICE FROM THE FRONTIER

The most important source for this chapter is Missouri Powell Propst's "Essay on Women," used with the permission of descendants, notably Janet Haltom Ames, Bellevue, Washington, youngest great-grandchild of Missouri. I am indebted also for the use of Sid and Missouri Propst's letters from Colorado, 1874–1876, courtesy of the late Frank Propst, grandson, Bay Minette, Alabama. Other primary sources include "On the Last Frontier," the account of the Powell family in Colorado, by Susan Powell deVeau, who came to Colorado in 1875; and extensive interviews with Lena Propst Woolman Emery, 1866–1963, who arrived at Buffalo, Colorado, in 1876.

A helpful background source was *The Methodist, Evangelical, and United Brethren Churches in the Rockies, 1850–1976,* ed. J. Alton Templin, Allen D. Breck, and Martin Rist, the University of Denver Department of History Series: The West in American History, No. 6 (Denver: The Rocky Mountain Conference of the United Methodist Church, 1977), pp. 33, 64.

An ironic pleasure has come with the publication of Missouri's complete essay almost 100 years after rejection by the Methodist *Christian Advocate.* It can be found in the quarterly, *Methodist History,* ed. Louise L. Queen (Lake Junaluska, North Carolina: General Commission on Archives and History, The United Methodist Church, vol. 20, no. 2, January 1982).

V.   THOSE STRENUOUS DAMES

This chapter is based partially on interviews with the following: Hildegarde Kloeckner Aeschlimann; Naioma Benson; the late Webster Davis and his sister Avah Davis Whitney, now in her nineties and living in Boulder; Margaret Garner; the late Anna C. Petteys; Robert Petteys; Genevieve Manuello Sanders and Mrs. Newton Sanders, for information about Georgia Sanders McRoberts; and Isabelle Sullivan. Correspondence was received from Dr. Ruth Hull Bennett, now living in Sandy Spring, Maryland, courtesy of Cleo Smith, Ovid; Kathleen Painter Littler; and Bertha Boger Wear, Burlington.

Further information about Margaret Garner came from "Centennial Mental Health News," Fall 1980; the Sterling *Journal-Advocate,* May 27 and 29, 1981; and nomination material for Channel 9, Denver, KBTV, annual "9 Who Care" award. Elda Lousberg, Logan County commissioner, researched women county commissioners; and information about women legislators came from the Legislative Council Office at the Colorado state capitol, Denver. Shirley Dickinson McCune's accomplishments were researched by Amy Dickinson Worthley.

Good stories were found in articles and brochures: the Sterling *Journal-Advocate,* September 24, 1965 (Daisy Littler); Julesburg Chamber of Commerce brochure, "Mail Services and Postmasters in Julesburg," prepared for the dedication of a new post office, April 10, 1964; Nancy M. Peterson, "When the Ladies Voted in 1871," *Empire Magazine,* November 20, 1977; and the Pratt family genealogical records.

Helpful books included *The Crowley County History;* Jones, *The History of New Raymer;* Koenig, *Pawnee Country;* and John Stands-In-Timber, *Cheyenne Memories,* ed. and co-author, Margot Liberty (New Haven and London: Yale University Press, 1967).

VI.   PICTURE BRIDES

This chapter is based on interviews and extensive correspondence with the five daughters of Tomi and Minosuke Noguchi; and their parents' poems are included with their permission. An interview with Kay Russell provided the Mary Hamano story; correspondence with Betty Urahama Shimamoto, Sedgwick, brought her story; with Hisa Shimabukuro, the story of her mother, Some Kosuge; with Tomiko Takeda, who gave information about her mother, En Watada, and provided some of her poetry for use in the book. En Watada's poetry was translated by Lucille Nixon. Other assistance with Japanese poetry came from Lori Schott Gill, Merino and Sandy Nitta, Hawaii.

Further assistance came from Lena Mori, who was the research

coordinator for the Japanese section of "The New Americans,"
the ethnic section written by Nell Brown Propst for *The Logan
County Ledger* by Dale Wells; the Sterling Arts Council Collection of Japanese-American Family Histories, copies of which were
donated to area libraries and museums in 1979; and *The Crowley
County History.*

VII.   MY CHILDREN, MY BLOOD

This chapter was based on information from Carmen
Prado Torres and interviews with Tom and Dorothy Torres,
great-grandchildren of Celedonia.

VIII.   YOU CAN'T LAY YOUR HEAD ON
MOTHER NATURE'S BREAST

Stories recounted in this chapter came from interviews with
Gladys Shull Brewer and Helen Sherwin Parr, and from the unpublished manuscript, "Black Dust," by the latter, courtesy of
Marguerite Sherwin Donovan. Graphic details also came from
experiences related by Etta Shannon Monroe in her unpublished
memoirs.

I am especially indebted to a book that gave an on-the-spot
view of the horrors of nature in the Greeley Colony during the
1870s and 1880s: Mrs. A. M. Green, *Sixteen Years on the Great
American Desert* or *The Trials and Triumphs of a Frontier Life*
(Titusville, Pa.: Frank W. Truesdale, Printer, 1887), reprint,
Windsor, Colorado: Coren Printing 1980, by great-grand-
daughters, Mary Alice Rice Lindblad and Virginia M. Rice
Lindblad.

Other helpful books were Jones, *The New Raymer History;*
Koenig, *Pawnee Country;* and Lehrer, *Up the Hemline,* with especial
contributions by Teresa Lee, Edith Stout, and Laura E. Weaver.

The Kate Slaughterback story came from an undated article,
"Rattlesnake Kate — Life in the City Not for Her," *The Greeley
Tribune,* from the collection of Opal Lingelbach Houghton.

IX. THROUGH THE VALLEY OF THE SHADOW

Stories in this chapter came from interviews with Barbara Smith Armstrong, granddaughter of Elizabeth Jane Weir Lanphere Mathews; Joseph Davis, son of Lizzie Davis; Marguerite Sherwin Donovan, Adeline Estelle Monnette story; Dallas Landrum, Jr.; and Lew and Ted Sindt and Mary Sindt Vallier, Adeline Monnette story.

I am especially indebted for the story of Mary Red Kettle from a valuable book by Emily H. Lewis, *Wo' Wakita, Reservation Recollections. A People's History of the Allen Issue Station District on the Pine Ridge Reservation of South Dakota* (Sioux Falls, South Dakota: Center for Western Studies, Augustana College, 1980).

The Jacob Deabald story came from Flora Allison, *My Autobiography.*

X. WHAT ONE WOMAN CAN DO

Carter "Pat" Merrell, who grew up on a homestead on the old Valley Station site on the South Platte Trail, told the story of his heroic mother, Christie Merrell, and provided pictures for this chapter. The book that he and his son Jim wrote, *The Merrells,* provided a graphic view of a Logan County homestead during the late nineteenth and early twentieth centuries, as well as the personal tragedies of Christie.

Other information was told by Amy Dickinson Worthley.

XI. GRASPING THE LEAD REINS

Several subjects of this chapter were interviewed in person: Lorraine Dalgleish Hays, Judee Lea McGuire, and Edith Steiger Phillips. Relatives interviewed included Jennie Gill Dixon, b. 1893, and the late Whitford Gill, b. 1900, niece and nephew of Bruce Johnson, who told the story of the Swedish housemaids; and Edna Price Kellogg, daughter of Mary Price. Details about the life of Mary Ann Dickens Allen were provided by Lawrence Allen of Berthoud, a grandson, and by his collection of family

history, including a letter by his father, A. W. Allen, which told
the story of Mary Ann's coming west. Helen and Paul Budin,
daughter-in-law and grandson of Barbara Budin, told of her life.

Marie Couch, president of Colorado Women in Banking, and
Elsie Erickson of Greeley gave information about women
bankers. Anne Thompson's story was provided by corespond-
ence and use of her curriculum vitae, as was Bertha Boger
Wear's. Information about Mrs. Wear was also given by Perry
Brewer and others in Burlington. Some material in this chapter
came from the Edna Weir Westlake letters.

Other sources included *The Crowley County History* and Mrs.
A. M. Green's *Sixteen Years on the Great American Desert.* For a more
complete account of Clara Hilderman Ehrlich, see "My Childhood on the Prairie," *The Colorado Magazine,* S/2 Spring 1974;
and Timothy Kloberdanz' "People Without a Country" in the
ethnic section of *The Logan County Ledger.* A helpful article was
"Career Women Found Success in Greeley" by Karen Krieg,
The Greeley Daily Tribune, March 10, 1982.

XII. YEAST FOR THE DAILY BREAD

Earlier writing and further study of talent in eastern Colorado
was prompted by the derogatory remark about rural people by
a Colorado legislator, which was quoted in a May 1978 issue
of *Roundup,* entertainment section of *The Denver Post.*

Many people in this chapter are known personally, and their
stories are told from years of observation, as well as from their
records of accomplishment. They are: Faye Tanner Cool,
Madeleine Davis Greenawalt, Sue Josties, Margaret Martin,
the late Anna C. Petteys, Chris Petteys, Jessie Whitney Scott,
and Celena Smith.

Correspondence and study of articles and memorabilia added
to the information about these women and their careers. Early
accounts and pictures testified to the remarkable fame of
Madeleine Greenawalt. Much information about Margaret Martin was located in the nomination form for a Channel Nine "9
Who Care" competition.

Books by Lora Conant were the best clue to her life and attitudes: *As the Wheel Turns* (Dallas: The Story Book Press, 1955) and *Things as We See Them* (Dallas: The Story Book Press, 1950). Information about the Garner daughters (Jerri Lines and Jo Boatright) was gleaned from programs, professional resumes, and articles, particularly "Musical America" in *High Fidelity Magazine* and *Ovation,* the magazine for classical music listeners, March 1982.

Laura Gilpin's accomplishments were found in a Chris Petteys interview with her in her Santa Fe studio, June 1978; through use of the Chris Petteys collection; study of Laura Gilpin's books; and articles, including "Laura: Grand Lady of Santa Fe" by Katie Dean, *Contemporary,* October 21, 1979.

Hazel Johnson's material came from correspondence, use of her memorabilia, and study of her writings, especially "Out of the Past"; Maxine Firestack Lampshire's, from an interview in Annandale, Virginia, correspondence, and her resume, plus the booklet of The National League of American Pen Women, Inc., updated and revised by Margaret T. Rudd of the Alexandria, Virginia, branch.

The account of Phyllis McGinley's years in northeastern Colorado is based on interviews with Dorothy Lutin Curlee, Frances Swedensky Reed Garfield of Colorado Springs, Veronica Foy McKenzie, and Laurence Ramey; on newspaper clippings, including a column by Harold Hamil about her guest appearance at the Lyndon Johnson White House and subsequent cover article in *Time Magazine;* the *Time* article, June 18, 1965; and study of her books, particularly *The Province of the Heart* (New York: The Viking Press, 1959), *Saint Watching* (New York: The Viking Press, 1969), and *Times Three, Selected Verse of Three Decades* (New York: The Viking Press, 1961), and other poetry.

Sister Michael Marie's story was revealed by interviews with her mother, Veronica Schell Kaiser, and her sister, Mildred Kaiser Marostica; by articles from *The Denver Post;* and by reading her books, *Songs for a Journey* (Brownsville: Springman–King Company, 1980) and *You Have Filled the Days* (Boston: Bruce Humphries, Inc., 1949).

Material about Mary O'Farrell was located in "Colorado's First Woman Artists" by Chris Petteys, *Empire Magazine,* May 6, 1979. Mary Stanley's story came from interviews with her granddaughter, Auriel Oram Sandstead, and extensive correspondence and use of her collection of articles, pictures, and memorabilia. The source of the Grace Smith material was articles from the collection of Gladys Shull Brewer.

A helpful article was "Meeker Women" by Catherine Devereaux, *The Greeley Daily Tribune,* March 11, 1982.

XIII.   CHAMPION LADY RIDER OF THE WEST

Sources for Bertha Kaepernik Blancett material included interviews with the late Billy Armour, Marguerite Sherwin Donovan, Mary Fonte Kaepernik, and Clifford Sherwin; articles in the Sterling *Journal–Advocate* and one by Willeta Regan of Portersville, California, quoted in the *Advocate.*

XIV.   COLORADO'S MARVEL OF A BIRD GIRL

Primary sources for information about Marvel Crosson include a handwritten biography, probably written by Marvel, courtesy of Mary Davis Weidner, a cousin, Denver; interview with Lt. Col. Dan Hofmann, second member in seniority of the Civil Air Patrol in Colorado; interviews and correspondence with relatives and friends of the Crosson family, particularly Edward Bryan Davis, Colorado Springs; Margaret Davis, California; Alice Landrum Reynolds; and Mary Davis Weidner; and research at the Overland Trail Museum, Sterling.

Articles include: "All About Alaska's Airplane Grocery Girl— How 'Pollyanna of the North' Dares Death to Spread Sunshine and Scatter Watermelons over the Yukon's White Wastes," Newspaper Feature Service, unidentified clipping, 1929; Marvel Crosson, "How I Learned to Fly," *Country Gentleman,* September 1929; "Marvel Crosson's Kid Brother Flies On," *Everyweek Magazine,* 1929; Klondike Nelson, "I Was a Bride in the Arctic," *Saturday Evening Post,* December 22, 1936; and *New York Times, Mid-Week Pictorial,* June 22, 1929, cover.

Newspaper articles include: *The High Plains Daily Journal,*

Sterling, Colorado, September 19, 1953; *The Sterling Advocate,* September 16, 1953; and an unidentified San Diego clipping, 1940.

The following books were helpful: Colby, Merle, *A Guide to Alaska, Last American Frontier* (New York: The MacMillan Co., 1943); and Thomas, Lowell, *Sir Hubert Wilkins* (New York, Toronto, London: The McGraw–Hill Company, 1961).

XV.   MABEL'S CHILDREN

The chapter about Mabel Landrum Torrey is based on interviews with the late Webster Davis, a cousin; with Bob McKay and the late Lorena McKay, nephew and niece of Mabel; and with other relatives; and on the book by Gladys Hamlin, *The Sculpture of Fred and Mabel Torrey* (Alhambra, Calif.: Borden Publishing Co., 1969).

Other material includes undated articles: "Wynken, Blynken, and Nod, Tough Sailing in Denver Park," *The Denver Post;* and clippings from the Sterling *Journal–Advocate.*

XVI.   THE NOGUCHI SISTERS

The Noguchi sisters' story is based on interviews and correspondence with Tsune, Sugi, SuZan, Yoshi, and Kisa Noguchi and with C. F. Poole and Clella Rieke Best; and on material from the Sterling Arts Council Collection of Japanese-American History. Bill Hosokawa's editorial appeared in *The Denver Post,* April 22, 1979. Poetry is quoted with the permission of the five sisters.

XVII.   ONE YEAR OF MY LIFE

This chapter is based on interviews and correspondence with Helen Brecht Drissel and on records and photographs provided by her.

XVIII.   GOOD GIRL, LOU!

The amazing athletic career of Lou Piel was documented with interviews and correspondence with Lou and her father, Arnold, plus access to an extensive collection of clippings, articles, trophies, and awards.

XIX.   THE GIANT STEPS OF DOCTOR PORTIA

Doctor Portia's story is based on interviews and correspondence with her friends and her daughter, Portia Lubchenco Curlee Whitaker; collections, letters, clippings, and mementos; and Doctor Portia's own writing, especially the essay, "State of My Nation." Of special value was the book that she authored with Anna C. Petteys, *Doctor Portia* (Denver: Golden Bell Press, 1964).

XX.   ANNA C. PETTEYS, CATALYST FOR THE PLAINS

The writing of Anna C. Petteys' story is based on long years of admiration and friendship; on interviews and correspondence with her son Robert; on study of the family collection of clippings, mementos, photographs, writings, and awards; and on the reading of her column, "Post Scripts."

INDEX